D1713654

Violence and the Latin American Revolutionaries

A Foreign Policy Research Institute Book

This book is part of a series of works sponsored by the Foreign Policy Research Institute in Philadelphia. Founded in 1955, the Institute is an independent, nonprofit organization devoted to research on issues affecting the national interest of the United States.

Violence and the Latin American Revolutionaries

Edited by
Michael Radu

Transaction Books
New Brunswick (USA) and Oxford (UK)

A Foreign Policy Research Institute Book
Copyright © 1988 by the Foreign Policy Research Institute

Library of Congress Catalog Number: 87-19169
ISBN 0-88738-195-2
Printed in the United States of America

Library of Congress Cataloging-in-Publication Data

Violence and the Latin American revolutionaries.

"A Foreign Policy Research Institute book"—T. p.
verso.
    Includes index.
    1. Latin America—Politics and government—
1948–   . 2. Revolutionists—Latin America—History—
20th century. 3. Government, Resistance to—Latin America—
History—20th century. 4. Terrorism—Latin
America—History—20th century. 5. Communism—Latin
America—History—20th century. I. Radu, Michael.
F1414.2.V54 1987   980'.03   87-19169
ISBN 0-88738-195-2

Contents

Acknowledgments   vi

List of Acronyms   vii

1. Introduction: Revolution and Revolutionaries   1
   Michael Radu

PART I   Patterns of Revolution

2. Revolutionary Warfare   15
   William Ratliff

3. Ernesto "Che" Guevara and the Reality of Guerrilla Warfare   37
   Ernst Halperin

4. The Changing Role of Revolutionary Violence in Nicaragua, 1959 to 1979   56
   Antonio Ybarra–Rojas

5. Strategy, Flexibility, and Violence   78
   Douglas Payne

PART II   The Practitioners of Revolution

6. Communist Orthodoxy and Revolutionary Violence   83
   Vladimir Tismaneanu

7. Revolutionary Elites   108
   Michael Radu

8. The Appeals of Revolutionary Violence   126
   Paul Hollander

9. Toward a Reassessment of Insurgency, Violence, Revolution, Communism, and Assorted Ailments   150
   Irving Louis Horowitz

About the Contributors   155

Acknowledgments

The editor wishes to express his gratitude to all those on the FPRI staff whose help has made this volume possible. Special thanks are due to Joanne Tomazinis for her editorial help, and to Monique Skruzny and Masroor Khan for the time-consuming support they have provided in proofreading the text.

List of Acronyms

AGEUS	Asociación General de Estudiantes Universitarios de El Salvador: General Association of Salvadoran Students
ARO	Alianza Revolucionaria Popular: Popular Revolutionary Alliance (Argentina)
CISPES	Committee in Solidarity with the People of El Salvador (USA)
CPUSA	Communist Party of the United States of America
EGP	Ejército Guerrillero de los Pobres: Guerrilla Army of the Poor (Guatemala)
ELN	Ejército de Liberación Nacional: National Liberation Army (Bolivia)
ERP	Ejército Revolucionario del Pueblo: People's Revolutionary Army (Argentina, El Salvador)
FAR	Fuerzas Armadas Rebeldes: Rebel Armed Forces (Guatemala)
FARC	Fuerzas Armadas Revolucionarias de Colombia: Revolutionary Armed Forces of Colombia
FARN	Fuerzas Armadas de Resistencia Nacional: Armed Forces of National Resistance (El Salvador)
FDR	Frente Democrático Revolucionario: Democratic Revolutionary Front (El Salvador)
FER	Frente Estudiantil Revolucionario: Revolutionary Student Front (Nicaragua)
FLN	Frente de Liberación Nacional: National Liberation Front (Peru)
FPL	Fuerzas Populares de Liberación: Popular Forces of Liberation (El Salvador)
FPMR	Frente Patriótico Manuel Rodríguez: Manuel Rodríguez Patriotic Front (Chile)
FSLN	Frente Sandinista de Liberación Nacional: Sandinist National Liberation Front (Nicaragua)
GAR	Grupos de Acción Revolucionaria: Groups of Revolutionary Action (El Salvador)

JCR	Junta Coordinadora Revolucionaria: Revolutionary Coordinating Committee
JSN	Juventud Socialista de Nicaragua: Socialist Youth of Nicaragua
M-19	Movimiento 19 de Abril: Movement of April 19 (Colombia)
MAP-ML	Movimiento de Acción Popular Marxista-Leninista: Popular Action Movement-Marxist-Leninist (Nicaragua)
MAS	Movimiento al Socialismo: Movement Toward Socialism (Venezuela)
MCR	Movimiento Campesino Revolucionario: Revolutionary Peasant Movement (Chile)
MIR	Movimiento de la Izquierda Revolucionaria: Movement of the Revolutionary Left (Bolivia, Peru, Chile)
MLN Tupamaros	Movimiento de Liberación Nacional-Tupamaros: National Liberation Movement (Uruguay)
MPR	Movimiento de los Pobres Revolucionarios: Movement of the Revolutionary Poor (Chile)
MR-13	Movimiento Revolucionario del 13 de Noviembre: Revolutionary Movement of November 13 (Guatemala)
MRTA	Movimiento Revolucionario Túpac Amaru: Tupac Amaru Revolutionary Movement (Peru)
OLAS	Organización de Solidaridad de América Latina: Latin American Solidarity Organization
ORPA	Organización Revolucionaria del Pueblo en Armas: Revolutionary Organization of People in Arms (Guatemala)
PC de N	Partido Comunista de Nicaragua: Communist Party of Nicaragua
PCB	Partido Comunista de Bolivia: Communist Party of Bolivia
PCB-ML	Partido Comunista de Bolivia-Marxista-Leninista: Communist Party of Bolivia-Marxist-Leninist
PCCh	Partido Comunista de Chile: Communist Party of Chile
PCES	Partido Comunista de El Salvador: Communist Party of El Salvador
PGT	Partido Guatemalteco de Trabajo: Guatemalan Labor Party
PLO	Palestine Liberation Organization
PO	Palabra Obrera: Worker's Word (Argentina)
PRT	Partido Revolucionario de los Trabajadores: Revolutionary Workers Party

PRTC	Partido Revolucionario de los Trabajadores de Centro América: Revolutionary Party of Central American Workers (El Salvador, Honduras)
PSN	Partido Socialista de Nicaragua: Nicaraguan Socialist Party
PSP	Partido Socialista Popular: Socialist Popular Party (Cuba)
Sendero Luminoso	Partido Comunista (del Peru en el Sendero Luminoso de José Carlos Mariátegui): Peruvian Communist Party on the Shining Path of José Carlos Mariátegui
SWP	Socialist Workers Party (USA)
UNO	Unión Nacional Opositora: National Opposition Union (Nicaragua)
URNG	Unidad Revolucionaria Nacional de Guatemala: National Revolutionary Unity of Guatemala

———

1

Introduction:
Revolution and Revolutionaries

Michael Radu

One of the most amazing things about the abundant bibliography on Latin America's revolutionary traditions and movements is the almost total absence of a serious analysis of the revolutionaries themselves. Going through most of the volumes on revolution south of the Rio Grande, one is hard–pressed to find an in–depth analysis of the makers of revolutions. The overwhelmingly dominant approach to revolutionary phenomena in Latin America, shared by authors with the most diverse ideological biases, is to treat them in an almost abstract manner. In most instances it is the "cause" of revolution that attracts most attention; in some isolated instances it is the "how," the modus operandi, of the revolutionaries. Almost never is the question "Who makes the revolution?" addressed. At best, the answer is provided as a secondary product of an author's specific approach to the issue of the "causes" of revolution; if those "root cases" are found to be "poverty, social injustice and oppression," then naturally the revolutionaries are "the people" subjected to such conditions. Seldom is any satisfactory definition of "the people" offered. If the "cause" of revolution is seen as external (for example, communist subversion), the revolutionaries are simply defined as "Communist," again without further explanation. Sometimes in the maze of analyses of revolutionary movements in Latin America one finds a glimpse of the actual leaders, but even their background is seldom seen as very relevant to their activities.

But is an understanding of the revolutionary phenomena in Latin America, particularly since the Cuban Revolution, possible without examining the nature and mentality of the makers of revolution? This question raises the additional issue of the impact the revolutionaries' background, as a group, has and has had on the nature and evolution of revolutionary movements. What, then, is the collective background of the Latin American revolutionaries, if indeed they do have a clear group identity and if such an identity is strong enough to cross borders from the Río de la Plata to the Rio Grande? Furthermore, what is the impact of the revolutionary individual and leadership group on the specific nature of their revolutionary movement? It is the answers to these questions that this volume tries to approximate.

Even a cursory reading of the different writings of Ernesto "Che" Guevara on revolutionary tactics and strategy amply indicates the highly voluntaristic nature of his approach to revolution. More than Lenin, Guevara was unprepared to wait for the right conditions for revolution or, in Leninist parlance, for a "revolutionary situation" to exist. Che's famous dictum "The duty of the revolutionary is to make revolution" perfectly proves his voluntaristic approach. It is enough to compare it with Kautsky's claim that "the Socialist Party is a revolutionary party; it is not a party that makes revolution. We know that our aims can be realized only through a revolution, but we also know that it is not in our power to make a revolution, any more than it is in the power of our opponents to prevent it."[1] It is the individual, in other words, who makes the revolution, and the revolution–making is a matter of choice, not of historic determinism. Obvious as it may appear—and it was obvious to Guevara's innumerable epigones—the fact that revolutions are made and are made by human beings has so far escaped the attention of Western academia. How else can one explain the obsession with the "root causes" of revolution at the expense of the makers of revolution? Guevara would probably have laughed at his scholarly admirers and at their hiding behind "sophisticated" economic, sociological, or political analysis "explaining" what for Che and so many others was simply a matter of individual, and perhaps lonely and painful but free, choice to become a revolutionary. In Latin America, as well as elsewhere during this century, a revolutionary starts by being more free than his fellow citizens, since he *acts* on his putative freedom and decides to break ties with society, his social group, often his family; he does not merely think about it. But by this very fact the revolutionary is also a loner, an isolated rebel. In the circumstances of Latin America, particularly of rural (and always Indian) as well as of Roman Catholic Latin America, such a loner comes almost exclusively from a few select social groups, those groups with a head–start advantage compared with the rest of the society. That means they have the economic freedom to be able to become a professional revolutionary—the only kind that could succeed in the twentieth century, as proved by a long list of leaders from Lenin and Hitler to Castro and Guevara themselves. It also means a weaker–than–usual tie with the two pillars of social cohesion in Latin America: Catholicism and community (village, tribe, family) membership. Furthermore, such a head start also means access to education—higher education, that is, the only education that provides the theoretical framework essential for a revolutionary to justify and legitimize, if not to choose, his option for revolution.

These requirements for a revolutionary choice, and most often career, in

Latin America are bound to produce a certain uniformity among the revolutionary leadership and core cadres throughout the continent. They also explain the disproportionate number of middle– and upper–class elements among the Latin revolutionaries, the equally disproportionate over–representation of ethnic minorities, and the domination of university–educated individuals. The membership in an ethnic minority speaks by itself, but in a still largely illiterate, or barely literate, society, university education, albeit partial in most cases, is a privilege of the few (although their number is increasing). As for economic independence, that is the even greater privilege of even fewer. The ineluctable conclusion, supported by all that is known about contemporary revolutionary leaders in Latin America, is that revolution is made, or at the very least led, by the middle classes, with heavy inputs from "traitorous" scions of the upper classes; in short, it is an elite phenomenon. A "typical" profile of the Latin American revolutionary leader or important cadres—since the phenomenon applies to far more numerous members of the revolutionary movements than the handful of supreme leaders (in fact applies to *most* cadres)—would include the following characteristics: (1) middle– or upper–class social origin, (2) some university–level education, (3) a far–above–average likelihood of belonging to an ethnic minority (Jewish, East European, mostly Croatian, Japanese, Basque), and (4) a far–wider–than–average knowledge, often firsthand, of other countries, whether in Latin America or elsewhere. In addition, to be a revolutionary in Latin America, U.S. liberal dreams notwithstanding, means to be a Marxist–Leninist—more the latter than the former, but always some of both.

Being a middle–class phenomenon and often a phenomenon of the intelligentsia, the revolutionary profession in Latin America is highly admired in the West by similar groups. In a way one can speak of a global intelligentsia solidarity. Thus, when Nicaraguan secret police boss Omar Cabezas writes a well–written book, he is naturally accepted as a fellow and admirable member of the global fraternity of intellectuals and receives the accolades of a Günther Grass or a Susan Sontag, both of whom presumably would be reluctant to so treat an Andropov or a Beria. The difference, most often, is that the Western elites are more vicarious in their "participation" in revolutionary change at home than they are in supporting it abroad—hence the implicit paternalism of their position. Fundamentally, what Doctorow, Vonnegut, Mailer, Sontag, Sartre, Genet, and Grass are saying is that communism is bad for the Russians, with some going as far as to admit that it is also bad for the Poles and even, *horrible dictu*, for the Vietnamese, but is needed for Latin Americans—if it is promoted by such intellectual luminaries as Omar Cabezas, Ernesto Cardenal, Gabriel García Márquez, or other self–proclaimed "talents of the revolution," even such minor ones as Roque Dalton, Otto Castillo, Javier Héraud, or Daniel Ortega.

The superficial, fashionable, and largely empty admiration that Western intellectuals and literati have for Latin revolutionaries should not obscure the very real similarities between some of those revolutionaries and their Western European or American counterparts. The modus operandi of the Uruguayan Tupamaros, the Argentine Montoneros, or the Nicaraguan Sandinistas was as strikingly similar to that of the Baader–Meinhof Gang in West Germany, the Weather Underground in the United States, or the Red Brigades in Italy as was their background. Indeed, Roque Dalton's Internado San José in San Salvador, Julio Mezzich's (of Sendero Luminoso fame) private Jesuit school in Lima, and many others are not different in fame and elitism from Kathy Boudin's Bryn Mawr or Daniel Cohn–Bendit's Sorbonne. Who learned from whom may be an impossible question to answer. All one can say is that the almost unanimously positive and admiring reception in Western Europe and the United States of Costa–Gavras' apology for Uruguayan terrorism in *State of Siege* was probably not due to the cinematographic performances but to the feeling of belonging that so many young Western rebels have; the "heroic" Tupamaros of the movie were indeed *like them*. The presence of Carlos Marighela's *Minimanual of the Urban Guerrilla* in the hideouts of the Baader–Meinhof, the Weathermen, or the Red Brigades implied more than the need to learn basics of terror; it also implied a brotherhood of aims.

Existentially, the Latin American revolutionary is a rebel—often in Camus' sense—an individual unable and unwilling to accept, let alone adapt to, the prevailing social conventions of his class or group. What makes him different from an anarchist—and the difference is not always clear, considering the strong anarchist influence over such prominent Latin revolutionaries as the Tupamaros, Montoneros, and the Chilean MIR—is his strong, even desperate, belief that other groups, mostly the peasants and the "poor" in general, hold similar or at least compatible values. Deep inside his ego, the Latin revolutionary needs to believe that the *campesino* is like himself in his hopes and goals, even if the latter lacks the revolutionaries' "consciousness," that is, the educational dogmatism and the ideological commitment. Perhaps nowhere was this phenomenon more clear than in Guevara's own fantasy, that the Bolivian peasantry would follow his banner in the name of the continental revolution. That Guevara paid with his life for that delusion is a fact; it is also a fact that his followers never understood the peasant any better. In certain cases, such as in Guatemala of the late 1960s, such hopes were the immediate cause of the guerrillas' collapse. The peasants simply did not go along with them. In the case of the EGP in the late 1970s, however, the peasants did go along and rapidly discovered that the revolutionaries could not feed them, protect them, or provide land for them. In Paraguay the peasantry was even less inclined to follow the siren song of the Left, and the "shoeless" (py–nandi)[2] of the Colorado Party were and still are the main bastion of defense of the Stroessner dictatorship (which seems to have copied more from the Leninist book than the latter may ever admit). In Nicaragua, the realization that the peasant is not a reliable follower of the revolutionary process dawned on the Sandinistas after they took power, when the peasantry of northern Nicaragua flocked to the banner of the "Contras."[3] In all these cases the revolutionaries may well be the victims of the relative truth of their own ideology. The class gaps between peasantry and urban, educated middle classes is too deep for well–mannered and apparently well–wishing outsiders to bridge, revolutionary promises not withstanding.

In the treatment of the peasantry, as well as in many other issues, the Latin American revolutionaries paid, and still pay, a heavy price for their own sanctification of Guevara. Indeed, instead of seeing Che as a marginally useful martyr, a very unoriginal theoretician, and a thoroughly discredited practitioner of guerrilla warfare, they have sanctified him and thus became bound to repeat the saint's very earthly errors. Moreover, to make things worse still, many of Guevara's epigones have repeated his totally erroneous interpretation of the importance of the Cuban Revolution as a model for Latin America as a whole. Being a revolutionary means being a believer. Belief gives strength and courage, but it also blinds. Thus the fact that Batista's Cuba was a country with a totally decadent regime and a larger–than–usual middle class, and, most important, the fact that Castro and his colleagues did not defeat Batista militarily, resulted in strengthening that omnipresent Latin American revolutionary disease: "triunfalismo." Triunfalismo is the inability to admit the existence of serious obstacles on the path to revolution, to admit the possibility of not winning, and the tendency to badly underestimate the capability of the enemy. The best example of the disastrous results of triunfalismo may be Guatemala. There, during the late 1960s, the guerrillas managed to convince themselves that the "ruling classes" were hopelessly decadent and small, that the Ladino peasantry of Zacapa and Izabal would naturally follow the insurgents of the Sierra de las Minas—and none of this happened. On the contrary, the peasants followed the leadership of the military and their own interest as landowners, and the so–called death squads, together with Colonel Arana Osorio's troops, finished off the guerrillas. Later, during the past eight years, the ORPA, the EGP, and the FAR tried to use the Indians for their aims, but the Indians proved to be intelligent enough, as a community, to realize that those foreigners making promises were just that, foreigners making empty promises. Between belonging to village self–defense groups, including their friends, cousins, and brothers, albeit armed by the military, and submitting themselves to orders of former intellectuals of Guatemala City in the name of an ideology alien to them by its very nature, the Indians naturally opted for the former. The guerrillas are now dying out in the highlands of Guatemala.

The cult of revolution and of violence is not a Marxist–Leninist invention in

Latin America; it pre–dates Castro, and even Marx. In fact, in many countries the term "revolution" is used as a label for any unconstitutional change of government. Each Bolivian colonel or general who ever took power labeled his coup a "revolution" and in at least some instances military coups did result in revolutionary changes, even if not always of a Leninist type. The 1964 Brazilian coup and Pinochet's coup in 1973 in Chile were not ordinary coups, since they both ushered in dramatic and painful restructuring of the society.

What the Guatemalan guerrillas of the 1960s and again during the late 1970s and early 1980s could never understand was the strong nationalist reaction of the military and business elites, made even more virulent by the internationalism of the guerrillas. In fact, it may be that nationalism is the strongest obstacle facing the Leninist left in Latin America. This appears to come in direct conflict with the natural and historic internationalism of the Left and with the Bolivarian dreams of the Latin intellectuals in general. The dreams of a united Latin America, ranging from the Tierra del Fuego to the Rio Grande, often overlaps with regional unity illusions, Morazanism in Central America, for instance. For well–traveled intellectuals and professional revolutionaries, *their* Latin America does naturally appear as gratuitously divided into seventeen mainland states, since they feel equally at home in Buenos Aires and Mexico City, Lima and Caracas. The question whether the same applies to the ordinary Chilean, Argentine, Brazilian, Salvadoran, or Panamanian does not appear to have occurred to them. It thus seems as if the internationalism of the guerrillas and their intellectual supporters clashes head on with the nationalism of the military, and one may suggest, unorthodox as the suggestion may be, that the latter is more representative of the populace. Furthermore, the internationalist threat represented by Leninists of all varieties, including Castroites, often tends to force cooperation between otherwise incompatible forces—such as between the Salvadoran and Honduran armies or between those of Peru and Chile or Argentina and Chile, against guerrillas. The Latin guerrilla is thus caught in a dramatic dilemma. Unless he attracts popular support in a massive way, he cannot normally hope to win, but in order to gain such support he must give up or at least hide internationalism, one of his most cherished and natural parts of being a revolutionary in the first place.

The first possibility seldom happened—becoming a nationalist is so incompatible with being a Leninist as to be impossible—which is why the truly nationalist revolutionaries in Latin America in this century, from the Mexicans of 1910 to Augusto César Sandino himself, have rejected Marxism–Leninism. The second does happen quite often: witness the nationalist show of the Sandinistas prior to their taking power, of Castro until 1961, and so on. Conversely, former internationalists, and Marxist–Leninists like Victor Haya de la Torre in Peru, renounced their Leninism as they moved closer to the realities of their countries and realized that popular support depends not only on reforms but also on their being perceived as consistent with the national interests.

The archetype of the elitist, internationalist, arrogant, and unrealistic Latin American *guerrillero's* nature and approach was provided by Guevara himself in his Bolivian adventure. In his own words he wanted to fight the Vietnam War all over again in Latin America. The Andes became in his imagination the continental Sierra Maestra, and the continent became a larger version of Cuba. Whether the Bolivians, from the peasants to the communists themselves, had a different opinion was irrelevant—witness Che's haughty refusal to allow even the Bolivian communists any leadership role in the whole enterprise. Pathetic as it was, Guevara's end in Bolivia was also indicative of the permanent strength of his beliefs and of his dedication to his own artificial world. The contradiction between the guerrillero's desperate attempts to "become one with the people", to move to the people and to assimilate himself into their universe, and his inner nature as fundamentally *different* from the masses is best defined by Rodrigo Asturias in Guatemala. As leader of the ORPA, he took the nom de guerre "Gaspar Ilom", after an eighteenth century Indian rebel, and his organization has always tried to root itself among the Indians. On the other hand, he has to take his books, including Plato, into the hills around Lake Atitlán. He is forever divided between his intellectual background, including the family tradition that has given Guatemala its only Nobel prize winner, and his revolutionary pretensions, beliefs, and needs. Similarly, Abimael Guzmán Reynoso, alias "Camarada Gonzalo", alias "The Fourth Sword of Marxism" (after Marx, Lenin and Mao), wrote his doctoral dissertation on Kant's theory of space but is now, as Sendero Luminoso's supreme leader, forcing the Indians of Peru back into pre–Columbian times by cutting off the fingers of those who vote, closing down village markets, destroying banknotes, and blowing up electrical installations. The difference between this behavior and Guevara's attempt to make the Bolivian peasant the spearhead of continental revolution is minimal, if it exists at all. In both cases the strength of the metaphysical beliefs tries to impose itself on reality by force—hence the peculiar nature of much of the revolutionary violence of Latin American revolutionaries. Indeed, it is understandable to the citizen if the land–owning oligarchy or military officer uses force to accomplish economic or political goals, but it is incomprehensible to see force used for the sake of remote, quasi–messianic, "idealistic" revolutionary goals.

None of the foregoing considerations really applies to the chances for the revolutionary to gain victory, much to the discomfort of many Western liberals, whose belief in democracy is often stronger than is their understanding of Latin American realities. In fact, the revolutionary does not have to care about popular beliefs and values, particularly those of the peasants. It may well be that the difference between revolutionary winners and losers, between Castros and Guevaras, lies in the ability to compromise ideals for the sake of expediency, to accept the radical dichotomy between tactics and strategy or, bluntly, to lie. What the revolutionary has to care about is, more often than not, the attitude of the United States and that of the urban groups in his country, or at least those in the capital. He also must take advantage of the smallest open political or social space allowed by those in power, because this allows fronts to flourish. The front is the best example of revolutionary deception, and in a war—and revolutionary action is a war—deception is not only encouraged but also essential.

More often than not, the most solid basis for the guerrillas' ability to attract public support is also the only strong emotion they and the ordinary Latin American (at least in the cities) generally share: anti–Americanism, a profound and complex distrust of the United States often bordering on hatred. In many respects, anti–Americanism is rooted in an irrational, Freudian transfer of responsibility for the real and imagined ills of Latin America. Perhaps the best brief analysis of this phenomenon is provided by Peruvian novelist Mario Vargas Llosa: "One of our worst defects—our best fictions—is to believe that our miseries have been imposed on us from abroad, that others have always had the responsibility for our problems, for instance, the Conquistadores."[4] That such feelings are irrational only facilitates their manipulation by revolutionary professionals but the manipulators could also be the most intelligent among anti–revolutionaries. It is thus natural that radicals on both sides of the political spectrum use anti–Americanism for their purposes—from Roberto D'Aubuisson and Pinochet to the Sandinistas. The fact that the former accused the Carter administration of being "communist" and the latter attacked Ronald Reagan for being "anti–revolutionary" only demonstrates the protean character of anti–Americanism in Latin America.

The ability of revolutionaries to establish viable fronts and coalitions with non–Leninist groups and organizations does not lie exclusively with the manipulation of anti–Americanism. Further impetus is provided by the very personalism that has dominated Latin political culture ever since the times of Pizarro and Cortés, an Iberian import with long–lasting consequences. Whether called *caudillismo* or personalism, the cult of the ruler dominates even democratic countries south of the Rio Grande. Whether institutionalized as a "six year–monarchy" as in Mexico, or de facto life–presidency as in Cuba or Paraguay, the role of the caudillo has changed little since the time of Bolívar. The reverse is that opposition to the caudillo, that is, traditional opposition, becomes so obsessed with the person in power as to neglect all other implications of the caudillo's possible fall. This is precisely what happened in Nicaragua, where the anti–Somoza opposition never managed to be more than strictly negative in its approach—with the exception of the Sandinistas themselves, the only ones with a clear program of government for the post–Somoza era. The same situation may now occur in Chile, where the opposition, from the traditional Right and Christian Democrats to the more moderate Socialists, seem to be so obsessed with the person of Augusto Pinochet that they may be repeating the errors made by the Cruzes, the Robelos, and the Pastoras of Nicaragua: form a coalition with the Communists and the MIR without realizing that the latter have the same advantage over them that the FSLN had over Nicaragua's "bourgeois" opposition in 1978–79—tight organization, a clear program, external ties and resources, and manipulative skill.

What makes Latin America radically different from previous areas of Marxist–Leninist activities is precisely the strong personal color of even the revolutionary elites. No matter how much Castro may be controlled by Moscow—and following chapters in this book make it clear that he is controlled to a very decisive extent—it is impossible to confuse Fidel with the faceless apparatchiks ruling Eastern Europe since 1945, with Honnecker, Husak, Kadar, Jaruzelski, or even with Asian communist rulers like Ho Chi Minh or Le Duan, even Kim Il Sung, all remote figures, almost abstract in their exercise of absolute power.

The persistence of caudillismo even in communist Cuba, or in the almost communist Chile of Salvador Allende, makes Nicaragua's FSLN seem odd in comparison. Moreover, as Antonio Ybarra–Rojas points out in this volume, even the historic founder of the FSLN, Carlos Fonseca Amador, never enjoyed the unquestioned authority over his fellow Sandinistas that Castro wielded within the "July 26 Movement," and Fidel had quite strong comrades, not least among them Guevara himself, Cienfuegos, and Matos. When he was "expelled" by a minority faction under the Ortega brothers, Fonseca literally died in the solitude of the Zinica mountains. Unlike Cuba, the apparatchiks had won in Nicaragua even before power was within reach, a point well made by Ybarra–Rojas, and one that may explain the "East European" flavor of Managua today as well as the relative weakness of Tomás Borge, sole survivor of the founding group of the FSLN. Colorful leaders were definitely not in vogue in Managua, judging by the colorless figure of Daniel Ortega and his very powerful brother, Humberto. Whether this peculiar character of the Nicaraguan leadership explains the rapid (compared to Cuba) alignment of Managua with the Soviet bloc, or whether it is the result of an alignment prior to 1977 (at the latest) is a question that will probably remain unanswered. What is Latin American is the nature of the FSLN *nomenklatura* today. Nowhere is the elitist background and self–limited origin of the revolutionary leadership in Latin America clearer than in the corridors of power in Managua. Obscure middle–class professional revolutionaries like the Ortegas and Borge share power with the rebellious scions of the aristocratic families of Granada and León, marry their daughters and adopt their claims to intellectual accomplishments as well as their taste for Gucci eyeglasses. At least the Sandinistas made public their "bourgeois" tastes after conquering power as self–appointed "representatives of the people." The Argentine Montoneros, or at least their supreme leader Mario Firmenich, made the passage from Kalashnikov to Gucci before and despite being unable to win.

At the end of this volume, Irving Louis Horowitz raises the perfectly legitimate question of the contributors' self–imposed preoccupation with the unrepresentativeness of the revolutionary elites in Latin America in relation to the society as a whole and points out the limitations of a psychological–sociological approach to the study of revolutionary elites in general. Those limitations are clear, but so is the fact that such an approach was seldom used. The problem, however, is that to say correctly that the reasons ethnic minorities are over–represented in revolutionary leadership circles are complex only serves to turn the focus of discussion once again to the complexities of sociopolitical causality, when the basic facts of the nature of revolutionary elites have been neglected or obfuscated for so long. Thus, the attention given by some chapters in this volume to the facts of the background of the revolutionary elites is justified by the absence of the topic in the literature. Once those facts are known, complex and complicated analyses of their significance will at least have the benefit of being based on concrete data rather than neglecting the question altogether or assuming the data. That a sociology and psychology of contemporary revolutionary elites is necessary and still not in sight appears evident to this author. Hence the hope that some of the chapters in this volume will provide the spark for a more complete treatment of the issue.

The following chapters make it clear that Latin American revolutionary elites are a peculiarly unrepresentative group, that anti-Americanism is one of that group's major beliefs, and that the issue of revolution in today's Latin America cannot be seriously examined outside the general set of issues related to the global role of the Soviet Union, the nature of contemporary world communism, and the role of the original interpretation of Leninism which was made in Cuba by an Argentine non–practicing doctor by the name of Ernesto "Che" Guevara. Once again, it is important to notice the seldom–mentioned fact that all those involved in the articulation of "Guevarism" were culturally and emotionally separated from the communist world, or at least from that part of it dominated by the Soviet Union. Guevara himself was an Argentine whose revolutionary experience was largely dominated by events in Guatemala in 1954, in Cuba in 1957–1959, in the Congo and Guinea–Bissau in the early 1960s, and in Bolivia at the time of his death in 1967—that is,

"Third World" events. Régis Debray, whose name appears on the formal articulation of the Guevarist doctrine, is a Frenchman whose practical experience was limited to Cuba and Bolivia, and "Rolando Morán", who played an essential role in providing Debray with his essential understanding of revolutionary warfare in Latin America, was a Guatemalan friend of Guevara with long experience in Argentina and Cuba in addition to his native land. If one adds to this combination the well–known inputs from Frantz Fannon, a Caribbean Negro intellectual involved in the Algerian war, Vo Nguyen Giap, and ultimately Mao, it becomes clear that "Guevarism" was a Third World interpretation of Leninism, owing even less to Marx than did Leninism itself. Based on the voluntarism of Spanish America, originating in the actions and thoughts of Pizarro as well as Simón Bolívar, "Guevarism" appealed to other areas of the Third World far more than did the stale, semi–European, semi–Asiatic, and heavily bureaucratized ideological banalities originating in Moscow. The Latin American communist parties, as Tismaneanu points out in this volume, were natural followers of Moscow, largely because their leaders and few members were themselves living in a bureaucratic frame of mind (in El Salvador the PCES was known during the 1960s as the "caviar and vodka set"); they were therefore largely irrelevant and often dangerous to the cause of revolution. Indeed, one may wonder if Roque Dalton, often mentioned as a legitimate martyr of the Salvadoran revolutionary cause, was not the archetypical Latin American communist. The scion of a rich family, well–educated, well–connected enough to romance Andréy Gromyko's daughter, he was accused (by fellow revolutionaries) of being an agent of the KGB and of the Cuban intelligence, and murdered by his comrades. Dalton has spent years in Prague and at the *World Marxist Review* and it was for that reason despised by "true" revolutionaries, who saw themselves following in the steps of Bolívar. Once dead, however, Dalton has become a fashionable martyr for those who murdered him.

It is revealing that Bolívar, the elitist ruler and maker of revolution, is accepted by Latin American Leninists as a legitimate model, the wealthy and contemptuous of the "castas" (half–breeds, illiterate followers) Creole aristocrat from Caracas being recognized as the natural predecessor of the equally elitist, urban aristocrats or well–off scions of bourgeois families now ruling Nicaragua and Cuba, or of Free Mason Allende.

It is an example of Soviet flexibility and ideological pragmatism that, at least since Cuba has proved its commitment to Soviet global goals by having its people killed in Angola, Ethiopia, and Mozambique, Moscow has practically left the management of Latin American revolutionary groups in Havana's charge and has raised no questions since the collapse of Allende and the implicit defeat of the Soviet line of electoral attempts and coalitions for the sake of coalition. On the other hand, the lessons of Guatemala in the late

1960s, of Guevara's death in Bolivia itself, and of the collapse of the Tupamaros, Montoneros, and the Argentine ERP have taught Havana the virtues of building broad "united fronts" and the risks of relying on all–out violence à la "Che." In other words, since 1975 the tactics, strategies, and theories of Havana and Moscow have converged, with Castro being the major but constrained winner. Some typical pro–Soviet communist parties have taken the road of violence, and many "Castroite" groups—at least those that have survived their belief in Che's tactics—have followed the Sandinistas' "broad front" tactics. Thus, as Ernst Halperin makes clear, while Guevarism is dead, the deep impulses that made it possible, strong, and influential survive. On the other hand, Stalinism, as the institutional face of Leninism, (Ybarra–Rojas's definition) has penetrated the hearts of the formerly "idealistic" and romantic revolutionaries of Latin America, sometimes without their noticing it, and has definitely marked the Nicaraguan revolution. Altogether, these developments demonstrate the vitality, the adaptability, and, therefore, the dangerous nature of the Latin American revolutionary phenomenon in contemporary times. It is a dangerous phenomenon for Latin American would–be democrats and nationalists, and it is deadly for U.S. interests as well. For these reasons, if for no others, this volume hopes to raise the awareness of those involved in both policy making and in the serious study of the future of the many and complex societies lying south of the Rio Grande.

Notes

1. Karl Kautsky, quoted in Michael Lowy, *The Marxism of Che Guevara* (New York: Monthly Review Press, 1973), p. 19.
2. See Michael Radu, *Origins of the Nicaraguan Insurgencies, 1979–1985*, ORBIS, Winter 1986, pp. 821–840.
3. Paul H. Lewis, *Socialism, Liberalism, and Dictatorship in Paraguay*, (New York: The Hoover Institution, Praeger, 1982), pp. 128–129.
4. Mario Vargas Llosa, "Latin America: Fiction and Reality," Conference lecture delivered at Georgetown University, Washington, D.C., May 16, 1986.

PART I
PATTERNS OF REVOLUTION

2

Revolutionary Warfare

William Ratliff

For the past quarter century Latin America has been a hothouse for guerrilla movements. Dozens have been planted, one or more in almost every country in the region, to be tended by hundreds of revolutionary gardeners. Most have failed to prepare the soil, and the plants have withered and died, sometimes rooted out by opposing political and military strains. But a few of these revolutionary gardeners, with green thumbs of their own and helpful friends abroad, have raised plants that have smothered out everything around them in their countries and then have shot out runners into neighboring lands.

Here we will look at some of these guerrilla movements, to demonstrate their variety and suggest why so many have died and only a few have thrived. The focus is on guerrilla movements in five countries that reflect Castroite, Trotskyist, Maoist, and Cuban/Soviet influences: the Castroite National Liberation Army (ELN) in Bolivia, the Trotskyist–Castroite People's Revolutionary Army (ERP) in Argentina, the Castroite Movement of the Revolutionary Left (MIR) in Chile, the Maoist Shining Path in Peru, and the Cuban–Soviet influenced Sandinistas in Nicaragua. But the discussion also will touch in some detail on the deep Cuban involvement in the region, with reference beyond the Bolivian adventure with Che Guevara; on the failures and successes of movements with ties to pro–Soviet communist parties and to the Soviet Union itself; on other influential guerrilla strains, such as the urban guerrilla National Liberation Movement (MLN, Tupamaros) in Uruguay.

Cuba and Its "Vietnam War" in Latin America

Guerrilla movements have been a feature of Latin American life since before the area became Latin America. And some guerrilla and broader military struggles have long had revolutionary objectives. What is more, since the early nineteenth century there has been a strong precedent for international involvement in the national revolutions of the region. It was no coincidence that a large portrait of Simón Bolívar was prominently displayed at the Latin American Solidarity Organization (OLAS) conference in Havana in August

1967, for example, for Bolívar had carried revolution against Spain from one country to another during the first third of the nineteenth century. But the concept of continental revolution with international support did not become a major issue again until after the overthrow of Fulgencio Batista in Cuba in January 1959. The new Cuban leader, Fidel Castro, made it his business to advocate and promote a continental revolution against "United States imperialism", which he charged had replaced the despotism of Spain. Castro's determination to confront the United States was not the result of U.S. opposition to his government during the 1959–1961 period, as many have claimed. It had, rather, been his objective long before he seized power. In 1958, while he was still fighting Batista and proclaiming the virtues of Western–style democracy, Castro wrote a confidant about his true destiny as the bane of the United States: "When this war is over, a much wider and bigger war will begin for me; the war I am going to launch against them [the United States]. I am saying to myself that is my true destiny."[1] Although Castro supported some efforts to "liberate" individual Latin American countries from his first months in power, his major support for revolution abroad began in the mid–1960s and reached its peak in 1967. That year brought three important events, with widespread and long–term ramifications that will be examined in this chapter:

- Publication of Régis Debray's "Revolution in the Revolution?"—a revolutionary tract that purported to be a summation of the lessons of the Cuban Revolution against Batista, published in Havana in January 1967 by the government–backed Casa de las Americas. It was in fact a gross oversimplification of the Cuban experience which eliminated the critical aspect of widespread domestic and international support for the revolutionary movement.
- The OLAS Conference, attended by many of the most radical guerrilla fighters and others from around the continent, which called for revolutionary warfare throughout the hemisphere.
- Che Guevara's effort to make a "Vietnam" out of Latin America, with its center in Bolivia.

The essence of the Castroite line pushed throughout the continent was that a small group of military fighters, the *foco*, could begin struggles around the continent and by their actions draw ever–wider support leading to the eventual downfall of the hemisphere's governments. The critical breaks with Marxist–Leninist tradition were the beliefs (1) that the vanguard of the revolutionary struggle need not be the country's communist party—indeed, in most countries it *could not* be the communist parties since they had become part of the establishment—and (2) that the true Marxist revolutionary was often made during the struggle. One critical result of this Castroite line was the scornful rejection—always in practical terms and sometimes in theoretical terms as well—of the general need for the kind of broad popular support that brought victory to the Cuban Revolution against Batista.[2]

Castro supported revolutionary movements in Latin America in many ways during this period, but his great effort to launch the continental revolution, the supreme example of misguided Castroism in practice, occurred in Bolivia.

A "Vietnam War" Centered in Bolivia

The Bolivian undertaking was turned over to Che Guevara, a native of Argentina who had a special interest in spreading revolution to the South American continent. He and his aides founded the Bolivian National Liberation Army–ELN, a curious misnomer for the band of international revolutionaries not under Bolivian control which had the unshaken objective of igniting a Vietnam War in all the Americas from a center in Bolivia. Never had Castroite expectations been higher; never was the outcome more disastrous.

At the height of their revolutionary fervor in the mid–1960s, Castro and Guevara, the latter recently returned from Africa, decided to make Bolivia the center of the "Vietnam" they sought to launch in the Americas to "liberate" the Latin American people from the "U.S. imperialists" and their regional henchmen. Guevara elaborated the overall strategy in his "Message to the Peoples of the World," released in Havana on April 23, 1967, a month to the day after his first military encounter at the head of the ELN in Bolivia.

> Our every action is a battle cry against imperialism, and a call for the people's unity against the great enemy of mankind, the United States of America . . . What a luminous, near future would be visible to us if two, three or many Vietnams flourished throughout the world with their share of death and their immense tragedies, their everyday heroism and their repeated blows against imperialism obliging it to disperse its forces under the attack and the increasing hatred of all the peoples of the earth![3]

Guevara's obsession with trying to create one of those "Vietnams" in America was reflected in the words of Pombo, a Cuban aide in Bolivia, who wrote in his diary: "Bolivia will sacrifice itself so that conditions [for revolution] can be created in neighboring countries. We have to make another Vietnam out of America, with its center in Bolivia". The Cuban–supported plan to launch a continental war was widely realized in revolutionary circles, although the choice of Bolivia as a staging area was not known for sure until Guevara's adventure had begun.[4]

To understand why Guevara made some of the fateful decisions he did before and during his time in Bolivia, it is essential to keep these continental objectives in mind. Ironically, Guevara's insistence on his personal leadership of the guerrilla war, which of course raised the level of international support for the campaign, also precluded any significant backing for the ELN from the pro–Soviet or pro–Chinese communists in Bolivia. These alienated groups, among others, could have supplied fighters to the ELN and given a national cast to the movement. But during much of the time, the majority of ELN members were Cubans, and many were from other countries; the Cubans always dominated the leading positions. Guevara's army at its peak consisted of fewer than fifty fighters, only slightly more than half of them Bolivians.[5] Not one Bolivian peasant ever joined the ELN, despite guerrilla efforts to woo some of them and frequent comments in published statements and diaries that mass support was essential for revolutionary victory.

Guevara had established contacts with several Communist Party of Bolivia (PCB) members before the formal split into pro–Soviet and pro–Chinese groups in 1965, and some, in Castro's own words, "worked with him on diverse tasks for several years". Castro's talks with Mario Monje, who became the leader of the pro–Soviet PCB, seem to have begun in January 1966 at the Tricontinental Conference in Havana. Monje visited Guevara at his camp in Nancahuazu on December 31, 1966. He believed that Bolivians—the PCB under his leadership—should be in charge of the struggle, but Guevara told him, "I was to be military chief and I would not accept any ambiguities on this matter". In his "Introduction" to the Cuban edition of Guevara's diary, Castro charged that Monje had entered into "shameful, ridiculous and unmerited claims to power". After the meeting in Nancahuazu, the PCB provided no support for, and in some ways obstructed, Guevara's effort.[6]

Castro also launched a bitter criticism of Oscar Zamora, the leader of Bolivia's pro–Chinese Communists, "Who had once promised to work with Che on the organization of an armed guerrilla fight in Bolivia" but then "withdrew his commitments and cowardly folded his arms when the hour for action arrived". Zamora responded in a long open letter to Castro reminding the Cuban leader that though Guevara had criticized many Bolivians in his diary, he had never criticized him. Zamora went on to say that at the end of 1964 he went to Cuba to tell Guevara that he and some other Bolivians had decided to set up a revolutionary vanguard separate from the PCB: the PCB Marxist–Leninist (PCB–ML). Zamora claimed that Guevara agreed to support him, but after Castro "sold out" to the pro–Soviet Communists at a Havana conference in November 1964, all Cuban contacts with the PCB–ML were terminated. Castro is correct, however, that the PCB–ML gave Guevara no help, though a dissident Maoist, Moises Guevara (no relation to Che), and several of his followers, did join the ELN.[7]

Guevara and Castro planned to launch a revolution on a continental scale from the southern cone for several years before they settled on starting in Bolivia. Guevara evidently visited the country in disguise for a short time at the beginning of 1966 and then sent several advance agents and guerrillas to prepare for his arrival at the end of the year. Among those arriving in advance were Haydée Tamara Bunke Bider (who became known as "Tania the Guerrilla") and Pombo.[8]

Guevara himself arrived at the beginning of November. The discussion with Monje came in December, and during early 1967 the guerrillas put their camp in shape, brought in stocks, and took a long and not very successful training march through the region.

Early in March, while the ELN was on its training trek, the Bolivian military raided the Nancahuazu camp, having already been alerted to its existence by guerrilla defectors, suspicious neighbors, and a mistake (or sabotage) by Tania, who turned out to be working for the Soviet KGB, which did not approve of Guevara's adventure, as well as for Cuban intelligence. One of the guerrilla defectors, and photographs and other materials found in the guerrilla camp, confirmed Guevara's presence as leader of the guerrilla band, which Guevara formally named the ELN on March 27, when it consisted of thirty–eight fighting men.

Although Guevara had stressed the importance of careful planning for the guerrilla war and expected the insurrectional stage to take up to ten years, he foolishly took the first opportunity to attack government forces. This battle came on March 23, when the government lost eight men and Guevara invited immediate government retaliation. The second battle occurred on April 10, when the government suffered nineteen casualties. On April 17 the ELN accidentally split into two sections, one led by Guevara and one by Joaquín. The two never got together again, and Joaquín's group was wiped out by government troops on August 31. Encounters with government troops continued and on July 31 Guevara lost his tape recorder, which had been used to decode messages sent by radio from Havana, thus becoming isolated from Cuba.

The next major battle for Guevara's group occurred at La Higuera on September 26, with several guerrilla fatalities. The final battle occurred on October 8 at Quebrada del Yuro, when six guerrillas were killed. Guevara was captured and executed on October 9. Three Cubans and three Bolivians escaped, though one of the Bolivians was killed soon after.

Shortly after Guevara's death, one of the Bolivian survivors, Inti Peredo, describing himself as the "accidental heir to the last and most valuable teachings of the greatest revolutionary genius of Latin America", proclaimed the continuation of the ELN. The group operated under Peredo, who repeated Guevara's call for a new Vietnam in Latin America. Peredo led the ELN until his death but, though others followed, the group never regained its status in the world of Latin American revolutions. In 1974 the ELN became one of four members of the new Revolutionary Coordinating Committee (JCR).[9]

Trotskyism and Castroism in Argentina

One of the most widely reported guerrilla organizations in Latin American history was the Argentina People's Revolutionary Army (ERP). Its policies by the end of the 1960s had been strongly influenced by Guevara's adventure in Bolivia and by the Uruguayan Tupamaros, perhaps the most successful urban guerrilla group in Latin American history, at least during the late–1960s and early–1970s. But in the beginning the ERP also had close ties to international Trotskyism.

The followers of Leon Trotsky have had a strange history in Latin America. Lenin's former rival and partner had moved to Mexico after Stalin took power in the Soviet Union. He lived there until 1940, when he was assassinated by one of Stalin's henchmen. Trotskyist parties and organizations have been found in many Latin American countries, sometimes representing three factions of the Fourth International, but they have played a significant role in only two countries: in Bolivia off and on since the 1940s, and in Argentina from the late 1960s to the mid–1970s.

The ERP was one of the most effective guerrilla groups in Latin American history, if we measure effectiveness in terms of destructiveness. Between 1969 and 1976 it was a major revolutionary force, with fighters in urban and rural areas, and a primary cause of the Argentine military's "dirty war" of the mid–1970s, the repercussions of which were still shaking Argentina a decade later.

And yet the ERP was not really Trotskyist in any ideological sense during its period of greatest power. Formed as a full–fledged member of the United Secretariat of the Fourth International, it never worked effectively toward the mass proletarian base Trotsky thought was essential. Ironically, it was from the beginning above all a Castroite organization. It was Castroite because the United Secretariat, in its buoyant enthusiasm for revolution in Latin America in the late 1960s, had enthusiastically endorsed the impatient ultraleftist guerrillaism Castro had promoted since his seizure of power—as in the OLAS conference and Guevara's adventure in Bolivia. In 1972 the main ERP leaders told the Chilean Castroite journal *Punto Final* (August 1972) that the organization, Marxist–Leninist in ideology, was inspired by Mao Zedong, Ho Chi Minh, and Che Guevara, among others, in addition to Trotsky.[10]

The roots of the ERP can be traced back to the early 1960s, when a guerrilla–oriented faction emerged within the Trotskyist Palabra Obrera (PO) headed by Nahuel Moreno. In 1964 the PO merged with the Frente Revolucionario Indoamericanista Popular, headed by Mario Roberto Santucho, to form the Revolutionary Workers Party (Partido Revolucionario de los Trabajadores, PRT), a member of the United Secretariat faction of the Fourth International.

During 1967 the United Secretariat threw itself behind what it saw as an all–out Cuban effort to develop guerrilla warfare in Latin America. "Che's guerrilla struggle would be the beginning of this continental civil war," Moreno recalled several years later, a war that would be "similar to the one on the Indochinese peninsula". Moreno concluded that in that continental civil war "we had to fight with and under the 'military, not political, discipline' of the Cubans and OLAS". Support for continental and even Argentine Castroism disappeared among Moreno's followers in the PRT after Guevara was killed and Cuba withdrew its active support for continental warfare.[11]

But in 1968, the year before the watershed 1969 Congress of the United Secretariat, the PRT split into two sections, one headed by Santucho, who was still an ardent Castroite. They were the PRT (*Combatiente*), the majority under Santucho, which remained the Argentine branch of the United Secretariat, and the PRT (*Verdad*), the minority under Moreno, classified as a sympathizing organization of the Fourth International.

The Santucho faction had its tactics and strategy endorsed by the United Secretariat at its turbulent 1969 Congress. In fact, in its "Resolution on Latin America", the congress adopted the full–fledged Castroite line discussed above.[12]

In August 1970 the PRT held a congress and emerged with the slogan "Ready for the Battle, All for War". The congress reaffirmed the PRT belief in mass work through agitation, revolutionary propaganda, and education in armed resistance. But the congress resolution further declared: "The only justification for recognition [of the majority PRT] as the unquestionable vanguard is our role in combat". In practical terms, the most important result of the congress was the formation of the ERP, which defined a mass organization as one seeking to develop "revolutionary civil war" against "the dictatorship and imperialism".

For a while the ERP promoted a Robin Hood image, much as the Uruguayan Tupamaros had done at first. In 1971 the ERP kidnapped Stanley Sylvester, manager of the Swift meatpacking plant in Rosario, and released him only when Swift distributed $57,000 worth of food and other supplies in Argentine slums.

But ERP activities soon became largely terrorist. In particular, armed robberies and assassinations, in addition to kidnappings for ransom, were carried out by small bands of fighters. Santucho always argued that ERP actions were "armed propaganda", in line with the 1969 resolution, and intended to cultivate mass support. In the *Punto Final* interview, after the kidnapping and murder of Oberdan Sallustro, director of Fiat Argentina, Santucho said that ERP military actions were "basically harassment". He gave examples of what he meant: "Such an operation would be to surround a police station with members of the repressive forces inside, offer them a chance to surrender, and if they refuse, open fire on them, try to confiscate their arsenal, and disperse rapidly. It would also include ambushing repressive patrols". In 1972 ERP activities were largely urban and Santucho looked with enthusiasm to the "qualitative step forward in the development of revolutionary civil war" when the ERP would launch the rural guerrilla war, which actually came during 1974.[13]

Early ERP activities were centered in Rosario and Córdoba, and later spread to Buenos Aires, Tucumán, and many other parts of the country. Military estimates placed the total number of ERP "effectives" at their peak strength in late 1974 early 1975 at one thousand or less, with perhaps up to four hundred in Tucumán. ERP relations with the armed Peronists, most importantly the Montoneros, improved somewhat after Peron's return to power but were off and on at best. ERP and Montonero guerrilla activities became so disruptive by 1975 that the government took law enforcement out of the hands of the inefficient police forces and turned it over to the army. A major army counterinsurgency program during much of 1975 and early 1976 virtually obliterated the ERP.

Notable among later ERP activities was the dramatic jail break from the Rawson Prison in Patagonia in mid–August 1972, which ended in the escape to Chile of Santucho and five other guerrilla leaders, but resulted in the death of eleven ERP members and others in the "Trelew massacre"; an attack on two Ford Motor Company officials, one of whom died from wounds received, in May 1973; the kidnapping and ransom (for $3 million) of John Thompson, director of Firestone operations in Argentina, in June 1973; the assassination of John Albert Swint, director of a Ford subsidiary, in November 1973; and the kidnapping and ransom (for $14.2 million) of Victor Samuelson, manager of Esso Argentina, in December 1973. The Samuelson kidnapping brought the ERP's ransom earnings for 1973 actions to more than $30 million and stacked a bank account that, even after the ERP had ceased to operate in Argentina, helped fund the international Revolutionary Coordinating Committee and guerrilla operations in other countries.

Other ERP urban activities included the takeover of an army medical headquarters in a five–hour gun battle in September 1973, an attack on an armored cavalry garrison in January 1974; and attacks on a Córdoba arms factory and the Catamarca paratroop garrison in August 1974. All were spectacular operations and took many guerrilla and other lives. A large–scale attack by several hundred guerrillas on a military base and other targets in the Buenos Aires region on December 23–24 left more than one hundred guerrillas dead, and dozens of civilians died when the guerrillas took refuge in a shantytown.[14]

In 1974 the ERP turned much of its attention to building a rural army in the northeastern province of Tucumán, which ERP leaders called the "Cuba of Argentina". Earlier, Santucho had been very critical of the "caricature of the

Cuban experience'' conveyed by the "focoist" theory expounded by Castro, Guevara, and Régis Debray around 1967.[15] But by 1974, as ERP activities became increasingly terrorist and farther from attracting mass support, ERP policies had more and more in common with the focoist line.[16]

Still, a recognition of some of the extremes of "focoism" remained. This was evident at the founding of the Revolutionary Coordinating Committee in February 1974. The ERP was thriving at the time, with tens of millions of dollars gained from kidnapping in its bank accounts, while the other three participating guerrilla groups have been decimated: the Uruguayan Tupamaros, the Chilean MIR, and the Bolivian ELN. The founding document of the JCR is in some ways more sophisticated and realistic than the raw Castroism of the late 1960s, though it too is grossly exaggerated, simplistic, demagogic, and warmongering.[17]

Castroism Subverts a Revolution: Chile

The most important Castroite movement in Chile, and one of the most interesting and influential Castroite movements in Latin American history, was the Movement of the Revolutionary Left between its founding in 1965 and the collapse of Chilean democracy in late 1973. During those years the MIR developed one of the most extensive and varied programs ever created by a guerrilla–oriented organization. Its actions had a strong Castroite quality and throughout that period they were opposed by the country's strong pro–Soviet Communist Party.

The MIR never seriously challenged the government of Christian Democrat Eduardo Frei (November 1964 to November 1970), but ironically it was one of the main reasons for the overthrow of Salvador Allende's Marxist Popular Unity government in September 1973. The MIR was founded by leftists of socialist, Trotskyist, and other inclinations. Its line became radicalized under the inspiration of the guerrilla warfare espoused at the OLAS conference in Havana in 1967 and it began advocating and pursuing the armed road to power. Several of the older founders resigned in protest, and the group fell entirely into the hands of the OLAS Castroites, based mainly at the University of Concepción. In early 1969 the group went underground; it took over buildings at the University of Concepción and carried out armed robberies and other actions that led to many arrests of MIR militants. The party condemned the "electoral circus" (which subsequently resulted in the election of Allende) and proclaimed: "We have decided to follow the example of Lenin, Fidel, and Che. We are going to proclaim the armed revolution". MIR leader Miguel Enriquez claimed that the group's "revolutionary expropriations" should not be confused with robberies by common criminals, because only "exploiters" were ever "expropriated".[18] MIR policy put it at odds with the

Communist Party, much of the equally strong but factionalized Socialist Party, and other sectors of the left which constituted the Popular Unity coalition. During 1970, the year Allende was elected president at the head of the Popular Unity ticket, the MIR continued its bank robberies, and led peasants, workers, Indians, and the unemployed in seizures of public and private lands.[19]

After Allende's inauguration in November 1970, Miristas imprisoned during the Frei period were released. Rivalry with the Communist Youth led to a battle that left one Mirista dead. For a short time after that, the MIR threw its grudging support to the president—and provided him with his bodyguard. But the MIR always believed it was an illusion to think the socialist revolution could be carried out within the confines of "bourgeois democracy", even with an Allende in the president's chair.

By mid–1971 the MIR was again charging that the revolution had stalled, and it again found itself working at cross–purposes with the Communists and the more moderate wing of the socialists. From then until the president's fall, the MIR, despite its small size, played an important role on and beyond the left–most fringes of the government.

Relations with Allende and his government deteriorated rapidly in 1972, and by the end of that year, while the president and the Communists were calling for "consolidation" of revolutionary gains, the MIR demanded pushing ahead without compromise. In June 1973 the MIR paper *El Rebelde* charged that the "revisionist" Popular Unity had "hit bottom," and it called for reliance on "power to the people" and for the formation of "dual power," a base of "people's power", in contradistinction to Allende's government.

From its base of strength in the universities, particularly Concepción, the MIR developed activities on three fronts: among the Mapuche Indians and peasants, particularly in the South, mainly through the Revolutionary Peasant Movement (MCR); among workers through the Revolutionary Workers Movement (MTR); and among the unemployed through the Movement of the Revolutionary Poor (MPR).

The main MIR guerrilla–type activities in the outskirts of cities, particularly Santiago, consisted of forming armed slum encampments (*campamentos*), run under strict discipline, which were out–of–bounds for the national police or military. Commando squads were sent out from these encampments to organize many of the thousands of land seizures (*tomas*) the MCR led in the countryside among Indians and peasants. Though it is impossible to know exactly how many MCR members there were, Robert Moss estimates about 1,200 in the Cautín province alone at the beginning of 1972. Key leaders of the *tomas* included "Comandante Nelson" in Nuble and "Comandante Pepe," who is thought to have controlled seventeen estates covering 350,000 hectares of the finest timber country around Lake Panguipulli by the beginning of 1972. These land seizures, carried out in violation of Allende land reform policy, created widespread unrest in the countryside. The Communist Party condemned them as ''ultraleftist'' and charged that they played into the hands of the Popular Unity's enemies, which they did. The MIR played a major role in establishing the extremist–controlled industrial belts (*cordones industriales*), which mobilized many of the workers in the cities, particularly Santiago, in the nation's leading industries and were expected to provide much of the armed muscle for ''dual power'' of the real Chilean revolution.

As time went on, the activities of the MIR and its allies brought increasing levels of confrontation with the Allende government and presented an increasingly open threat to what the Marxists–Leninists called the ''bourgeois'' and ''reactionary'' sectors of society. The competing policies and activities of the Left created enormous and uncontrollable political, economic, constitutional, and international contradictions with which Allende and his Popular Unity government could not cope. In time the Popular Unity's inability to govern the country united the opposition of the Center and the Right and precipitated the military overthrow of Allende in September 1973 and the formation of the Pinochet government which followed.[20] The MIR was decimated after the military coup, but it retained a core structure mainly outside the country. By the mid–1980s the Communist Party had thrown its continuing organization and greater weight behind armed struggle against the military government, and the potential effectiveness of the MIR in future revolutionary activities was uncertain.

The Shining Path in Peru

One of the most unusual guerrilla organizations in Latin American history is the Shining Path in Peru. Maoist parties have existed in the hemisphere since the early 1960s, but no Maoist guerrilla force has ever caused nearly as much unrest and destruction as this originally provincial group from the Andes.

The Peruvian Communist Party split into pro–Soviet and pro–Chinese factions in 1964, and the Maoist sector itself split in the years that followed. For many years the most vocal Maoists were in the universities, though they demonstrated little knowledge of Mao—or of Marxism–Leninism, for that matter. Like most student Maoists around the world, for them, the pro–Chinese appellation seemed to be a political–ideological tag which meant they considered themselves more revolutionary than anyone else.

The pro–Chinese parties generally criticized pro–Soviet groups for restricting their activities to those that fell within the realm of ''bourgeois legality,'' for refusing to let party members train for guerrilla warfare, and for turning leadership of the revolutionary united front over to "bourgeois nationalists". At the same time, the Maoists blasted the pro–Cuban groups, which, they said, derived from adventurist, romantic, individualistic, ultraleftist, and anti–Marxist origins, were led by small nonproletarian cliques, took on all enemies at once, and rejected proletarian party leadership. In practice few Maoists made any serious effort to follow the Maoist line of the time: to develop rural base areas and build the protracted, peasant–based war. Among Latin American Marxists–Leninists who claimed any indebtedness to Mao, only Marco Antonio Yon Sosa, in Guatemala during the mid–1960s, had demonstrated any practical grasp of Mao's support of rural base areas.[20]

But the Shining Path—the Sendero Luminoso—was different. It can be traced back to the early 1960s in the National University of San Cristóbal de Huamanga in Ayacucho, with its many students of peasant Indian background. Philosophy professor Abimael Guzmán Reynoso and his followers—some fifty students and faculty by 1964—became the Huamanga command of the National Liberation Front (Frente de Liberación Nacional, FLN). In 1965 the FLN split because of the Castroite style of guerrilla leaders Luis de la Puente Uceda and Héctor Bejar. Guzmán and his Huamanga followers became part of the Maoist Peruvian Communist Party—Red Flag—though they were expelled between 1968 and 1970 and adopted the name "PCP por el Sendero Luminoso de José Carlos Mariátegui" (Peruvian Communist Party in the Shining Path of Mariátegui), alluding to José Carlos Mariátegui, who founded the first communist party in Peru in 1928.[22]

Sendero Luminoso spent the year prior to 1980 developing a strong rural base in Ayacucho, an area long neglected by the government. Its strength seems to have come in part because it focused specifically on the Indian communities, both through university programs and outside activities. According to Woy–Hazleton, ''it created liberated zones in which it imposed its antitechnological, subsistence peasant model by brutal methods, destroying farm equipment, crops, closing regional markets, and killing informers and reluctant supporters''. These tactics, and the open warfare launched in 1980, set it not only against the government but also against Peru's large legal and parliamentary Left.

More than six thousand lives were lost in the Shining Path insurgency between 1980 and 1985. Many were people killed by the guerrillas, and many were guerrillas killed by the government, but many were also peasants caught between the warring camps.[23]

Although the level of Sendero activity ebbs and flows, the following can be taken as typical of the group's activities: bombing of the oil pipeline between the Amazon and the Pacific, destruction of bridges linking the central highlands to Lima, and bombing of industry and burning of storehouses. Sendero caused $15 million worth of losses in electricity in 1984 alone. Sendero guerrillas often attack military bases, patrols, and civilians, sometimes simultaneously in several parts of the country. Between 1980 and the end of 1984, sixty–four officials of all parties were killed, including ten mayors in 1984. By February 1986, nineteen provinces were under emergency decrees and, in response to twenty–six attacks in one week, a state of emergency had been declared in the capital of Lima.

Sendero seems to have no international ties; even its friendship with China was directed toward Mao Zedong rather than the present Chinese leadership. In fact, one of several embassies dynamited in Lima in February 1986 was that of the People's Republic of China. Nor does it seem to have significant domestic ties, either with the broadly–based United Left or with groups that search them out to join their guerrilla struggle. This last characteristic is altogether consistent with the Chinese practice of the mid–1960s which won Guzmán over. The Maoism propagated by Chinese leaders at that time was a dogmatic little recipe—as Venezuelan guerrilla Douglas Bravo described Debray's Castroite foco of almost the same period—which had only a superficial relationship to the rich Chinese revolutionary experience. Above all, like the foco, it often failed to recognize in practice, if not in theory, the need to cultivate all sorts of allies in the early stages of the struggle.[24]

Cuba, Nicaragua, and a Model of Revolution for the 1980s

Régis Debray called his influential little 1967 tract "Revolution in the Revolution?" His question was something like: Is it possible to break with (what he regarded as) the stale revolutionary stereotypes, the ineffective revolutionary formulas of the past, and just go out and, as it were, make the revolution? Hadn't Fidel repeatedly remarked that the hemisphere was "ripe for revolution" and said in his 1962 "Second Declaration of Havana" that "the duty of every revolutionary is to make revolution", a phrase that became the official slogan of the OLAS conference? So there you are. That, Debray told his readers, is what Fidel and Che had done. "Go thou", he said, "and do likewise".

Many tried, before and after the OLAS conference and Che's Bolivian adventure, but it did not work. Most who tried ended up dead, in jail, or endlessly tramping through the outback of countries around the hemisphere. In time, even Castro withdrew his support for them.

Of course it didn't work because it is *not* what Fidel and Che had done in Cuba, where a broad front of anti–Batista forces had over thrown the dictator. Instead, during the height of the "Castroism" period, Debray and Castro advocated a go–it–alone revolutionary elitism, with almost exclusive reliance on militarism. In practice, this denied the importance of cultivating cooperation with major sectors of the domestic population, with domestic political parties, or even with potential allies abroad—China, the Soviet bloc countries, the pro–Soviet or pro–Chinese or Trotskyist parties of Latin America. This was the most extreme and mindless Castroism, an instantly ossified dogma that cultivated ties only with the tiny ultraradical and unrepresentative groups in the hemisphere's countries.

As Douglas Bravo subsequently said, Debray's foco was "the tactic of the shortcut, the tactic of underestimating the organization of the party, of the front, of the working class, and of the peasants". What is more, it was "a distortion of what occurred in Cuba, a distortion that unquestionably resulted in defeats of great magnitude in Latin America, culminating in the destruction of the guerrilla nucleus in Bolivia and particularly in the death of Comandante Ernesto Guevara". Focoism, wrote revolutionary strategist Abraham Guillén, is "an insurrectional movement for piling up cadavers".[25]

It is not clear why Castro promoted these tiny, suicidal guerrilla movements in defiance of Cuban history as well as the policies of the Soviet Union and most pro–Soviet parties in the hemisphere. Did he really think the continent was ripe for revolution and that the masses would fall into line if the foco in the countryside would but show the way?[26] Certainly there was no historical evidence to support this foco interpretation of the Cuban experience. If he believed in it, why did he revise his views in the late 1960s? Because of the obvious defeats of foco movements—Guevara in Bolivia being only the most obvious example—or because his domestic economy was falling apart and he needed vastly increased support from the Soviet Union to pull through, support that could come only if Cuba fell into the Soviet line on foreign policy? Or was his support for those groups altogether cynical? Did he know the groups were insignificant, that they couldn't win, but conclude that their mere presence throughout the hemisphere would draw the attention of the United States from him in Cuba, that they would pose the threat of the "two, three, many Vietnams" Guevara had called for in his 1966 "Message to the Tricontinental" and dissipate U.S. power?

Whatever the reason or reasons, Castro did withdraw support for these factionalized groups in the late 1960s and early 1970s and for all practical purposes stopped promoting guerrilla warfare in most of the hemisphere's countries. And many Latin American revolutionaries, like Bravo, looked for other ways to make the revolution. Some turned to urban guerrilla warfare. The first widely read book on urban guerrilla warfare by a famous practitioner, *Minimanual of the Urban Guerrilla*, by Brazilian guerrilla Carlos Marighela, was even circulated by the Cuban government. During the late 1960s and early 1970s the urban guerrillas had their heyday with the Tupamaros in Uruguay, the ERP and Montoneros in Argentina, and the MIR in Chile. They collected money by robbing banks, kidnapping for ransom, and similar activities. All were crushed by military forces and their activities resulted in the imposition of severe military governments in Chile and Uruguay, upsetting longstanding democratic traditions. All these groups, in varying degrees, suffered from the problems of the Debray—Guevara focos elitism and militarism.[27] Others, in time, turned back toward the true example of the Cuban Revolution. This turn was a major factor in the victory of the Sandinist National Liberation Front (FSLN)—the Sandinistas;—in Nicaragua in July 1979.

The return to broad–front revolutionary policies came in the wake of other major developments, including the increasing isolationism that came upon the United States in the wake of the defeat in the Vietnam War and the Watergate scandal. These events, along with such other developments as the overthrow of Salvador Allende's government in Chile, all encouraged the Soviet Union, together with its close Cuban ally, to undertake a more aggressive international policy in the Third World. The first two major joint ventures occurred in Africa—in Angola and Ethiopia—and the next in Central America. When Cuba turned its eyes again to Nicaragua at the end of the 1970s, the Soviet Union was prepared to provide support for the Sandinista revolution, at first indirectly and subsequently directly as well. Carlos Fonseca Amador and other Nicaraguan Communists formed the Sandinista movement in 1961, long before Guevara went to Bolivia, under the inspiration of the Cuban Revolution. Ties were formed immediately with Castro and Guevara in Cuba and with other revolutionary leaders in Europe, Asia, and the Middle East. The Sandinistas passed through many years of insignificance, suffering several almost terminal military setbacks, and in the mid–1970s split into three competing factions.

One of these factions, the so–called "Terceristas", was under the intellectual leadership of Humberto Ortega, brother of Daniel Ortega, who became president of the country in a much disputed 1984 general election. This is what Ortega saw in 1977: the suicidal fiasco of the guerrilla foco; the debilitating impact of factionalism within the FSLN; the unmistakable groundswell of anti–Somoza sentiment in Nicaragua and a surge in the activities and popularity of moderate democratic forces in the country, which if allowed to continue would render Marxist–Leninist opposition to Somoza unnecessary; and a fundamental shift in Cuban and Soviet attitudes toward revolution in the Third World.

And so Ortega and the Terceristas came to the obvious conclusion that the Sandinistas should adopt a revolutionary strategy that would put all these lessons and elements to work for the FSLN. And they set out to form a broad alliance with virtually any individual or group in the country who opposed Somoza, overtly or covertly.

As Guillén had noted fifteen years earlier—and Mao had seen decades before that—this front would have to be built on a broad program of a nonsectarian type.[28] In practical terms, this meant taking such steps as:

1. Turning to a more practical—a less militantly and mindlessly ideological—approach to revolution.
2. Adopting the General Political Military Program of May 1977 which called for a broad anti–Somoza front, explained within the FSLN movement as a "tactical and temporary alliance", muting the noisy Marxist–Leninist rhetoric in favor of calls for support of a popular democratic revolution.
3. Formation of "The Twelve", a group of prominent Nicaraguans who gave the movement a strong democratic cast.
4. Recruitment of social democratic guerrilla leader Edén Pastora, in 1977, which not only greatly strengthened the military movement but also opened the door to extensive support from abroad, particularly from Venezuelan President Carlos Andrés Pérez.
5. Unity of the three factions in December 1978 as a result of strong pressure from Cuba stipulating that the Sandinistas had to get together if they wanted the extensive military aid they would need—and eventually got—from Cuba in the final months of the war.[29]

Thus the war against Somoza took place on many levels, particularly after the assassination of *La Prensa* editor Pedro Joaquín Chamorro in January 1978. A broad–based political front worked to galvanize anti–Somoza activity in Nicaragua and abroad. This meant wide–ranging cooperation among most sectors of the population in Nicaragua, and diplomatic pressure on Somoza from governments abroad, the most important being those of Venezuela, Panama, Costa Rica, Cuba, and the United States.

After victory in July, the Nicaraguan revolution became the "model" for revolution in Latin America and a similar broad–based political front intending to give legitimacy to a united front of guerrilla armies appeared in El Salvador. The model was explained by Manuel Pineiro, head of the Americas Department of the Cuban Communist Party, which is in charge of Cuban support for revolutionary movements in the Americas. Addressing delegates to a conference of communist parties in Havana in 1982, Pineiro said the Nicaraguan experience combines guerrilla warfare and a broad united front, "taking advantage of any, even the smallest opportunity of winning a mass ally, even though his ally is temporary, vacillating, unstable, unreliable and conditional". It reaffirms "the critical value of the unity of the vanguard as the nucleus providing cohesion and orientation to the anti–dictatorial, democratic, anti–imperialist and revolutionary forces as a whole".[30]

The Varieties of Latin American Guerrilla Tactics

The Latin American revolutionary hothouse has produced a remarkable variety of political and military tactics over the past twenty–five years. Groups have claimed inspiration from innumerable sources—from Bolívar to the Palestine Liberation Organization, but mainly from Marx, Lenin, Mao, Castro, Guevara, and a variety of national revolutionaries. Some tried to tie their group into a national or regional legacy with names, among them the Tupamaros, the Montoneros, the Sandinistas, while other took one of several standard guerrilla names used throughout the hemisphere, like the Movement of the Revolutionary Left or the National Liberation Army.

The most successful organizations—even if for only a period of time before ultimate defeat—have combined foreign inspiration, and foreign training and aid, with domestic resources. The vast majority of the groups either were taken in by dogmatic little recipes from abroad, which were pasted on a domestic situation without regard for local conditions, or just muddled along with no particular modus operandi whatsoever. It is no wonder they withered, were torn out by their shallow roots, or persisted indefinitely as sufferable nuisances.

Over the past quarter century, guerrilla struggles in Latin America have generally been guided by what the fighters themselves took to be some form of Marxism–Leninism, though what they said and how they acted would often have seemed ridiculous and juvenile in the extreme to either Marx or Lenin. They were generally led by middle–class elements, as Michael Radu shows elsewhere in this volume. And they tended to fall into several sometimes overlapping categories:

1. Varying forms of armed struggle by small revolutionary groups trying to seize power directly or, by their very radicalism, hoping to ignite a general conflagration that would propel them to power.
2. Combined armed and nonarmed struggle built on at–least–temporary unity of the radical and moderate left in pursuit of more moderate, short–term goals.
3. Armed conflict centered in the countryside.
4. Armed conflict centered in urban areas.

Specifically, some of the groups best representing different tactics have been:

1. *The Bolivian ELN.* The ELN, headed by Guevara, ignored most domestic conditions and forces in an effort to create a "Vietnam War" in the Americas, to sacrifice one country to create a continental war with its pri-

mary target the United States. Guevara planned to wage military struggles
in Bolivia and to draw in similarly oriented groups in other countries,
among them the ERP in his native Argentina, while waging political struggle around the world against the United States. The Bolivian experience
demonstrated the need to build the guerrilla's base of support prior to engaging the military forces of the country. Guevara, who had insisted on
the necessity for solid groundwork in his writings on guerrilla warfare,
demonstrated typical Castroite impatience in his premature attacks on the
Bolivian military. The defeat of the ELN can be traced to these factors,
among others: exclusivity, disregard of domestic conditions and peoples,
absence of good supply routes either within the country or abroad,
Castroite impatience, and emphasis on military at the expense of political
struggle.

2. *The Argentine ERP*. The ERP experience during the 1969–1976 period
   represented an effort to combine the Castroism and Trotskyism of the
   United Secretariat, the urban Castroism of the Uruguayan Tupamaros, and
   a rural foco Castroism in Tucumán, the latter buttressed temporarily by
   limited residual political support held over from activities of its parent
   party a decade earlier.[31] Whereas ERP leaders spoke of needing broad support, their early Robin Hood image was swamped in the later terrorist activities, as had happened to the Tupamaros. Once the military cracked
   down, the ERP was quickly decimated, in contrast to the Montoneros,
   who survived a bit longer, in part because they had a broader political
   base. The failure of the ERP and Montoneros to work together was a typical failing of groups following the arrogant supremacy line of 1967
   Castroism.

   The formation of the Revolutionary Coordinating Committee in 1974, under the direct leadership of the ERP, marked the first major effort by Latin
   American guerrilla groups to form an international alliance largely independent of Cuba, though by then three of the four groups had been crushed
   at home and existed primarily abroad. The committee's founding document demonstrated some realization of the fatal mistakes of the Castroite
   road but still lacked a grasp of historical realities or sophisticated revolutionary and tactics.

3. *Peruvian Shining Path*. The Shining Path, the only somewhat legitimately
   Maoist organization in the Americas, has developed a rural guerrilla war
   strengthened by close ties to certain Indian communities, at first in an isolated province. But it is weakened by its at times almost "Pol Potian"
   mistreatment of natives and its evident inability to broaden its base to include other groups in other provinces. By the mid–1980s it had expanded
   its activities to urban areas and its area of operations to provinces around
   the country.

4. *The Chilean MIR*. The MIR had an unusually broad scope of contacts
   among peasants, including Indians and others, the unemployed and home-

less, a few workers, and some intellectuals, including many radical Socialists. However, despite an effort to develop support across the range of the Chilean intellectuals, workers, and the poor, it demonstrated typical Castroite impatience by effectively sabotaging a socialist/communist government that at a more gradual pace might have achieved unchallenged power and imposed a socialist/communist order by wearing down the opposition without provoking a military coup.

5. *Pro–Soviet Guerrillas.* Prior to the late 1970s, the Soviet Union supported few guerrilla groups in Latin America. Among the interesting exceptions was the Revolutionary Armed Forces of Columbia (FARC), which has been dominated since the mid–1960s by the pro–Soviet Communist Party of Colombia. For years the Colombian Communists have been able to combine, in some degree, the armed and unarmed to pressure successive Colombian governments. Neither the FARC nor the Colombian Communists have achieved significant success, however, though they have doggedly demonstrated their ability to survive years of conflict.

6. *The Nicaraguan Sandinistas.* In strategic and tactical terms, the Sandinistas, with support from the ''reformed'' Castro and his allies, have demonstrated the effectiveness of the broad antidictatorial united front, combined with a significant guerrilla movement having major foreign support. The breadth of domestic support facilitated victory at home, in part by fostering cooperation among moderate governments and groups abroad. What is more, repeated stress on moderate objectives disguised the hardcore Marxist–Leninist objectives of the Sandinista *comandantes*, who since victory in July 1979 have gradually consolidated their control over all domestic opposition. The Sandinista model has provided a strong challenge to governments in El Salvador.

In the mid–1980s Latin American guerrilla movements, which for some time were found throughout the hemisphere, were concentrated primarily in Central America. With Soviet and Cuban guidance and assistance, they focus much more on winning political support at home and abroad, among moderate as well as revolutionary individuals and groups, as an essential factor in developing their military challenge. Thus guerrilla forces, which without broad support tend only to stagnate, if they survive at all, are more likely to be viable fighting units.

In 1967, at the OLAS conference, the Cubans proclaimed the elitist go–it–alone foco model as the wave of the future. But the only two successful Marxist–Leninist revolutions in Latin America as of the mid–1980s—Cuba in 1959 and Nicaragua in 1979—were broadly based prior to the seizure of power. They are the real world refutations of the foco, and now they themselves have been proclaimed the wave of the future by Marxist–Leninist revolutionaries in Latin America.

Notes

1. Quoted in Hugh Thomas, *The Cuban Revolution* (New York: Harper Torchbooks, 1977), p. 278.
2. See William Ratliff, *Castroism and Communism in Latin America* (Washington, D.C.: American Enterprise Institute/Hoover Institution, 1976), pp. 28–34. This chapter distinguishes between the focoist "Castroite" policy, which peaked in 1967, and the very different sort of Cuban support for and influence on Latin American revolutionaries beginning in the mid to late 70s.
3. *Granma*, (Havana), weekly English. ed., April 23, 1967; reprinted in *Yearbook on International Communist Affairs* 1969 (Stanford, Calif.: Hoover Institution Press, 1969), pp. 855–60.
4. Pombo is Harry Villegas Tamayo, one of three Cuban ELN survivors of the war. See entry of November 15, 1966, in *The Complete Bolivian Diaries of Che Guevara and Other Captured Documents*, ed. Daniel James (New York: Stein and Day, 1968), p.287. See also comments in the next section on support for continental war by the United Secretariat of the Fourth International and the Argentine People's Revolutionary Army.
5. Ibid., pp. 35, 324–27; Daniel James, *Che Guevara: A Biography* (New York: Stein and Day, 1969), pp. 248–49, where the numbers vary slightly.
6. Castro's comments are found in Fidel Castro, "A Necessary Introduction", in *The Diary of Che Guevara*, ed. Robert Scheer, the authorized Cuban edition (New York: Bantam Books, 1968), pp. 13–14; Guevara's statement is in *Complete Bolivian Diaries*, p. 96; see also James, *Che Guevara* pp. 188, 224–26.
7. Castro, "Necessary Introduction", p. 14. Oscar Zamora, "Partido Comunista de Bolivia (ML) responde a Fidel Castro", *Causa Marxista–Leninista* (Santiago, Chile), January-February 1969, p. 36. See also Ratliff, *Castroism and Communism*, pp. 95–96.
8. The account in the next few paragraphs comes largely from the diaries found by military forces, collected in *The Complete Bolivian Diaries*, and James, *Che Guevara*, pp. 178–273.
9. Inti Peredo, "Guerrilla Warfare in Bolivia Is Not Dead: It Has Just Begun," special supplement to *Tricontinental* (Havana), undated but published in 1968. See also Ratliff, *Castroism and Communism*, pp. 126–128. On the JCR, see below.
10. Mario Santucho, "Armed Struggle Is the Only Road to the Liberation of Argentina," *Internal Information Bulletin (IIB)*, November 1972, p. 22. The *IIB*, the *International Internal Discussion Bulletin*, the *The Internal Discussion Bulletin*, and *Discussion Bulletin* are publications of the United Secretariat of the Fourth Internal produced for internal consumption only. English language editions are published in New York by the American Socialist Workers Party.
11. Nahuel Moreno, "A Scandalous Document: A Reply to Germain", *International Internal Discussion Bulletin* (New York), January 1974, pp. 31–32.
12. The Fourth International took a torturous route to the Castroism it adopted in 1969. European members of the Trotskyist movement were reluctant to adopt the Cuban revolutionary model in the early 1960s, but American Socialist Workers Party (SWP) Latin America specialist Joseph Hansen, and the majority of his party, promoted the Castroite road for almost a decade. As a SWP dissident wrote, "The Cuban guerrilla warfare line (adopted by the United Secretariat in 1969) originated with the SWP as a sympathizing organization to the Fourth International and was 'sold' to the European section . . . by Comrade Hansen and

company''. Tom Cagle, ''An Historical and Dialectical Criticism of Comrade Hansen's Document'', *Discussion Bulletin*, January 1971. Ironically, by 1969 the SWP had changed its mind and generally opposed the line it had promoted so relentlessly even two years earlier, before the death of Che Guevara.

13. *Internal Information Bulletin*, November 1972, pp. 21–27. See also Ratliff, *Castroism and Communism*, pp. 143–146.

14. See Guy Gugliotta, ''Argentina's Dirty War,'' *AFP Reporter* (New York), Fall 1985, p. 28; *Yearbook on International Communist Affairs 1970–1971* (Stanford, Calif.: Hoover Institution Press). In 1980 an ERP remnant took credit for the assassination of deposed Nicaraguan dictator Anastacio Somoza. *Yearbook 1982*, p. 66; Richard Gillespie, *Soldiers of Perón* (Oxford: Clarendon Press, 1982), p. 254.

15. Santucho interview, *Internal Information Bulletin*, November 1972, p. 26.

16. Gugliotta, ''Argentina's Dirty War,'' pp. 27–29; Gillespie, *Soldiers of Perón*, p. 195.

17. The JCR founding document is translated in Ratliff, *Castroism and Communism*, pp. 209–215; see also pp. 153–154.

18. *Punto Final* (Santiago), July 1, and September 9, 1969.

19. See Ratliff, *Castroism and Communism*, pp. 155–188, and my chapters on Chile each year from 1969 through 1974 in *Yearbook on International Communist Affairs*.

20. The most useful discussion of the MIR's activities is by Robert Moss, *Chile's Marxist Experiment* (London: David and Charles Newton Abbot, 1973), esp. pp. 98–122. Moss covered the Allende period for *The Economist* of London. For the view from within the MIR, see the group's paper *El Rebelde*, esp. the 1973 issues dated February 27–March 5, June 19–26, and July 11–16; see also Ratliff, *Castroism and Communism*, pp. 155–188, and annual articles in *Yearbook on International Communist Affairs*. Two good studies of the Allende period are Robert J. Alexander, *The Tragedy of Chile* (Westport, Conn.: Greenwood Press, 1978); and Paul Sigmund, *The Overthrow of Allende and the Politics of Chile* (Pittsburgh: University of Pittsburgh Press, 1977).

21. See Ratliff, *Castroism and Communism*, pp. 93–97, 117–118.

22. Much of the detail for this section comes from David Scott Palmer, ''The Sendero Luminoso Rebellion in Rural Peru,'' *Latin American Insurgencies*, ed. Georges Fauriol (Washington, D.C.: National Defense University Press, 1985), pp. 67–96; and from Sandra Woy–Hazleton, ''Peru,'' *Yearbook on International Communist Affairs 1985*, pp. 120–127.

23. *Los Angeles Times*, October 12, 1985.

24. Shortly after Guevara's death, Debray admitted that the ''so–called foco theory in its simplest, most skeletal form'' was ''certainly a utopian notion,'' but he maintained that ''people's war'' was not. Debray then wrote that Latin American revolutionaries could learn a great deal about alliances from Mao. See Régis Debray, *Prison Writings* (New York: Random House, 1973), pp. 125–126, quoted in Ratliff, *Castroism and Communism*, p. 36.

25. Bravo interview in *Marcha* (Montevideo), May 15, 1970, and Abraham Guillén, *Desafío al pentágono* (Montevideo: Editorial Andes, 1969), pp. 74–75.

26. According to K. S. Karol and others, Debray wrote his book ''after long private discussions with Fidel Castro, who . . . himself revised and corrected the proofs.'' K. S. Karol, *Guerrillas in Power* (New York: Hill and Wang, 1970), p. 374.

27. Abraham Guillén criticized the Tupamaros, the first widely admired urban guerrilla group, for these and other failings in ''El pueblo en armas'', in Donald C.

Hodges, *Philosophy of the Urban Guerrilla: The Revolutionary Writings of Abraham Guillén* (New York: Morrow, 1973), pp. 263–277. When the Tupamaros held their first legal congress in Uruguay in December 1985, the remnants of the movement admitted many of these mistakes. The two most important were "the failure to establish ourselves thoroughly within the masses, which implies some degree of contempt for the Uruguayan people" and the lapse into "militarism that caused us to forget the eminently political substance of our action". *La Vanguardia* (Barcelona), January 5, 1986, in *Foreign Broadcast Information Service* (Latin America), January 15, 1986.

28. Guillén, *Desafío*, p. 163.
29. This program and these policies, among others, are what Douglas Payne has called *The Democratic Mask* (New York: Freedom House, 1985). On this policy, see also David Nolan, (FSLN), *The ideology of the Sandinistas and the Nicaraguan Revolution* (Miami: University of Miami, 1984), esp. pp. 60–75; and Shirley Christian, *Nicaragua: Revolution in the Family* (New York: Random House, 1985), esp. pp. 34–97. The importance of unity within the revolutionary leadership, no matter what the tensions and differences, was affirmed in early 1986 in the Interior Ministry magazine *Bocay*. Unity, it said, "is the magic formula, the greatest secret we Sandinistas have." Quoted in *The New York Times*, March 19, 1986.
30. Manuel Pineiro, in *New International: A Magazine of Marxist Politics and Theory*, New York, Spring–Summer 1984, pp. 124–125. See also William Ratliff, "The Future of Latin American Insurgencies," in *Latin American Insurgencies*, ed. Georges Fauriol (Washington, D.C.: National Defense University Press, 1985), esp. pp. 174–179.
31. Gillespie, *Soldiers of Perón*, p. 195.

3

Ernesto "Che" Guevara and the Reality of Guerrilla Warfare

Ernst Halperin

The very essence of Ernesto "Che" Guevara's theory of guerrilla warfare is formulated in the following sentences in the opening chapter of his guerrilla manual, *La guerra de guerrillas* (*Guerrilla Warfare*):

1. The people's forces can win a war against the army.
2. It is not always necessary to wait until all the conditions for revolution are present; the insurrectionary nucleus can actually create their fruition.[1]
3. In the underdeveloped Americas, the countryside must be the basic terrain for the armed struggle.[2]

A fourth important point is made in the chapter having to do with the *guerrilla as social reformer*:

> We have also already said that under the present conditions, at least in the Americas and indeed in nearly all countries with poorly developed economies, the places that offer ideal conditions for the struggle are rural, and because of this the basic social demand voiced by the guerrillas will be for a change in the structure of agrarian property. The banner of the struggle throughout this period will be the agrarian reform.[3]

Nowhere in his writings does Guevara explain why revolution is necessary and desirable. He was a typical Latin American leftist intellectual and simply took this for granted. He was solely concerned with the *how*, the way to bring about the revolution. And the promise to give land to the peasant is made for tactical reasons: to win the peasant's support, which is all–important, while the armed struggle is being waged in the countryside. Once the revolution is victorious, the peasant will receive land. But that does not mean that at a later stage of the revolution it will not be taken away from him, expropriated in order to form giant state farms or collectives.

The stated aim of a socialist revolution is the abolition of private property and the nationalization of the means of production. In Che Guevara's view (if not already that of Fidel Castro), the Cuban Revolution was to be a socialist revolution, for he was a dedicated Communist, even if not an orthodox pro–Soviet one. In 1960, the same year in which *Guerrilla Warfare* was published, Guevara also wrote "Notes for the Study of the Ideology of the Cuban Revolution", in which he said that "one must be 'Marxist' as naturally as 'Newtonian' in physics and 'Pasteurian' in biology" and then rendered homage to the successors of Marx and Engels, "Lenin, Mao Zedong and the new Soviet and Chinese leaders".[4]

After unfurling the banner of agrarian reform, the guerrilla must incessantly woo, cajole, and propagandize the peasants: "The peasant must always be helped technically, economically, morally, and culturally. The guerrilla will be a sort of guardian angel descended upon the zone".[5] And "the guerrilla, as a social reformer, not only must always provide an example by his personal life but must also incessantly provide orientation in ideological problems".[6]

Guevara's lucid and elegantly written manual makes guerrilla warfare appear not only idealistic and heroic but also relatively easy. It was an instant best seller on university campuses across the American continent. In the first years after its publication it inspired groups of young men and women of urban, middle–, and even upper–class extraction to take to the hills in nearly all the countries of Latin America. Most of these "rural" guerrilla campaigns of the 1960s were instigated and at least partially financed and armed by the revolutionary government of Cuba. Some of them were quickly defeated. Others dragged on for years. All of them failed. Gérard Chaliand lists failures in Paraguay, Colombia, Ecuador, the Dominican Republic, Argentina, Peru, Brazil, Honduras, Mexico, Bolivia, Venezuela, Guatemala, and Nicaragua.[7]

One of the rural guerrilla bands active in the 1960s has survived and managed to continue its guerrilla activities until today, although it has never come anywhere near victory—the FARC in Colombia. This guerrilla band is an exception also in not being of urban, middle–, and upper–class origin. From the beginning it was of genuinely peasant composition, and it was founded not under the inspiration of the Cuban Revolution but at an earlier date. The FARC is linked to the pro–Soviet Communist Party of Colombia, but it originated in the civil war among peasant supporters of the liberal and conservative parties in the Colombian countryside in the 1950s.

One of the organizations founded under Cuban inspiration in the early 1960s has indeed achieved its goal in seizing power: the FSLN in Nicaragua. But the Sandinistas' attempts at revolution through rural guerrilla warfare in the 1960s failed miserably. It was only after transferring their main theater of operations to the cities in the late 1960s that their fortunes changed.

The guerrilla failures of the 1960s culminating in Guevara's own failure and death in Bolivia in 1967 demonstrated that his theory of *foquismo*— revolution through the activities of a guerrilla nucleus—was deeply flawed.

The basic flaw in Guevara's theory was his assumption that guerrillas can win peasant support with the slogan of agrarian reform. This assumption is the product of urban upper–class arrogance and ignorance. It presupposes:

(1) That because they are illiterate, it has never occurred to the peasants that they would be better off if they owned more land, and that it would thus be a revelation to them and fill them with enthusiasm and gratitude, if they were informed of this by a group of city–dwellers.
(2) That the peasants would trust an ill–armed little group of city–dwellers, people of a different culture, ethnic provenance, and, in the Andean countries, even of different language, first to lead them to victory against the police and the army and then, in the highly unlikely event that victory was achieved, actually to fulfill their promise and give them land.

Latin American peasants may be illiterate, but they have gone through the hardest of all schools and are anything but naive. From their perspective, they were being asked to sacrifice their lives so that the guerrillas could replace another set of city–dwellers behind the desks of government offices.

One might ask how, in the face of this peasant distrust, Fidel Castro had been able to achieve his astonishing, even miraculous victory in Cuba. Was the small band with which he landed in a mangrove swamp on the shores of Oriente Province on December 2, 1956, not composed of city–dwellers? The answer is that Fidel Castro owed his *final victory* to his own genius, but he owed the *survival* of his tiny, harried band in the crucial first months of his guerrilla campaign to somebody else—not an idealistic young city–dweller, but a man of the people, an old man in his sixties, a denizen of the countryside who was intimately familiar with the terrain on which the campaign was being waged and close to the peasants who lived there: Crescencio Pérez.

Crescencio Pérez was an organizer of the sugar workers' union, and in the years of democracy before Batista's coup of 1952 he had been a *sargento político*, an electoral agent of President Prio Soccaras's ruling Auténtico Party. When a country doctor's daughter who was a member of Castro's July 26 Movement, Celia Sánchez, asked for his help in preparing for a friendly reception—by the peasants—of Castro's landing party, he sent a message to Havana asking the highest Auténtico Party official still in Cuba for advice. Some years later that official, Rubén de León, who had been President Prio Soccaras's defense minister, ruefully told the present writer that in order to make trouble for Batista he had given Crescencio permission to cooperate with the Castroites even though Castro had been a member of the Ortodoxo Party, the main opposition party under the previous Auténtico regime.

Crescencio's electoral district had been the western part of the Sierra Maestra, precisely the region to which the handful of survivors of Castro's landing party fled after they had been ambushed at Alegría de Pio three days after the landing. Crescencio knew every path and every peasant in his territory. His brother Mongo had a farm there, and it was at that farm that Fidel Castro's little band found a first safe hiding–place after the disaster at Alegría de Pio. Crescencio also had several unofficial households in the Sierra Maestra. It appears that Guevara, a strict moralist, disapproved of this, and that is probably the reason he only mentions Crescencio in passing, without even hinting at the importance of his role, in his account of Castro's guerrilla campaign, *Reminiscences of the Cuban Revolutionary War*.[8]

In *Guerrilla Warfare* the need for preliminary contact with the peasantry, so well demonstrated in the Cuban case by the example of Crescencio Pérez, is not mentioned at all. The consequences of this omission for all those who followed Guevara's precepts were disastrous.

The Practice of Guerrilla Warfare

In practice it does not suffice to woo the peasants with apparently good deeds and mobilizing propaganda. Their silence when the army comes must be assured. Those who have informed must be punished, prospective informers must be eliminated, and the population must be made to fear guerrilla retribution even more than it fears the brutality of army interrogators. *Guerrilla Warfare* offers only obscure hints in a few passages dealing with the punishment of informers, not spelled out. Thus, in the chapter on guerrilla tactics Guevara writes of the need for "absolute implacability toward all the despicable elements who resort to informing or assassination".[9] His chapter "The Guerrilla as Social Reformer" states:

> The guerrilla will be a sort of guardian angel who has descended upon the zone always to aid the poor and to molest the rich as little as possible in the first phase of the development of the war. But the war will follow its course, contradictions will continually grow sharper, and there will come a moment when many of those who hitherto regarded the revolution with a certain sympathy will go over to a diametrically opposed position; they will take the first step into battle against the people's forces. At this moment the guerrilla must go into action and become the standard-bearer of the cause of the people, bringing to justice any betrayal.[10]

Terror against civilians is a necessary and inevitable component of guerrilla warfare. Only in his last work, the diary of the Bolivian campaign found on him when he was captured in October 1967, did Guevara spell this out with brutal frankness. In his summary of the operations in May 1967, he wrote:

> The army announced the arrest of all the peasants who collaborated with us in the Masicuri zone; now comes a phase in which terror against the peasants will be employed by both sides, even though with different objectives; our triumph will bring with it the qualitative change needed for a leap in their development.[11]

The guerrillas will thus terrorize the peasants for their own good, for a leap forward in their development. Guevara's statement is a classic example of the paternalistic mentality of the Latin American upper class.

The way terror was practiced by Castro's guerrillas in the Cuban campaign is described in one of the most valuable sources on that war, Neill Macaulay's *A Rebel in Cuba*. Macaulay, a veteran of the Korean War, had gone to Cuba to join Castro's movement in August 1958 because, as he frankly explained, "It was a good cause . . . and I had nothing better to do".[12] In the recruiting office on Amsterdam Avenue in New York, Macaulay met an American adventurer named Soldini, who had served with Raúl Castro on the Second Front, located in the Sierra Cristal in northeastern Oriente Province. Soldini complained that Raúl Castro had been reluctant to commit his troops to action:

> All Raúl did was sit around on his ass and send patrols out after the *chivatos*. *Chivatos* are people who are for Batista they give information to the army. Raúl's patrols would take these guys from their houses and bring them to Raúl's camp and Raúl would string 'em up. Once in a while Raúl would send a patrol out to attack a *cuartel*—that's an army post—and that's how I got this bullet in my shoulder. Raúl got pretty pissed off at me, Soldini continued. I kept telling him that I wanted action. Finally he kicked me out of his camp and told me not to come back.[13]

In Cuba, Macaulay was sent to a new guerrilla front that was being opened up in Pinar Del Río, the westernmost province of the island. He soon learned that the elimination of informers was an essential ingredient, indeed *the basic ingredient*, of guerrilla warfare. His commander in Pinar del Río was a guerrilla named Claudio, whose task was described by Macaulay as follows:

> Claudio's mission was, first, to survive, which meant eluding and if possible destroying any pursuing soldiers; and, second, to bring the entire population of the highlands east of Pan de Guajaibo under rebel control. Once all the batistianos and chivatos were cleared out of the mountains, he could begin striking into the lowlands.[14]

The key words here are "to bring the entire population . . . under rebel control". This is the prerequisite for the survival of a guerrilla band. In his graphic description of the execution of one government supporter (*batistiano*, *chivato*), Macaulay gives an example of how it was done in Cuba,

> One suspected informer, a fairly prosperous colono who lived beside one of the Mercedita rail lines, knew he was in danger and had sent his family away. When the guerrillas arrived to search his house before dawn one morning, it was deserted. The man, a middle aged Negro, was found sleeping in a tool–shed in the yard. When told that he was going to be executed, he asked only for permission to urinate. After he finished and broke wind two or three times, he was

hanged from one of his own shade trees. He must have thought it all a nightmare from which he would awake at any moment.

"He is no informer," Pipilo said to Alberto and me, speaking of the dead man in the present tense. A batistiano, yes, but an informer, no. Nevertheless, Claudio had decided that a known Batista sympathizer should not live among our supporters. His body was cut down from the tree and hoisted twenty–five feet to the top of a concrete frame—a structure that straddled the tracks and supported the pulleys, that, during the harvest season, lifted sugar cane onto railcars. Then we returned to our camp in the mountains. When the sun rose, the dangling corpse could be seen from the nearby highway. Afraid to expose themselves to possible sniper fire, the police and Rural Guards refused to cut it down. Not until late afternoon did the batistiano mayor of Cabanas appear to remove his friend's body personally.[15]

The hanging of government supporters as practiced in Cuba is a relatively mild method of intimidating the population and thus bringing it under control. Another Latin American guerrilla leader, Augusto César Sandino, used more imaginative methods. In *The Sandino Affair*, Macaulay described these methods:

Sandinista justice was administered by several *cortes*—a Spanish word that can mean either "courts" or "cuts". The most famous of these was the *corte de chaleco*, the "vest cut": the offender's head was lopped off with a machete, after which his arms were severed at the shoulders and a design was etched on his chest with machete slashes. Pedrón invented the "vest cut" and applied it often until he tired of it in 1930 and ordered that all "traitors" should receive the *corte de cumbo* instead. This *corte*, the "gourd cut", was applied by an expert machete man who sliced off a portion of the victim's skull, exposing his brain and causing him to lose his equilibrium and suffer hours of agony and convulsions before death. Less sophisticated was the *corte de bloomers*, by which the victim's legs were chopped off at the knees, eventually producing death through bleeding. "Liberty is not conquered with flowers", Sandino declared in 1931; for this reason we must resort to the *cortes* of vest, gourd, and bloomers.[16]

In some guerrilla wars, the population is brought under control in a preliminary stage, before the actual fighting even begins. According to Eqbal Ahmad,

In the early years of the Algerian revolution it took the FLN from two months to a year to kill a popular but quisling village chief without incurring the liability of the village or tribal hostility, and that was an anticolonial war. Therefore, it is amazing to learn that in Vietnam about 13,000 local officials were killed between 1957 and 1961. The number seems unusually large for a country which then had a total of some 14,000 village units.[17]

In order to survive, the guerrillas must eliminate civilian support for the opposing side in the contested area. Therefore, guerrilla warfare is first and foremost warfare against the civilian supporters of the opposing side. Harassment of the enemy forces is only a secondary objective.

The guerrillas cannot hope to prevent the enemy army from entering and sweeping through the territory in which they have brought the civilian population under their control. Indeed, one of the basic rules of guerrilla strategy is to avoid being pinned down in positional warfare. What they refer to as "liberated territory" is therefore *not* territory rendered inaccessible to enemy forces. In guerrilla parlance, "liberated territory" is territory in which the guerrillas have established and continue to maintain total control over the civilian population in spite of the intermittent or even permanent presence of enemy forces. To reconquer that territory, the enemy will either have to evacuate the civilian population into areas under his control or to regain control over the population by a "pacification campaign", that is, a combination of political, economic, and social measures and police action for which regular army units are not usually trained and are therefore ill–suited.

However, while the establishment and maintenance of control over the civilian population is essential for the survival of the guerrillas, it is not enough for their victory. Thus, a 1976 Swiss report on the guerrilla war in Eritrea stated:

> Having suffered heavy losses during some "mopping up" operations against the partisans, the Ethiopian forces are now refraining from offensive activities and remain more or less passive at their bases. The fighting consists mainly of guerrilla attacks against Ethiopian supply convoys and troop movements. The Ethiopian air force is very active, however, flying sorties almost daily in support of ground units, bombarding partisan positions and bringing supplies to isolated government posts. But its direct successes are very slight, since the guerrillas operate in a highly decentralized fashion. Nevertheless, the presence of the air force exerts heavy pressure on the two liberation organizations.

> In those areas controlled by the army, the partisans try to demoralize the government troops through frequent terrorist attacks. On the whole the initiative at present seems clearly with the liberation groups, while the Ethiopian forces take the offensive only in the air. Most of Eritrea today is under the influence, if not the control, of the guerrilla organizations. The army controls only those segments of the population resident in cities and villages with military bases—less than 20 in number. . . .

> The Ethiopian army finds itself in a difficult and possibly hopeless situation, since it cannot defeat the guerrillas militarily, is faced by a hostile Eritrean population and has serious problems to deal with in other Ethiopian provinces as well.[18]

Today, more than nine years after this report was published, the situation in Eritrea is to the best of our knowledge still more or less the same. Control over the civilian population is essential for the survival of the guerrilla band, but it is not sufficient for its victory.

Achieving Victory—The Role of Outsider Support

How, then, do guerrillas win a war? In *Guerrilla Warfare*, Guevara provides the orthodox Maoist answer:

> It is well established that guerrilla warfare is a phase of war that in itself does not offer opportunities for final victory; it is, furthermore, one of the first phases of war and will continue to develop until the Guerrilla Army, by its constant growth, acquires the characteristics of a Regular Army. At that moment it will be ready to deliver decisive blows to the enemy and to achieve victory. The final victory will always be that of a Regular Army, even though its origins may be those of a Guerrilla Army.[19]

Yet in reality guerrilla wars are *not* won by the guerrilla groups getting stronger and stronger until they are capable of confronting and defeating the enemy army in pitched battle. Even the guerrilla campaign that inspired Guevara to write his manual, the Cuban campaign of Fidel Castro, was not won in this way. All the "battles" described in Guevara's *Reminiscences* are minor engagements. His confused account of the final "battle of Santa Clara" shows that the alleged battle consisted of a guerrilla group ambushing a train and a series of street fights and sieges of buildings in which small contingents of Batista soldiers were holed up. The main position of the army, the Leoncio Vidal Barracks, was still holding out when news arrived that the dictator had fled the country.

There is indeed one, and only one, known case of guerrilla groups being converted into a regular army: that of the Chinese communist forces that after World War II confronted and defeated the battle–scarred armies of Chiang K'ai–shek. But this was not the result of a gradual, step–by–step development. It was made possible by a sudden, massive influx of arms when the Japanese armies in Manchuria capitulated to the Russians, who handed over the Japanese equipment to their then ally Mao.

The Contemporary Aspects of Guerrilla Warfare

The outcome of guerrilla wars is often determined by events elsewhere in the world, by decisions made in some distant capital. Therefore guerrilla warfare is first and foremost political in outcome. Military activities are largely secondary.

Walter Laqueur gives a long list of nineteenth– and twentieth–century guerrilla wars in his book *Guerrilla*.[20] In studying his list, one discovers an extraordinary phenomenon: throughout the age of imperialism, right up to World War II, the resistance of colonial peoples to the colonizers, which usually took the form of guerrilla warfare, was almost always unsuccessful. The only exceptions were Ireland after World War I and a number of cases of interventions by foreign powers in favor of the guerrillas: Cuba in 1898 and earlier interventions by European powers in favor of the Balkan (Greeks, Bulgarians) peoples struggling against the decrepit Ottoman Empire.

Since World War II, on the other hand, nearly all risings of colonial peoples against the colonizers have been successful. Only in the most recent cases—Afghanistan for instance—is the issue still in doubt. On the other hand, risings against domestic governments, whether separatist or otherwise politically motivated, are usually unsuccessful, even if the government in question is quite unpopular. The explanation for this phenomenon is simple: the outcome of World War II brought about a drastic, worldwide change of the political climate.

During the nineteenth and early twentieth centuries the educated, politically influential strata in the United States and Europe took the biological superiority of the white race for granted. The works of liberals and even of radicals like George Bernard Shaw show that even they accepted the major tenets of the day termed "Social Darwinism" but in their time was simply known as science. The sordid spectacle of World War I cast considerable doubt on the doctrine of the superiority of the white man, but then an exponent of the most virulent racism took power in Germany. In rereading *Mein Kampf* this author found to his great surprise that it is a lucid, absolutely logical, and well–thought–out exposition of Social Darwinism—a Social Darwinism carried to its most extreme consequences.

World War II was a war between the exponents of two ideologies: Social Darwinism and the ideology of the French Revolution: Liberty, Equality, Fraternity. It ended in total defeat for the exponents of Social Darwinism, and consequently that ideology has fallen into utter disrepute. Primitive racism is still very much alive, manifesting itself daily not only in the United States but also in the cities of Great Britain, France, and Germany. But in polite society it is no longer respectable to express racist opinions even in a sophisticated disguise. As several prominent academics have found out, writings that attempt to revive Social Darwinism in any form come under instant, fierce, and deadly attack.

It was the educated, politically influential strata of the metropolitan population that forced the largest colonial powers to dismantle their empires. The liquidation of the British Empire was decided in London. In Indochina, the French suffered just one major military defeat: Dien Bien Phu. But even that was an outpost in the backlands; the troops that held were mercenaries and therefore expendable, and the French still controlled Hanoi, Saigon, and the rich river valleys. Nevertheless, in faraway Paris the decision to withdraw was made.

Guerrillas can be politically victorious in spite of military defeat. "In strictly military terms, the Algerian War ended in defeat for the Front for National Liberation (FLN)'', wrote Gérard Chaliand. "On the eve of the signing of the Evian Accords in 1962 which ended the war, only a few thousand men were still holding on, mercilessly hounded down and barely managing to survive''.[21] The Mau Mau rebellion in Kenya was put down by the British. A few years later, the leader of the Mau Mau was the ruler of a free Kenya.

This writer has never regarded the Vietnam War as a colonial war, but many people in the United States and elsewhere did and still do. In that war, the United States never suffered a Dien Bien Phu. The *Tet* Offensive was a military disaster for the Vietcong, but psychologically, and therefore politically, it was a decisive victory for them. That war was not won and lost in Vietnam at all. It was won for the Vietcong on the campuses of the United States.

What does this mean for the guerrillas? It simply demonstrates the decisive importance of public opinion for victory in war—public opinion in the country where the war is being fought and also, or even more, in the homeland of the colonial power or in the country sponsoring the government that the guerrillas are striving to topple. There is no mention of this in Guevara's *Guerrilla Warfare*. The book has a chapter on propaganda, but it is most disappointing. In it, he stresses the need for a "national civic organization" operating outside the rebel zone, presumably clandestinely, and publishing periodicals, bulletins, and proclamations as well as specialized publications for various sectors of the population: peasants, workers, enemy soldiers. Other publications should be printed and distributed in the area already under guerrilla control. Finally and most important, the guerrillas should operate a radio station of their own. But there is no mention in that chapter or elsewhere in the manual of the possibility of using the media already existing in enemy territory and abroad for propaganda. This omission is all the more remarkable and significant because Guevara was serving under a leader who was a master at doing just this: Fidel Castro is a real genius at public relations. In fact it was through public relations rather than through victory on the battlefield that he won his guerrilla war.

One can catch only a glimpse of Fidel Castro's technique of media manipulation in Guevara's *Reminiscences* in the chapter entitled "The Second Battle of Pino del Agua". This "battle" was in fact just a series of skirmishes in the vicinity of a lumber camp manned by a company of soldiers. The guerrillas withdrew after inflicting some twenty casualties on the enemy and themselves losing perhaps half a dozen men. Guevara's description opens with these words: "Fidel felt it was important to strike a resounding blow to take advantage of the fact that censorship had now been lifted, and we prepared ourselves for this".[22] The army post was attacked not because of its strategic importance or because of the arms and supplies that might have been stored there, but in order to get into the news. Guevara apparently learned nothing from this. On another occasion he does show a glimmer of understanding. In describing the guerrillas' preparations for the "battle" of El Uvero (an army post with a garrison of fifty–three seized by the guerrilla band which at that time, late May 1957, numbered some eighty combatants) Guevara wrote:

> At this point we had an interesting discussion, led principally by myself and Fidel. I was of the opinion that we should not waste the opportunity to seize a truck and that we should concentrate specifically on ambushing them on the roads on which they passed unconcernedly up and down, but Fidel already had the action at El Uvero in mind and thought that it would be much more worthwhile and would constitute a much greater success if we went through with this action and captured the post at El Uvero, because it would have great psychological impact and would become known in the entire country, whereas this would not happen with the attack on a truck, which could be presented as a traffic accident with a few casualties, and although people would suspect the truth our effective fighting presence in the mountains would never become known. That did not mean that he totally rejected the notion of capturing a truck under favorable circumstances, but we should not make it the main goal of our activities.
>
> Today, several years after the discussion in which Fidel made that decision, but did not convince me, I have to admit that his judgment was correct and that it would have been much less productive for us to conduct an isolated attack on one of the patrols that rode in the trucks.[23]

Castro's first big propaganda coup in the guerrilla war was the interview he gave to *New York Times* editorial writer Herbert Matthews in February 1957. While still on the run with a band of eighteen men, Fidel had sent a messenger to Havana with orders to bring back a foreign reporter, preferably an American. The reporter who came was Herbert Matthew, who had arrived in Havana in search of a story. They had to meet in the dark of night, which should have made Matthews suspicious, but he was completely taken in, and that was no surprise to anyone who has ever met Castro and experienced his irresistible charm.

So Matthews published three reports on the situation in Cuba in the *New York Times*. The first began with the following lead:

> Fidel Castro, the rebel leader of Cuba's youth, is alive and fighting hard and successfully in the rugged almost impenetrable fastness of the Sierra Maestra. President Fulgencio Batista has the cream of his Army around the area, but the Army men are fighting a thus–far losing battle to destroy the most dangerous enemy General Batista has yet faced in a long and adventurous career as a Cuban leader and dictator.[24]

Later in the same report Matthews explains why Castro had kept absolutely quiet, not coming forth to contradict the government claim that he was dead:

"As I learned later, Señor Castro was waiting until he had his forces reorganized and strengthened and had mastery of the Sierra Maestra. This fortunately coincided with my arrival".[25] At the time Castro gave his interview to Matthews, his band numbered eighteen men. It did not have "mastery of the Sierra" but was on the run.

In *The Cuban Story*, Matthews described the interview with Castro as "the biggest scoop of our times".[26] He only admits to "a few minor errors",[27] such as overestimation of "the size of Fidel's forces"[28] in his *Times* story, which was published on February 24, 1957. That his story "came at the ebb tide of the flood that was to lead Fidel on to fortune" is also only counted as a "minor error".[29] Later, in his political biography of Castro, Matthews sourly gave a few details on how he was tricked:

> It has become a standard source of glee among the Cuban rebels who were there, from Fidel and Raúl Castro down, that they had fooled me into believing that they were a larger and stronger force than they really were. Fidel himself, with a slightly malicious gleam in his eyes, broke the news that he had only eighteen armed men. This was at a huge luncheon at the Overseas Press Club which I helped to arrange in New York in April 1959. In Carlos Franqui's book on *The Twelve*, Celia Sánchez, Guillermo García, Manuel Fajardo, Efigenio Almeijeiras and Vilma Espin all talk about their ruses. When I saw Raúl Castro in Havana in October 1967, he chortled about it once again.
>
> In Celia's words: "We prepared everything so that Matthews would get a good impression and believe that Fidel was in another camp." It seems that Raúl "passed up and back always with the same men". He is supposed to have told Fidel about news from "another column," and so forth. These tactics are so old as the history of warfare.
>
> It was all interesting as showing how anxious they were to make a "good impression" and get effective publicity—but if these things took place they made no impression of any kind on me.[30]

Two months later Castro staged another propaganda coup: a television interview by CBS reporter Robert Taber. In his *Reminiscences*, Guevara only briefly mentions the Matthews interview, pointing out that he himself had not been present, In fact, Castro had sent him away for the night, fearing that Guevara would not be able to contain his rabid anti–Americanism in the presence of the American reporter. Guevara did dedicate a chapter to the visit by CBS reporter Robert Taber, but he had nothing to say about its significance, except that Castro and his men tried "to demonstrate our strength to the North Americans and to avoid answering any question that was too indiscreet; we did not know who the journalists were".[31]

Lacking any understanding of the importance of publicity, Guevara failed to realize that the Matthews interview and its follow-up—the Taber interview that confirmed Castro's presence in the Sierra Maestra—together constituted a greater setback for Batista than any defeat on the battlefield. In spite of the favorable economic situation, the Batista government's standing abroad was greatly impaired by statements in that most reputable of newspapers, the *New York Times*, such as that Batista's troops were "fighting a losing battle" and that a rebel had "mastery of the Sierra Maestra". At home, the impact of the two interviews on Cuban public on can read to the Tet Offensive on American public opinion: a wide credibility gap developed, because government spokesmen, who had announced Castro's death after his landing in December 1956, now denounced Herbert Matthews' interview as "totally untrue due to the physical impossibility of entering the zone in which the imaginary interview took place". Thus the military commander of Oriente Province, General Díaz Tamayo claimed that "No one can enter the zone without being seen. In my opinion this gentleman has never been in Cuba. Someone furnished the imaginary information and then his imagination did the rest".[32] Batista's minister of national defense, Santiago Verdeja, denounced the Matthews interview as "a chapter in a fantastic novel".[33] The general, the defense minister, and other government spokesmen were given the lie by the CBS television interview two months later.

Then, in October 1957, Castro made the decision that was to win the war for him. Again, it was not a decision for some military move but for a move on the battlefield of propaganda and public opinion: Castro decided to send a lobbyist to Washington, D.C. A Caribbean guerrilla chieftain maintaining a lobby in Washington? This was not quite as strange and unique as it may seem. Castro is an educated man, well ready in the history of Cuba. He undoubtedly remembered from the history books that during both of the Cuban wars of liberation against Spain (1868–1878 and 1895–1898) the freedom fighters lobbied intensively in Washington.

Castro chose as his lobbyist a dedicated democratic opponent of Batista, a man who believed that with the fall of the dictator constitutional government would return to Cuba and who was bitterly disappointed by the actual turn of events. He was highly intelligent and able and soon won two key senators and two influential congressmen for the anti–Batista cause.

In March 1957, Senate Majority leader Mike Mansfield and Senator Wayne Morse, Chairman of the American Republics Subcommittee of the Foreign Relations Committee, and Congressmen Charles Orlando Porter of Oregon and Adam Clayton Powell of New York, moved that all further arms deliveries to the Batista government be suspended. Much to the distress of the Eisenhower administration, the motion was passed by both houses of Congress. That was Fidel Castro's decisive victory in the guerrilla war against the Batista dictatorship. It was won not on a battlefield in Cuba but in Washington, D.C., in the Congress of the United States.

It is true that Batista did not need the American arms, because the guerrillas posed only a very minor military threat. Should he need arms, he could easily buy them elsewhere, for Cuba was a wealthy country, and in spite of the guerrilla war 1957 had been one of the best years in its economic history. However, it was an axiom generally accepted in Cuba, and refuted only in the 1960s by Castro, that the country could not be ruled without the goodwill of the United States, and Batista had obviously lost that goodwill. Batista was utterly corrupt. He was in politics to make money and was surrounded by opportunists who had the same goal. These opportunists now rapidly left his sinking ship.

In the summer of 1958 the army made a final effort to wipe out Castro's guerrilla band. It had him surrounded in the mountains and somehow failed to press home its advantage. In August, after more than two months of fighting, the troops withdrew, totally demoralized. Now new guerrilla fronts were established, first in the western province of Pinar del Río and then in central Cuba. Political parties and even the military commander of Oriente Province sent liaison officers to the camp. In December the demoralized army failed to prevent the Castroite guerrilla groups of Guevara and Camillo Cienfuegos and the two rival groups of Gutiérrez Menoyo and Faure Chomon from cutting the Central Highway and railroad from Havana to the eastern province of Oriente. On the early morning of January 1, 1959, Fulgencio Batista left Cuba by airplane after a sad farewell party on his country estate.

Guevara's *Reminiscences* make no mention of Castro's lobby in Washington, let alone of the decision by the U.S. Congress to suspend arms deliveries to Batista. In all likelihood Guevara's ferocious anti–Americanism caused him to disapprove of Castro's wooing of the Congress of a country that he regarded as the imperialist enemy and exploiter of mankind. There is no mention in *Guerrilla Warfare* of the desirability of wooing public opinion in the foreign country that is sponsoring or supporting the government that the guerrillas are struggling to overthrow—this even though the manual was written primarily for readers in Latin America where such advice would be very appropriate. Thus Guevara's manual contains neither the formula for survival— preliminary contacts with the peasantry—nor the formula for victory. It paints a romantic picture of what is actually a cruel, dirty, murderous war directed mainly against civilians. It is useful as a recruitment pamphlet, but quite useless as a manual for waging a guerrilla war. Many of those who followed its prescriptions paid with their lives.

The Future of Guevarism

Does that mean that Guevarism, or *foquismo* as it is called in Latin America, is dead, that there will be no more attempts to spark off revolutions by the activities of a small guerrilla nucleus or focal point? On the contrary, there are likely to be more such attempts, and it is not at all certain that these attempts are doomed to failure, like those of the 1960s. The guerrilla campaigns of the 1960s failed because the guerrillas slavishly followed the prescriptions of Guevara's manual. It was shown above that there are two basic mistakes in the manual. In Central America today, the revolutionaries are rectifying both these mistakes. One of the two mistakes was Guevara's inability to discern, or refusal to accept, the importance of public opinion in the United States and the possibility of influencing it, and through it the U. S. Congress, in favor of the guerrillas.

CISPES, the Committee in Solidarity with the People of El Salvador, was set up in 1980 as the American branch of a "World Front in Solidarity with the People of El Salvador" on the initiative of an emissary of the Farabundo Martí National Liberation Front (FMLN), the umbrella organization of the Salvadoran Marxist–Leninist groups. It would be far beyond the scope of this chapter to describe the activities of CISPES and its network of relations with American radical leftist groups. Suffice it to say that it is engaged in manifold propaganda activities, such as sponsoring and co–sponsoring protest meetings against U. S. intervention in Central America, publishing pamphlets and a newsletter, and organizing letter–writing campaigns to Congress and directly lobbying congressmen. Considering their handicap in having to lobby for an openly Marxist–Leninist revolutionary movement, the performance of the CISPES lobbyists is remarkably proficient. From this one could infer that the Salvadoran guerrillas have carefully studied the history of the Cuban Revolution and drawn the right conclusions from their study—or perhaps they have a highly competent adviser, a mentor who is in a position to tell them, "Look, this is the way I myself did it in Cuba many years ago!"

In addition, the Marxist–Leninist or Castroite protagonists of revolution through guerrilla warfare have unexpectedly gained a powerful ally—which can be of great help to them in winning the trust and cooperation of the peasantry and thus in avoiding the second great mistake in Guevara's theory and practice, the mistake that cost him his life in Bolivia: neglect of the need for preliminary contacts with the peasants in the zone of operations. A sector of the Roman Catholic Church has declared itself in favor of violent revolution with the aim of constructing a new society in accordance with the tenets of Marxism–Leninism. This is the movement that calls itself "liberation theology".

The Roman Catholic Church in Latin America is severely understaffed. In the Catholic countries of Europe, a peasant class prosperous enough to give its children an education provides recruits for the priesthood, but in Latin America this class is almost totally absent. Candidates for the priesthood must be recruited from the middle and upper classes, and many members of these classes are not churchgoers. Consequently, the Catholic Church in Latin

America suffers from a severe lack of priests. There are not nearly enough priests for the urban shantytowns, and far too few for the rural parishes. These parishes are usually served by priests from the municipal centers, each of whom services five or six parishes, or in some regions even more village churches. In some cases they do not conduct regular services in the rural parishes at all, but appear only at infrequent intervals to conduct marriage services and baptisms, and to hear confessions if time permits. Sometimes there are intervals of many months between these visits.

In spite of this, and the consequent survival of pagan, pre–Colombian, and African rites in the countryside and shantytowns, the church enjoys considerable respect among the villagers. Indeed, the authority of the priests may even be enhanced by the rarity of their visits, which makes each appearance a very special event in the drab life of the peasants and laborers. Because of this, revolutionaries can use leftist–extremist clerics that precede or accompany them to overcome the peasants' distrust of the guerrillas. These clerics thereby act as guerrilla agents and recruiters among the peasantry. That is why the military in countries where guerrillas operate have become extremely suspicious of the presence of priests in the countryside. This provides the background for the bestial murder of four American women: two Maryknoll sisters, an Ursuline nun, and a lay sister in El Salvador. Already in December 1967 three Maryknoll priests and a Maryknoll sister were expelled from Guatemala accused of having established contacts with the guerrilla band of César Montes. In his history of the Catholic Church in Latin America, written from the point of view of "liberation theology," Enrique Dussel affirmed: "Apparently this small group of clergy desired to join the guerrillas in the northern part of Guatemala, but they returned to the United States and began a crusade against North American militarism in the Third World".[34]

Today, "liberation theology" is clearly dominant in the Maryknoll Order. The Maryknoll sisters whom this author has met in recent years were thoroughly indoctrinated. They were voluble in their denunciations of "American imperialism" and had complete command of the terminology of "liberation theology". Indignation at the foul murder of the four women and at the reluctance of the Salvadoran authorities to punish those who killed them is fully justified. But two important questions have not yet been raised: Who sent these poor women to their death in an area of intensive guerrilla activity, and why were they sent?

The leftist–extremism currently associated with "liberation theology" is usually—and plausibly—assumed to be the result of the priests' indignation at the deprivation and misery with which they are daily confronted in their work in the villages and the shantytowns surrounding the big cities of Latin America. However, this explanation does not square with the facts. "Liberation theology" was not created by Franciscans working among the poor. It was born in the universities.

The hero and martyr of "liberation theology" is Father Camilo Torres Restrepo, the son of two prominent colonial (i.e., aristocratic) Colombian families. He was chaplain and associate professor of sociology at the National University in Bogotá. In 1965, at the age of thirty–six, he left the priesthood (though not the church) in order to set up a legally operating front organization for the Castroite ELN guerrilla group, which was seeking to overthrow the constitutional government of Colombia. In October 1965 he joined the guerrillas. The following February he was killed in action while engaging in the not very Christian activity of ambushing an army patrol.[35]

Theory follows practice; ideology is the ex post facto justification of policy. In 1972 the Peruvian priest Gustavo Gutiérrez, a personal friend of Camilo Torres since their student days at the Catholic University of Louvain, published his *Teología de la liberación*, a book that has had a tremendous impact in Protestant as well as Catholic religious circles. In *Teología de la liberación* Gutiérrez unreservedly accepts the neo–Marxist *dependency theory* in its most radical version. According to this theory, the capitalist world system creates underdevelopment in the countries of the dependent periphery and is therefore responsible for "the situation of oppression and alienation in which the immense majority of mankind lives".[36] It follows that a global struggle to smash the capitalist system must be waged and won, if poverty, oppression, and alienation are to be abolished. Gutiérrez maintains that merely by abstaining from this struggle the church would be intervening on the side of the oppressors. And not only the church, but also the individual Christian, must join in the struggle against world capitalism, because this struggle is the road to salvation. Indeed, the road is open not only to Catholics, not only to Christians in general, but to anyone who participates in the struggle for a "just society," because "the building of a just society signifies acceptance of the Kingdom [of God] or, in terms more familiar to us, to participate in the process of the liberation of man is already, in a certain way, a work of salvation".[37]

Gutiérrez makes it clear that, in his view, acts of violence may be used to promote this "process of the liberation of man". He quotes, with approval, a statement by Latin American clerics demanding that "it must by all means be avoided that the *unjust violence* of the oppressors who support this 'evil system' be equated or confounded with the *just violence* of the oppressed who see themselves obliged to resort to it in order to achieve their liberation".[38]

With the exception of his last months, Camilo Torres spent his entire adult life in academia, first as a student, then as a chaplain, a teacher, and an administrator. Gustavo Gutiérrez is presently a professor of theology and social sciences at the Catholic University in Lima and adviser to the Peruvian National Union of Catholic Students. It is no coincidence that "liberation theology"—first the practice and then the theory—was created by two university teachers and student advisers. "Liberation theology" originated as the response of Catholic educators to the appeal of Marxism–Leninism to the youth of the Latin American elites after World War II. It might be called a "me too" reflex by these educators. Lacking the knowledge of economics needed to refute the Leninist doctrine of imperialism or the neo–Marxist Dependency Theory, smarting under the accusation that their church was the instrument of a ruling class of exploiters and oppressors, desperately seeking to retain, or regain, the respect of and authority over their charges, they began to argue that Catholicism is compatible with the acceptance of Marxist theory and revolutionary practice. From there it was only a small step to the assertion that to make a revolution is the duty of the Catholic.

In sum, according to Gutiérrez the revolutionary is well on his way to the road to salvation even without being a believer. He is fulfilling God's will by striving to replace capitalism, which is sinful per se, by a just—socialist—society in which there is no exploitation of man by man. One consequence of this preaching is that it allows the priest to associate with Marxist–Leninist, atheistic guerrillas without boring them with attempts at conversion. Why seek to convert them if they are already well on the road to salvation?

By serving as a link with the peasantry, the "liberation theology" priest is invaluable to the guerrillas as an aid to survival. But the "liberation theology" movement can also help the guerrillas achieve victory—their second task. It has been seen that guerrilla wars are won not on the battlefield but by the successful wooing of public opinion not only in the country in which the guerrilla campaigns is being waged, but also in other countries sponsoring or supporting the government the guerrillas are striving to overthrow. The "liberation theology" movement has already spread from Latin America to the United States and to Europe, from the Catholic Church to Protestant denominations and sects. It is emerging as a huge international propaganda and lobbying machine for leftist–extremist protagonists of violent revolution in general and revolutionary guerrillas in particular. And it has given a new lease on life to Guevarism, the doctrine of revolution through guerrilla warfare.

Notes

1. *El foco insurreccional*: the insurrectional focal point or hearth, i.e., the guerrilla band. Hence Guevara's recipe for revolution through guerrilla warfare is often referred to, in Latin America, as *foquismo*.
2. As quoted in Ernesto "Che" Guevara, *Obra revolucionaria*, 4th ed. (México D. F.: Ediciones ERA, 1971), p. 27. Translations from *Obra* are this author's.
3. Ibid., p. 47.
4. Ibid., p. 508.
5. Ibid., p. 47.
6. Ibid., p. 48.
7. Gerard Chaliand, *Revolution in the Third World* (New York: Penguin Books, 1978), pp. 44–45.
8. Che Guevara, *Reminiscences of the Cuban Revolutionary War* (New York: Monthly Review Press, 1968).

9. In Guevara, *Obra revolucionaria* (México, D. F.: Ediciones Era, 1968), p. 38.
10. Ibid., p. 47.
11. Translated from *El Diário del Che en Bolivia* with a prologue by Fidel Castro, 3rd ed. (México, D. F.: Siglo Veintiuno, 1968), p. 152.
12. Neill Macaulay, *A Rebel in Cuba* (Chicago: Quadrangle Books, 1970), p. 24.
13. Soldini, as quoted in ibid., p. 14.
14. Ibid., p. 60.
15. Ibid., pp. 79–80.
16. Neill Macaulay, *The Sandino Affair* (Chicago: Quadrangle Books, 1967), p. 212.
17. Eqbal Ahmad, "Revolutionary War and Counterinsurgency," in *Revolutionary War: Western Responses*, ed. David S. Sullivan and Martin J. Sattler (New York: Columbia University Press, 1971), p. 9.
18. "Eritrea's Silent War of Secession," *The Swiss Review of World Affairs*, March 1976, pp. 22–24.
19. In Guevara, *Obra revolucionaria*, p. 31.
20. Walter Laqueur, *Guerrilla: A Historical and Critical Study* (Boston: Little, Brown, 1976).
21. Chaliand, *Revolution in the Third World*, p. 69.
22. Guevara, *Reminiscences*, p. 228. Batista had formally adhered to the Cuban Constitution of 1940, which allowed him to impose censorship for only ninety days. When this period expired, Batista had to find a new pretext to reimpose censorship.
23. Guevara, *Obra revolucionaria*, p. 163–164.
24. Quoted here as reproduced in Herbert Matthews, *The Cuban Story* (New York: George Braziller, 1961), p. 27.
25. Ibid., p. 31.
26. Ibid., p. 45.
27. Ibid., p. 41.
28. Ibid.
29. Ibid.
30. Herbert L. Matthews, *Castro: A Political Biography* (London: Penguin Press, 1969), pp. 96–97.
31. Guevara, *Obra revolucionaria*, p. 153.
32. Quoted in Matthews, *The Cuban Story*, p. 48.
33. Ibid., p. 46.
34. Enrique Dussel, *A History of the Church in Latin America: Colonialism to Liberation* (Grand Rapids: William Eerdmans, 1981), p. 172. The translation from the 3rd Spanish edition of 1971 is by Alan Neely of Southeastern Baptist Theological Seminary.
35. See Germán Guzmán Campos, *El Padre-Camilo Torres*, 3rd ed. (México D. F.: Siglo Veintiuno Editores, 1969) p. 263.
36. Gustavo Gutiérrez, *Teología de la liberación*, 7th ed. (Salamanca: Ediciones Sigueme, 1975), p. 95. This and the following quotations are my translations from this 7th edition, published just three years after the 1st edition.
37. Ibid., p. 108.
38. Ibid., p. 130.

4

The Changing Role of Revolutionary Violence in Nicaragua, 1959–1979

Antonio Ybarra–Rojas

The success of the Sandinista revolution has been generally attributed to a movement toward the center in a social–democratic manner by the Sandinista National Liberation Front (FSLN). The main hypothesis of this chapter is that what actually occurred was a realignment of the FSLN to the Stalinist, communist strategy previously adopted by the Cuban leadership after 1975 and followed by the Sandinistas.

We will be looking at the changing role of violence within the successive ideological archetypes that have sustained the different strategic models followed by the Sandinistas from 1959 to 1979. This will help to identify the varying adaptations to the changing strategic models adopted by the Cuban Revolution. Integrating the historical development of the FSLN into the Cuban strategic forces explains the conditions that have permitted the Cuban Communist Party to direct the level of violence and ideology and the strategic line of the Sandinistas. The focus of this chapter is the changing role of revolutionary violence in Nicaragua as a result of the FSLN's on the Cuban leadership.

The PSN was established in 1947 as the country's first communist, pro–Soviet party. Despite its name, it is a full–fledged Marxist–Leninist organization having nothing to do, formally or otherwise, with the international socialist movement or principles.

The Sandinista Brotherhood Is Born in the PSN

In 1952, Jośe Manuel Fortuny, then secretary–general of the Guatemalan Labor Party stated that Guatemalan communists believed their country would have to continue for some time on the path of capitalism—a national and democratic capitalism, of course, for which the party counted on the collaboration of the progressive bourgeoisie and the army.[1] The 1954 defeat of the revolutionary government of Jacobo Arbenz raised serious questions about the viability of the strategy of gaining power under middle–class leadership. The defeat greatly influenced the views of Ernesto "Che" Guevara, who personally participated on the losing side of this struggle in Guatemala. Guevara focused his criticism on the illusions of building an alliance with the armed forces even if they were led by nationalist middle–class officers and the forces of the Communist Party.[2] He concluded that only a revolutionary army would guarantee the social gains of a popular revolution. The perspective at work was that a new field of political struggle would open up, and that the triumph of the Cuban Revolution would be confirmation that such an alternative was viable.

A new concept of revolutionary strategy was also being formulated. The empirical lessons of the defeat in Guatemala led Guevara to break with the Stalinist classical model of revolution by stages or phases, the view that a "phase" of democracy is required and that this phase necessitates capitalist bourgeois–democratic state institutions and a historical period of capitalist development.[3] For the Stalinist Latin American communist parties, however, the lesson from Guatemala was that a stronger alliance with the middle classes was required and would lead to the formation of a "Democratic Front". Since the late 1950s it has repeatedly split into increasingly radical factions, the most important of which are the FSLN, the Communist Party of Nicaragua (PC de N) which is all–out Stalinist, and the Popular Action Movement–Marxist–Leninist (MAP–ML), a Maoist group.

In Nicaragua by 1948, the political space working with the Somoza regime was closed to the communists because of Somoza's initial repression with the application of Cold War policies. Following the example of the Guatemalan Labor Party, the PSN set to work radicalizing the middle classes. The new relationship with radical middle sectors had a contaminating effect on the party, and its youth branch (the JSN), which led the effort of opening this new political space, became increasingly influenced by its new allies. As a result, among the leadership of the JSN, led by Guatemalan cadre Heriberto Carrillo, and by Silvio Mayorga, Tomás Borge, and Carlos Fonseca Amador,[4] there developed a new revolutionary archetype that would bring about an alternative strategic model, and with it the Sandinista Brotherhood.

The petite bourgeoisie started to become radicalized in Nicaragua after the defeat of a military uprising of April 1954 and the clear evidence that Somoza was going to seek re–election and not step down, as he had promised conservative leader Emiliano Chamorro in the 1950 pact. According to Eduardo Crawley,[5] the relationship between the middle classes and Somoza grew more hostile after the July 1955 currency devaluation. At that time, from the youth of the Independent Liberal Party, there emerged Rigoberto López Pérez, who had been forced into exile. According to Crawley,[6] while Rigoberto was in El Salvador he became convinced that if Somoza were assassinated, there would be a spontaneous uprising that would finish the job of demolishing the dictatorship. On September 20, 1956, Rigoberto assassinated President Anastasio Somoza García. Besides the direct accomplices, many others were involved. According to Andrés Pascal Allende,[7] Carlos Fonseca was imprisoned in connection with the assassination and was deported that year. In the repression that followed, Tomás Borge was also jailed for several years, and the incipient communist student movement was broken up.[8]

Rigoberto López had successfully introduced violence into the political struggle in Nicaragua. All previous acts of violence against the regime had ended in failure, but his self–sacrifice succeeded. His poem "Anxiety" expressed the feeling of the entire radical petite bourgeoisie of Nicaragua, which carried a "hero in their veins that seeks liberation".[9] The political explanation of Rigoberto's act would be expressed through another of his poems, "Nicaraguans," where he stated: "Finish off Somoza in the way that he imposed himself on us and that we know so well".[10] (Somoza had to kill Sandino in order to come to power.) This notion of gaining liberation through the killing of Somoza and martyrdom on the altar of the fatherland is the foundation of the Sandinista Brotherhood.

The same perspective also explains the words of Fonseca, quoted by Tomás Borge: "Sandino," he said, "is a path" initially taken by the first Sandinista of the Brotherhood, its quasi–mythical hero, Rigoberto López Pérez.[11] The archetype under which the Sandinista Brotherhood was born was a fraternity modeled on the ideal of martyrdom, in the shadow of unselfishness: Sandino and Rigoberto. The Sandinista Brotherhood sees itself as brothers of Rigoberto who will continue to kill the murderer of their father until they topple the regime.

For PSN leader Luis Sánchez Sancho' however, the communist strategy was to be directed toward building a "Democratic Front" against Somoza, but one that would not allow Chamorro's Conservative Party to gain hegemony.[12] In addition to the terrorist ideal of martyrdom, the Sandinista Brotherhood was also subjected to other ideological influences during its formative period. After being elected president of the student body of the Centro Universitario de la Universidad Nacional (CUUN) in 1957, Carlos Fonseca was a PSN delegate to the Sixth World Youth and Student Festival in Moscow.[13] In a pamphlet that related his impressions of the Soviet Union, entitled "A Nicaraguan in Moscow", he praised the practice of U.S.S.R.–style communism. According to Nolan,[14] Fonseca's uncritical apology for Soviet orthodoxy was best expressed when he explained how communism had solved both social and economic questions: "Now the answer is the States". Fonseca "believed that the Soviet State represented the people and that consequently the true owners of the factories are the people".[15] In a classic Stalinist pro–Moscow perspective, he failed to understand the difference between the independent organization of the working class and the bureaucratic dictatorship against the people of the Soviet Union.

A synthesis, a new strategic model, was developing, one that Rigoberto had brought to the forefront with his belief that a successful assassination would spark a spontaneous uprising. This belief resembled the assumption that the *foco* insurrectional strategy would bring about insurrection, based upon a claimed inference of what the Cuban Revolution was about. The substitution of armed struggle for attempts on the lives of the heads of government marked the transition to the new strategic mode.

The Sandinistas Split from the PSN

According to Ernest Mandel, the Cuban Revolution is the only victorious revolution that was not led by a force originating from the Stalinist Communist International or that was not heavily influenced by Stalinism.[16] The Cuban Stalinists strenuously opposed the early July 26 Movement, openly sabotaging Fidel Castro's strike call in 1958 and participating in Batista's fake elections.

The Cuban guerrilla struggle had an immediate impact in Nicaragua. In November 1957 a plot by Nicaraguan air force officers and conservative party members was uncovered in Honduras.[17] In September 1958 Ramón Raudales began an armed movement called the "First Liberation Army of Nicaragua", which included the old followers of Sandino and university students like Alejandro Martínez and Edén Pastora Gómez (Commander "Zero"). The survivors of that experience later founded the "Sandino Revolutionary Front".[18]

The rest of the opposition pursued armed struggle. In February 1958 Enrique Lacayo Farfán of the Independent Liberal Party and Pedro Joaquín Chamorro of the Conservative Party led an invasion from Costa Rica.[19] In March 1958, the signing of a minimal program led to the founding of a new communist political front, the "Republican Mobilization Party" (PMR); Fonseca was one of the co-signers.[20] In March 1959 the PSN called upon Silvio Mayorga and Carlos Fonseca to set up the youth branch of the PMR, the Juventud Democrática Nicaragüense (Nicaraguan Democratic Youth), later known as Juventud Patriótica.

However, after receiving the information that the Conservative Party was preparing an invasion in Costa Rica with the help of President "Pepe" Figueres, the PSN started organizing an invasion group of its own. This group went to Cuba and, according to the *New York Times*, was led by the "Nicaraguan Communist, Rafael Somarriba". Trained by Major Ernesto ("Che") Guevara in Havana, the group was then sent off to Honduras, where it was attacked and dispersed by the Honduran army at El Chaparral.[21] The guerrilla column was named "Rigoberto López Pérez". It was joined by Carlos Fonseca, who with the help of the local communist party was able to travel from Guatemala to Honduras and join the group that had just arrived from Cuba. In June, Fonseca was wounded, and left Tegucigalpa in September to recuperate in the Calixto García Hospital in Havana.[22]

The young Cuban leaders quickly learned to support the Stalinist line. From as early as 1959 they did not support any group that was not allied with the PSN. The *New York Times* reported that the group led by Chester Lacayo had gone to see Castro to ask for support of an invasion of Nicaragua and that they were told "by Premier Fidel Castro's brother, Major Raúl Castro, Commander–in–Chief of the Cuban armed forces, that a condition of aid was to form a '*popular front*' with the communists. They were also told to deal directly with Major Ernesto (Che) Guevara, commander of La Cabana Fortress in Havana, who was in charge of Caribbean affairs".[23] Cuba's support was also demonstrated by the training it provided to the "Rigoberto López Pérez" column, which also included an important number of Cuban fighters. Later the same month, the *New York Times* reported the arrival in Havana of twenty–eight Cubans captured by the Honduran authorities and flown back to Cuba from the battle of El Chaparral.[24]

When Carlos Fonseca returned to Nicaragua from Cuba, Tomás Borge explained Fonseca's effort to convince the "generation of Juventud Patriótica" of his new ideological learnings: "He attempted, though still a novice, to give the Juventud Patriótica [associated with the PSN] a new ideological content. He made a great impression on its leadership. The Socialist Party, of course, opposed such audacity".[25] Fonseca's new approach was to abandon the PSN's strategic model of revolution by stages. What he was really advancing was the Cuban version of "permanent revolution". This new line proposed the socialist revolution as the direct strategic objective, not a democratic, anti–imperialist, bourgeois revolution, like the one that had just failed in Guatemala. The empirical discovery of this strategic model was acquired in the company of Che Guevara with whom Fonseca had established a deep friendship. From Guevara he would hear about the notion of uninterrupted revolution, a revolution that does not go through "stages" or "phases" but grows directly into a socialist revolution. Central America's version of this new model was also present in Guatemala, where Fonseca was again deported in June 1960 and sent to El Petén in July. In El Petén he met and established a strong friendship with Lieutenant Luis Augusto Turcios Lima, the future head of the FAR of Guatemala.[26]

On November 29, 1960, Carlos Fonseca arrived in Havana, where he met up with Tomás Borge and Julio Jerez. This time they accepted a proposal by Guevara to organize an independent political organization, separate from the PSN, that would adopt the new Castroite strategic line of socialist revolution.[27] Fonseca did not try to separate the activity of his organization from the PSN for many years.[28] However, when PSN leaders rejected him, their own cadre, Fonseca, recently returned from Cuba, blamed the rejection on Che Guevara. In order to better understand the PSN's reaction to Fonseca's new strategic option, it is necessary to know what international communist lessons Cuba was propounding at the time.

In an interview with a Chinese journalist in April 1959, Guevara stated that the Cuban revolution was "of an uninterrupted development, that it needed to abolish the whole social system and its economic foundations".[29] But even the most open–minded communist leaders in Latin America had another understanding of the Cuban Revolution. For Rodney Arismendi,[30] leader of the Uruguayan Communist Party, the history of bourgeois–democratic revolutions in Latin America, such as the one in Cuba, demonstrated the need for construction of a "democratic front" that included the workers, the peasants, the middle sectors, and the most advanced sectors of the national bourgeoisie. Of course, the support of the national bourgeoisie would require that private property be temporarily respected and that the capitalist mode of production not be drastically changed.

The FSLN and Che Guevara

According to Guillermo Toriello Garrido,[31] the 1954 defeat in Guatemala occurred because of the unfavorable "correlation of forces" during that period. The Cuban leadership had a firsthand understanding of the role of the "correlation of forces", because in April 1961 they had faced the Bay of Pigs invasion. The understanding that their revolution was in great danger of a collapse led them, from their first day in power, to develop forces that would consolidate the revolution. Their conviction that the Soviet Union would ultimately not go to war with the United States on their behalf was only confirmed by the outcome of the missile crisis. From the start, revolutionary Cuba's national interest required the creation of forces that could continentalize the conflict should Cuba be faced with an armed U.S. intervention. Therefore, in every Latin American country possible, Cuba's foreign policy sought to create groups modeled on the Sierra Maestra guerrilla experience. Even if those forces did not achieve the overthrow of their governments, their manipulation by Havana would be an effective tool to convince the countries of the region that it was in their best interest to keep Cuba as a friend rather than to treat it as an agent of subversion.

In 1961, implementing Che Guevara's proposal, Carlos Fonseca Amador founded the "New Nicaragua Movement," a front organization that included the young cubs of the PSN and the non–communists of the "Sandino Revolutionary Front". In a July meeting in Tegucigalpa, the leadership decided to form the Sandinista National Liberation Front (FSLN).[32] The first task of the FSLN was to put into practice the teachings of Che Guevara. The modus operandi that characterized the formative period of the FSLN was largely a logistical operation, from Nicaragua to Cuba by way of Tegucigalpa and Mexico City. First Santos López was recruited, then Germán Pomares,[33] and to complete their claim to the property rights on the Sandinista label, Blanca Segovias Sandino, the very daughter of Sandino.[34] In addition, Nicaraguans from other countries were recruited and directed toward Cuba for training. Tomás Borge explained: "Silvio [Mayorga] went to Caracas and brought back a group of Nicaraguans to Cuba, where already there were other Nicaraguans joyfully walking the jubilant streets of Havana. Later there were the Sandinista guerrillas at Bocay and Rio Coco".[35]

The first foco of Bocay and Rio Coco was a total disaster; that first application of Che Guevara's guerrilla warfare theory had left the FSLN worse off than when it started, with only about twenty activists left in the cities and ten in the mountains.[36] For Guevara, the strategic objective of a socialist revolution had two implications: first, a successful socialist revolution would come about through armed struggle directed by a military revolutionary vanguard; second, socialism would be achieved only through the destruction of the military–bureaucratic apparatus of the capitalist state (as claimed by Lenin).[37] The role of the vanguard was to create the "subjective" revolutionary conditions through armed struggle. In order to achieve this miracle, only a small cadre of revolutionary fighter was necessary, as in the case of Cuba, where only twelve men survived the landing at Granma. The subjective conditions would be the aftermath of the foco, which would ignite a spontaneous spark of rural-based revolution. This theory of a spontaneous spark, or foquismo, was later elaborated by Régis Debray.[38] Che Guevara's strategy was to use guerrilla warfare to force the capitalist state, even if formally a democracy, to unmask itself, to reveal its repressive character.[39]

The Sandinista Front proclaimed itself to be the type of instrument that Che Guevara prescribed.[40] It decided first to become the needed "vanguard" and second to develop armed struggle to destroy the capitalist state. However, the strategic model of Guevara, after it was patterned, had other features that revealed a terrorist character. For Lenin, "the cult of spontaneity is the common route of all terrorists".[41] Accordingly terrorists think they can create the subjective conditions for the revolution merely by arousing the indignation of those intellectuals who are self-sacrificing, isolated individuals working to bring down the established order.

After the defeats of Bocay and Río Coco in 1962 and 1963, the FSLN retreated to the cities to start recruiting and building up its membership for a larger, better prepared foco. It recruited from among the youth of the PSN and from cadres in Moscow on scholarships, as in the case of Oscar Turcios, who became a member of the FSLN in Moscow in 1965 and then returned to Nicaragua.[42]

For Carlos Fonseca, however, the experience of this period of legal work would only confirm his conviction regarding the role of violence as a needed corrective element lacking during that phase. He stated: "The armed struggle is the only thing that can inspire the revolutionary combatant in Nicaragua to carry out the tasks decided by the revolutionary leadership, whether they be armed or of any other revolutionary character".[43] The practice of terrorism would be the key, while commitment to Marxist–Leninist ideology would come alive when armed struggle came alive. That would be the criterion that would distinguish between the "false" Marxist and the "true" Marxist.[44]

In this context, it is easier to understand Fonseca's line, which he presented to the FSLN:

> At the current time, it is necessary for us to strongly emphasize that our major objective is the *socialist revolution*, a revolution that aims to defeat Yankee imperialism and its local agents, false oppositionists and false revolutionaries. This propaganda, with the firm backing of armed action, will permit the front to win the support of a sector of the popular masses that is conscious of the profound nature of the struggle we are carrying out.[45]

Under this model, violence is propaganda, socialist propaganda through the armed actions of the vanguard—the same type of propaganda as the "martyrdom" of Rigoberto, who died while assassinating Somoza García. The violent act itself awakens the "consciousness of the popular masses to the profound nature of the struggle we are carrying out".[46] But *who* will perform this heroic task? Fonseca had an answer: "The sector of the people formed by students is the one that with great enthusiasm accepts this goal".[47]

The Cuban Strategic Forces Integrate the FSLN

For the Cuban leadership, the Somozas were the main American card in the region. The special effort put into developing the FSLN can explain why, besides just qualifying on the basis of a shared strategic model, this small group of terrorist students was invited to represent Nicaragua alongside the major organizations of the Left from the Third World in the First Tricontinental Conference in Havana in January 1966; Carlos Reyna was the official FSLN representative.[48] As the *New York Times* reported at the time, the Tricontinental Conference

> was an attempt by the most militant segments of the Communist parties of the world to organize a world Communist strategy that would confront the non–Communist particularly the United States, with a series of guerrilla wars. It was hoped that these would cause chaos in so many places at the same time that

even an interventionist and powerful government in Washington could not hope to deal with them.[49]

Who were these "militant Communist parties"? They were primarily the left–wing Stalinists of the Third World—North Korea, North Vietnam, and the newly formed Communist Party of Cuba. Application of this policy to Latin America would have to wait for clarification until the July 1967 meeting of the Latin American Solidarity Organization (OLAS).

According to the *New York Times*, the meeting of OLAS reassured the delegates that Cuba would meet her "revolutionary duty" to support the guerrillas of the continent.[50] The FSLN representatives, Casimiro Sotelo and Julio Buitrago, led the Nicaraguan delegation.[51] However, many communist parties declined the invitation, and some, like Chile's, ended up criticizing the meeting in *Pravda*, the newspaper of the Soviet Communist Party. The autonomy of the Cuban leadership with regard to the Soviet Union can be measured by the margin of dissent they expressed against their benefactor state. *The New York Times* reported that the conference approved a resolution condemning Soviet economic and technical assistance policy in the Western hemisphere.[52] It was also reported that the final resolution of the conference was seen as a "challenge to Moscow" because it proclaimed that the fundamental line of revolution of Latin America was armed struggle.[53]

The OLAS meeting concluded with a message of salute from Bolivia by Ernesto Guevara.[54] The meeting was actually an endorsement of the strategic model of Che Guevara, then on trial in the jungles of Bolivia. The strategy of the OLAS, for the Cuban government, was to try to create a second and third Vietnam in Latin America so that the isolation of Cuba could be broken and the enemy forces directed against Cuba would be dispersed and diluted. Bolivia seemed to be one of the best fortress nations of Latin America from which to resist an intervention and to propagate revolution. However, the fate of Guevara in Bolivia was paralleled on another battlefield of this continental war by the FSLN's foco of Pancasán.

The destinies of both intertwined. *The New York Times* of October 12, 1967, reported both defeats: the death of Che Guevara in Bolivia and the news that the FSLN guerrillas in northern Nicaragua had been smashed.[55] However, Cuba did try to cover the guerrillas' defeat in Pancasán in August 1967. The *Tricontinental Bulletin* of September 1967 reported that they were still fighting; the November issue reported their presence; the December issue denied Somoza's report of the defeat.[56] Even the January–February 1968 issue declared that the FSLN was well and fighting.[57] But the reality was otherwise. The FSLN was dead and had to be reborn—this time in Cuba. A year later, the *Tricontinental Bulletin* reported the fatal casualties of the foco of Pancasán.[58]

According to Casimiro Sotelo, in *Tricontinental Magazine*,[59] the FSLN had wanted to provoke a U.S. intervention in Nicaragua with the foco of Pancasán. The objective was to further Guevara's many–Vietnams strategy of dispersing the forces of imperialism by igniting a war throughout Latin America. The Pancasán foco was timed to be simultaneous with Guevara's Bolivian campaign. Every event was timed to coincide with Guevara's efforts, namely, the 1966 Tricontinental Conference and the 1967 OLAS meeting. The Cuban leadership's use of FSLN forces to launch an offensive in Nicaragua without the resources, strength, or popular support needed to confront the challenge not only of the National Guard but of a U.S. military intervention made their intentions clear. They wanted to subordinate the interest of Nicaragua's revolutionary objectives to the geopolitical interest of the Cuban regime. This experience demonstrated that the Sandinista front was no longer an autonomous Nicaraguan insurrectional organization but had been absorbed completely into the Cuban strategic forces.

Only the Cubans, and Che Guevara in Bolivia, could really benefit from the sacrifices of the Sandinista guerrillas. However, Guevara's strategy did pay off in part: the Somoza regime was forced to unmask itself. Guevara stated this goal in writing: "The dictatorship tries to function without resorting to violence, thereby masking its true nature".[60] The repression that followed Pancasán created tremendous suffering in the Nicaraguan countryside.[61] However, the FSLN was also "unmasked" as a force that was alien to the political reality of the Nicaraguan people, as an instrument of the Cuban strategic forces.

The Cuban Vanguard in the "Protracted Popular War" in Nicaragua

After Che Guevara's death in Bolivia, Fidel Castro accused the leader of the Bolivian Communist Party, Mario Monge, of being co–responsible for the defeat. He stated: "The Communist Party pretended to dispute with Che over the political and military position of head of the movement".[62] Monge claimed that he wanted to lead the struggle in his own country. Castro's reaction can be explained: the war was a war "in" Bolivia, not "of" Bolivia. He saw it as part of a continental war with many battlefields whose vanguard and headquarters were in Havana. A month later, César Montes of Guatemala's FAR would clarify this model of the vanguard role: "Those who are really ready to make revolution must build their vanguard organizations in the heat of battle, as the Koreans did with Kim, the Vietnamese with Ho, and the Cubans with Fidel".[63] Under this model of Third World Stalinism, not only is the Cuban Communist Party the vanguard for this continent, but Cuban–style leaderships should become the vanguards in every country.

The Nicaraguan version arrived quickly. In August 1968, Carlos Fonseca Amador blamed the "hypocrites who disguise themselves as revolutionaries" for the defeat in Pancasán. He ended by proclaiming: "The sacrifice of Major Ernesto 'Che' Guevara represents the firm resolve of Latin American guerrilla forces to engage in the battle that will lead to socialist emancipation".[64] Fonseca was a late starter in a process that already had its own history. Douglas Bravo had been expelled from the Venezuelan Communist Party after he rejected the party's authority and its "mass line".[65] César Montes, in Guatemala, had split from the PGT, declaring his independence from the party.[66] In March 1968, the PGT responded by raising the question of the vanguard.[67] It was necessary to identify the vanguard as well as the relationship between the vanguard and the groups that sponsor armed struggle. For Andrés Pascal Allende of Chile as late as 1979, Cuba was not a historic exception but the vanguard of the Latin American revolution.[68]

After the disaster of the foco of Pancasán and the losses in the city of Managua, where Casimiro Sotelo, Roberto Amaya, Hugo Medina, and Edmundo Pérez were killed, the FSLN prepared for its rebirth in Cuba. From 1968 to 1970 the new leadership of the FSLN was trained in Cuba and in other communist countries and prepared to become the alternative "vanguard" for Nicaragua and Central America under the Cuban leadership and the Cuban version of the "prolonged popular war" strategic model. The FSLN revealed its program of "popular war in Central America" in *Tricontinental Magazine* in May–June 1970,[69] with a model based on the following principles: (1) the spark of violence in the masses would generate a guerrilla war; (2) the new strategic concept of a close combination of political and military struggles would be used to develop a "protracted war"; (3) the political–moral factor (the accepted legitimacy of their cause among the people) would turn the balance of the "correlation of forces" in their favor; (4) the armed struggle would take place in rural areas, and the rural population would be the support base; (5) the strategic posture would be "offensive," because this was to be part of a "continental war" against the United States within a global "offensive" spearheaded by Vietnam; (6) the war would be a local war that would face or provoke a U.S. military intervention, a phase necessary to develop the general–insurrection stage of the war; and (7) the war would be fought in the whole of Central America, and for that purpose the FSLN would coordinate and develop the guerrilla movements of the other countries in order to create a second Vietnam.

The most revealing feature of the Cuban version of protracted people's war is the notion of an "offensive strategic" posture, not a defensive one. The theory of protracted popular war developed in Asia by Mao and Giap pinned strategy to a defensive posture based on Clausewitz's concept of the advantage of the strategic defensive in war—especially when one faces a large enemy force and the objective is to increase one's forces over time.[70] The Cuban version, adopted by the FSLN, was far from the view of General Giap, for whom "a conception born of impatience and aimed at obtaining speedy victory could only be a gross error".[71]

For Cuba, however, this new strategic model had its advantages, especially under the conditions of Soviet pressure to change course. A protracted people's war strategy could put Cuba's proxy on hold and, for the time being, have them "count" on their own resources in the development of their "own" forces. The showdown with the Soviet Union was under way, and the process of Stalinization of the Cuban Revolution would soon be complete.

Adoption of the people's war strategy did not mean a departure from Guevara. It meant following him in his own theoretical development, presented in his July 1957 paper on "The War and Peasant Population"[72] and in his review of Mao and Giap in his preface to Vo Nguyen Giap's 1964 book *People's War, People's Army*. For the Cuban leadership, the strategy of protracted people's war was a means of resolving the question of the vanguard to their advantage.

The FSLN Follows the Cubans Under the New Soviet Pressures

Irving Luis Horowitz has published a good view of the theory of the Stalinization of the Cuban Revolution.[74] External indicators were evident as early as 1968, when Castro publicly supported the Soviet invasion of Czechoslovakia. The Soviet grip grew even tighter, given their subsidization of the Cuban economy, and this dependence took a qualitative leap forward after the failure of the *Zafra*, the 10–million–ton sugar harvest. With regard to Latin America, the Soviet Union would not abandon the role of the vanguard to Cuba. The rift in Soviet–Cuban relations, under way for some time, became public in 1968 when Soviet military deliveries to Cuba hit an all–time rock bottom.[75] The following year the Soviets told the Cuban leadership that they must stop conflicting with Soviet strategy in Latin America, or they would get no more oil deliveries. The Cubans closed the guerrilla training camps. For the Soviet Union, other opportunities offered more promising returns in Latin America at the time. In Chile, Salvador Allende was on the way to being elected president; in Peru, General Velasco Alvarado was buying Soviet military supplies, and "progressive" changes were taking place in Argentina under Héctor Campora. It was not the time for Cuba to continue its "continental war" against the United States. A new realism descended on the Cuban bureaucracy. They understood that dependence on sugar cane was not that bad, and the monoculture under Soviet–style socialism was better than no socialism at all.

The Cubans did not leave their Sandinista Brotherhood completely out in the cold. The FSLN was provided with channels to survive the period of reaccommodation with the Soviets. The Cubans looked toward the PLO and the North Koreans to train the FSLN. In Mexico in 1969, a FSLN–PLO agreement was signed;[76] the PLO "ambassador" to Cuba coordinated the relationship with Tomás Borge.[77] As payment for their training in Amman (Jordan),[78] where Commander Pedro Arauz Palacios of the FSLN fought against King Hussein in September 1970, the FSLN helped the PLO in its terrorist campaign.[79] Juan José Quezada of the FSLN hijacked a British Overseas Airways plane on September 9. Patricio Argüello Ryan, with Leyla Khaled, attempted to hijack an Israeli El-Al aircraft, but the attempt failed and Argüello was killed.[80] Both operations were developed together with George Habash's, PFLP, a member of the PLO umbrella.[81] In 1969 a number of FSLN militants were trained by the PLO in Tyre, Lebanon, and others in PLO camps in Algeria.[82] After Fonseca was freed from prison in Costa Rica, he, Carlos Aguerro, and Humberto Ortega Saavedra led FSLN militants to training camps in North Korea.[83] The first battles of the "protracted popular war" were being fought in airplanes all over the world and in terrorist training camps overseas.

In Nicaragua, after the government took over the student association, the FSLN finally received the new recruits it needed to apply the protracted war strategy at home.[84] However, the new strategy brought only the same history of defeats. In 1969, Julio Buitrago and most of the internal resistance leadership were killed in Managua. In January 1970 Commander Leonel Rugama, the new head of the FSLN internal resistance, was also killed, along with his high command. In February the Zinica guerrilla column suffered many casualties. In April, Enrique Lorente and Luisa Amanda Espinoza were killed in León.[85] The worst blow came in December, when José Benito Escobar, Daniel Ortega, and fifteen other Sandinistas were captured, leaving Oscar Turcios, who had just returned from Lebanon, as the sole member of the National Directorate of the FSLN free in Nicaragua.[86] The month before, in November, Anastasio Somoza Debayle had reached a power–sharing agreement with Fernando Aguerro Rocha, head of the Conservative Party. The new pact was called the "Kupia Kumi".

The FSLN formulated a new characterization of the regime in power in Nicaragua, first in the July 1971 *Tricontinental Bulletin* and finally in the February 1972 issue, where the government was identified as "a liberal–conservative regime bathed in blood that hands the country over to North American imperialism".[87] That definition presaged a new approach to the type of struggle needed to confront the government of the united oligarchy of Nicaragua.

The stability of Somoza's regime was short lived. The earthquake of December 23, 1972, also killed the alliance with the Conservative Party, leaving the latter divided into three factions. For the FSLN, however, things also got worse. In September 1973, Oscar Turcios, Ricardo Morales, Juan José Quezada, and Jonathan González were killed by the National Guard in the neighborhood of Nandaime in Granada.[88] During that period, which was known in the FSLN as the phase of "silent accumulation of forces",[89] Fonseca was writing his "Notes on the Will of Rigoberto López Pérez".[90] But the Cuban security forces were devoted to another task. In April 1972, Camilo Ortega Saavedra arrived in Cuba for military training and surprisingly, at twenty–two, became the head "responsible" for the FSLN troops in Cuba.[91] The Cubans had earlier given that position to another young Sandinista leader, Fausto Amador, half brother of Carlos Fonseca Amador, who came to Cuba after the disaster of Pancasán. But Fausto did not work out as expected. He found it difficult to adapt to Stalinism, and after leaving Cuba in 1969 he joined the Trotskyist Fourth International (United Secretariat).[92]

What was Camilo up to in Cuba from 1972 to 1975? The official Sandinista biography of Camilo claims that he was involved in an intense study of revolutionary theory.[93] But why would the brother of Humberto and Daniel Ortega Saavedra be trained in theory for such a long time? Because from this process "the fundamental lines that permitted the first elements of what would be the strategy that led to the takeover of power in Nicaragua [were] to be drawn".[94]

What was going on in Cuba at that time was in fact the formulation of a new strategic model that would mean a total break with the strategy of "protracted people's war". The new strategic model would be more representative of the total Soviet control over Cuban Stalinism, and it would better reflect the new "correlation of forces" on a worldwide scale. The new strategy would be to in fact abandon Guevarism and the Cuban version of "permanent revolution" at the June 1975 Havana meeting of the Stalinist parties of Latin America.[95] But not all the FSLN leadership were able to adjust as the Ortega brothers had. In August 1975 Carlos Fonseca returned to the mountains of Nicaragua for the last time, determined to implement the "protracted popular war" strategy learned from Guevara and Luis Turcios Lima, under the banner of the strategic objective of socialist revolution without compromise with "Democratic Fronts" with the Nicaraguan bourgeoisie.[96]

The FSLN Rejoins the World Stalinist Movement

The 1975 conference of Latin American communist parties tried its best to help the Cubans save face.[97] However, the Cubans signed a declaration recognizing (1) that communist parties would lead the struggle in Latin America; (2) the legitimacy of "all forms of struggle"; (3) the independence of every party to choose the correct course of action; (4) acceptance of a selective policy of occupying different political spaces, including the formation of "democratic fronts''; and (5) the strategic option of a revolution by ''stages'' or ''phases.'' The document made clarified the implications for Nicaragua:

> In Central America . . . the formation of broad anti–oligarchic and democratic fronts in some countries, the existence of progressive elements in the armies of some countries, the formation of an alliance of banana–producing countries . . . and the growing isolation . . . of the Somoza dictatorship, the main watchdog of the imperialist interest in the region, are all indicators of unquestionable gains in the struggle.[98]

The conference also legitimized armed struggle led by the communist parties in cases like Chile and Nicaragua, but under a broad anti–oligarchic movement allied with the bourgeoisie.

The Stalinization of Cuba made even friends of the Cuban revolution recognize that ''one striking example of this is Havana's alignment, almost total, behind Kremlin policies in Latin America and behind the strategy of the Stalinist Communist parties of that continent''.[99] The FSLN, tied to Cuba's tail, followed Havana in its new course. The strategy for the overthrow of Somoza, which the Cubans were teaching the Ortega brothers of the new FSLN leadership, had already been elaborated with Moscow's blessing since 1968.

In February 1968, Luis Sánchez Sancho, who until 1985 was secretary general of the PSN, outlined the strategy for a successful overthrow of the Somoza regime. He presented the elements of this strategy ''as the objective of the entire present stage of the revolution, as the minimum program of anti–oligarchy—anti–imperialist and democratic government, the realization of which would open the way directly to the socialist tasks''.[100] The model includes (1) a minimum program that would be the basis of a broad ''Democratic Front'' that included the anti–Somoza bourgeoisie; (2) the preparation of a successful insurrection strategy by ''popular uprisings''; (3) raising the pressure in the ''boiler'' to the point that an explosion might take the form of a ''popular uprising''; (4) the hegemony of the vanguard of the working class in such an alliance; and (5) an urban–center theater of operations. It was precisely this strategy that Fonseca rejected in his ''Nicaragua: Zero Hour,'' and it was this strategy that the FSLN opposed when it presented its Cuban version of the ''protracted popular war'' in Central America. Consequently, it was not easy for the Cubans to impose their new strategy on the old guard of the FSLN.

The issue of the new Cuban strategic model led to the divisions the FSLN suffered from 1974 to 1977. The process practically required development within the FSLN of a faction led by the Ortega brothers that could become the dominant force with the help of the Cuban bureaucracy. According to a FSLN communiqué of December 1976, signed by Commander Pedro Arauz

Palacios, the Ortega brothers (Humberto and Daniel), Victor Tirado, and José Benito Escobar, in a special session the National Directorate of the FSLN in October 1976 "purged" Carlos Fonseca from his post as secretary general of the FSLN and from his position within the National Directorate.[101] The decision was reached without the participation of the rest of the National Directorate: Henry Ruiz, Carlos Aguerro, Tomás Borge and Pedro Arauz Palacios himself. The communiqué also stated that Commander Fonseca was left with the option of leaving with the guerrilla column headed by Humberto Ortega, out of the Zinica region and on to Cuba, or staying by himself in the mountains, where the National Guard was already aware of the guerrillas' presence. Fonseca decided to stay and tried unsuccessfully to contact the other guerrilla groups headed by Henry Ruiz and Carlos Aguerro. Accompanied by only three comrades, the almost–blind founder of the FSLN died in combat two weeks later, on November 8, 1976, during an attack by a National Guard patrol in the Zinica area.

In 1977 the new Cuban line was expressed by the insurrectional tendency of the FSLN of the Ortega brothers, which publicly abandoned the rural protracted war strategy in favor of the urban–based insurrectional model, as described by Luis Sánchez Sancho in 1968, in alliance with all the "democratic forces." The document that introduced the new strategy entitled "Politico–Military Platform of May 1977 of the Tercerista Insurreccional Tendency",[102] adopted all the basic elements required by the Soviet strategy for Nicaragua: the minimal program, the "Democratic Front", armed struggle as mass insurrections in the cities, even the "party" as the workers' vanguard. In addition, it assured the other Stalinist bureaucracies that the new FSLN was a party that intended to develop an iron fist. The document also stated that the transition to socialism had taken place, which translated into Stalinism. But, most remarkable, the new model of violence no longer advanced a war of national liberation but proclaimed a real Nicaraguan civil war.

The civil war took the form of an offensive against the Somoza regime, and it began in October 1977. Humberto Ortega explained: "This offensive took place as part of an insurrectional strategy, but it was not an insurrection, although we called for one. As it turned out, these operations served as propaganda for insurrection".[103] The goal of an insurrection was clarified by Humberto Ortega: the United States had a democratization plan for Nicaragua, and the offensive taken made it possible to defeat this "imperialist scheme".[104]

After the FSLN victory of July 1979, the FSLN "party" held its first Central Committee meeting, the Sandinista Assembly.[105] The document of that meeting stated: "We could say that the trap that imperialism and local reactionaries set for Sandinistas in 1933 and 1934 [the substitution of domestic for foreign intervention forces] enables today's Sandinism to draw imperialism and the reactionary bourgeoisie into an extremely effective ambush".[106] By the "trap" and the "ambush" the FSLN meant that in destroying the National Guard, it was "waving the unifying banner of anti–Somozism to rout out the military underpinning of the bourgeois system with the help of the bourgeoisie itself".[107]

The success of the Nicaraguan–FSLN strategy as an example of what can be achieved when revolutionary forces follow the Soviet–Cuban strategy has been used by the Cuban Revolution to instruct their remaining proxy forces in Latin America. In April 1982,[108] Manuel Pineiro Losada, head of the Americas Department of the Cuban Communist Party and former head of the General Directorate of Intelligence (DGI), set the "broad–front" technique that had made possible the FSLN conquest of Nicaragua a model for the entire hemisphere: "Taking advantage of any, even the smallest, opportunity, vacillating, unstable, unreliable, and unconditional".[109]

The lesson that the Cubans themselves had the credit of establishing in Latin American history, and that the FSLN was able to repeat, was that with a *manto*, or "veil" or cover,[110] of a "Democratic Front," and keeping the hegemony in armed struggle, a movement that wants to contribute to the world Stalinist revolution has two successful examples to follow. However, other "traps" and "ambushes" are feasible only if the same deception can be repeated.

The destinies of the Cuban and Nicaraguan revolutions are historically tied. The future of Nicaragua can be seen in the products of the Cuban experience. The FSLN learned its lesson well. The final, open integration of Nicaragua into the Soviet bloc is only a matter of approval by the "strategic allies" of the FSLN in Havana and Moscow, as Bayardo Arce Castano stated in 1984.[111] The path they will follow is out of their hands.

Conclusion

The common empirical ground for the relationship between the Cuban and Nicaraguan revolutions was found in the lessons of the failed Guatemalan Revolution of 1954. For Luis Cardoza y Aragón, the only salvation was the development of guerrilla warfare.[112] The difference between the two revolutions lies in the character of the revolutionary forces that brought the process to power. Even if Fidel Castro was a Marxist, he did not develop within a Stalinist Communist Party.[113] For the Nicaraguan leadership the story is very different. The ideological development of this group was under the Marxism learned in manuals of the Soviet Union. With writings by Konstantinov and texts by Georges Politzer, they were trained as Stalinists in an archetype of institutionalized state violence way before they ever dreamed of gaining power.

In Cuba, after almost ten years of struggle to keep the revolution from being totally captured by the Soviet Union, the Cuban leadership surrendered. In Nicaragua, the day the FSLN entered Managua on July 19, 1979, the pro–Soviet bureaucracy was already fully developed. Besides occupying the mansions and the Mercedes–Benzes of Somoza, the Sandinistas directed their brutal repression first to the revolutionary comrades at their left. Commander Edén Pastora Gómez revealed:

> In the jails the counter–revolutionaries rub elbows with the Marxist revolutionaries, the latter being punished for the grave offense of interpreting Marx by different criteria from those of their comrades in power. I have with sorrow seen that among my people there is anxiety, distress, fear, the bitterness of frustration and personal insecurity, when they see our Miskito, Sumo, Rama, Indians persecuted, jailed, or murdered, without a press or radio which might denounce to the world this reign of terror prevailing on the Atlantic Coast and throughout Nicaragua by the already feared state security.[114]

Marx observed that there is eternal recurrence in history, that events and personalities reappear: "On the first occasion they appear as tragedy; on the second, as farce".[115] After twenty–seven years, Cubans have placed themselves completely within the socialist bloc led by the Soviet Union, and they survive. After seven years, the FSLN in Nicaragua faces one of the largest opposition fronts that almost any Stalinist Third World bureaucracy has ever faced. One thing is certain: the FSLN will not have the same easy success as Cuba in the establishment of Nicaraguan communism. The opposition to Sandinista violence has steadily increased, and this trend will most likely continue.

Notes

1. José Manuel Fortuny, "Relatorio Sobre la Actividad del Comité Central al Segundo Congreso del Partido" (December 1952), quoted in Michael Lowry, *Dialéctica y Revolución* (S.A., México D.F.: Editorial Veintiuno, 1975), p. 172.
2. Che Guevara, *Textes Militaires* (Paris: Editions Maspero, 1968), p. 156.
3. Ernest Mandel, *Revolutionary Marxism Today*, ed. Jon Rothschild (London: NLB, 1979), p. 92.
4. Carlos Fonseca Amador, *Bajo la Bandera del Sandinismo: Textos Políticos* (Managua: Editorial Nueva Nicaragua, 1981), p. 92.
5. Eduardo Crawley, *Nicaragua in Perspective* (New York: St. Martin's Press, 1984), p. 114.
6. Ibid., p. 116.

74   Patterns of Revolution

7. Andrés Pascal Allende, "Mensaje a los Miembros del M.I.R. y a los Revolucionarios chilenos" (en el quinto aniversario de la muerte de Miguel Enríquez, Secretario General del M.I.R., Chile, October 1979), p. 29.
8. David Nolan, *The Ideology of the Sandinistas and the Nicaraguan Revolution* (Institute of Inter–American Studies, Graduate School of International Studies, University of Miami, Coral Gables, 1985), p. 20.
9. Eduardo del Río Rius, *Nicaragua for Beginners* (London and New York: Writers and Readers Publishing Cooperative, 1984), p. 83.
10. Ibid.
11. Quoted in Tomás Borge, *Carlos, the Dawn Is No Longer Beyond Our Reach* (Prison Journals of Tomás Borge remembering Carlos Fonseca Amador, founder of the FSLN (Vancouver, Can.: New Star Books, 1984), p. 20.
12. Luis Sánchez Sancho, "Nicaragua Communist in Van [sic] of the Liberation Movement," *World Marxist Review*, February 1968, Vol. II, No. 2, pp. 30–38.
13. Jiri and Virginia Valenta, "Sandinistas in Power," *Problems of Communism*, September–October 1985, p. 4.
14. Nolan, "Ideology," p. 20.
15. Carlos Fonseca Amador, "Un Nicaragüense en Moscou" (1985), in *Bajo la Bandera*, p. 45.
16. Mandel, *Revolutionary Marxism*, p. 100.
17. Nolan, "Ideology," p. 156.
18. Myrna Torres Rivas, "Los que Siquieron a Sandino," *Cuadernos del Tercer Mundo* (Mexico), August 1979, pp. 21–23.
19. Nolan, "Ideology," p. 156.
20. Fonseca, *Bajo la Bandera*, p. 434.
21. *New York Times*, August 23, 1959.
22. Fonseca, *Bajo la Bandera*, p. 435.
23. *New York Times*, August 23, 1959.
24. Ibid., July 4, 1959, p. 5.
25. Borge, *Carlos*, p. 30.
26. Fonseca, *Bajo la Bandera*, pp. 435–436.
27. Ibid., p. 436.
28. Carlos Fonseca Amador, "Nicaragua: Zero Hour," in *Sandinistas Speak* (New York: Pathfinder Press, 1984), p. 34.
29. Che Guevara, *Selected Works* (Cambridge, Mass,: MIT Press, 1969), p. 372.
30. Rodney Arismendi, "Problèmes d'une Révolution Continentale," *Recherches Internationales à la Lumière du Marxisme*, July–August 1962, pp. 22–58, quoted in Lowry, *Dialectica y Revolución*, pp. 175–176.
31. Guillermo Toriello Garrido, *A Popular History of Two Revolutions: Guatemala and Nicaragua* (San Francisco, Ca.: Synthesis Publications, 1985), p. 20.
32. Fonseca, *Bajo la Bandera*, p. 436.
33. Roger Vázquez B., 1970 interview with Germán Pomares Ordonez, *Ventana* (Managua), July 13, 1981, pp. 13–15.
34. Blanca Segovias Sandino, interviewed by the Sandinista Television System of Nicaragua on the 50th anniversary of General Sandino's death as part of the commemorative events in February 1984, according to videotape of the Nicaraguan information center (Saint Charles, Mo., 1984).
35. Borge, *Carlos*, p. 3.
36. Nolan, "Ideology," p. 25.
37. Guevara, 1985, "Guerrilla Warfare" with an introduction and case studies by Brian Loveman and Thomas M. Davis, Jr. (Lincoln and London: University of Nebraska Press), pp. 12–13.

38. Régis Debray, *Revolution in the Revolution* (New York: Monthly Review Press, 1967).
39. Guevara, "Guerrilla Warfare," p. 13.
40. Sandinista Front? 1984, "The Historic Program of the FSLN" in *The Sandinistas Speak* (New York: Pathfinder Press, 1984), p. 13.
41. Lenin 1974, p. 97. "Que Hacer" (Pekin: Ediciones en Lenguas Extranjeras–Jeras, 1974), p. 97.
42. "Oscar Turcios: Su Intensa Vida Revolucionaria," *Barricada*, September 18, 1983, p. 3.
43. Fonseca, "Nicaragua: Zero Hour," pp. 35–36.
44. Fonseca, "Nicaragua: Zero Hour," p. 35.
45. Ibid., p. 40.
46. Ibid., p. 40.
47. Fonseca, *Bajo la Bandera*, p. 137.
48. Nolan, "Ideology," p. 158.
49. "Latin Reds Open Parley in Havana," *New York Times*, August 1, 1967.
50. Ibid., p. 1.
51. Casimiro Sotelo, November 1967, p. 113; and "Héroes de la Revolución: Julio Buitrago," *Patria Libre* magazine, Padre de La Resistencia Urbana del FSLN, Managua, No. 6, August 1980, p. 40.
52. "Parley in Havana Rebuffs Moscow," *New York Times*, August 10, 1967, p. 1.
53. *New York Times*, August 11, 1967.
54. UPI cable from Havana, Cuba, August 10, 1967, in ibid., p. 14.
55. "Nicaraguan Rebels Believed Crushed" and "Cuba Ends Silence on Guevara Report," *New York Times*, October 12, 1967.
56. *Tricontinental Bulletin*, September 23, 1967, p. 30; November 1967, p. 44; December 1967, p. 46.
57. Ibid., January–February 1968, p. 43.
58. Carlos Fonseca Amador, "On the Road to the Struggle," in *Tricontinental Bulletin*, August 1968, pp. 18–21.
59. Casimiro Sotelo, "In Sandino's Footsteps," pp. 118–119.
60. Guevara 1985, "Guerrilla Warfare," p. 13.
61. Amaru Barahona Portocarrero, "Estudios Sobre la Historia Contempóranea de Nicaragua," *Revista del Pensamiento Centroamericano*, October–December 1971, pp. 40–43.
62. Fidel Castro, "Che: Universal Inspiration of Struggle," *Tricontinental Magazine*, September–October 1968, p. 103.
63. César Montes, "Turcios Lima: The Measure of Man," *Tricontinental Magazine*, November–December 1968, p. 114.
64. Fonseca, "On the Road," p. 21.
65. Quoted in Mercier Vegas, "Guerrillas in Latin America," p. 224, cited by Che Guevara, *Guerrilla Warfare* (1985), p. 16.
66. Eduardo Galeano, in "Guatemala: Clave de Latino America" (Interview, Montevideo, 1967), quoted in William Ratliff, *Castroism and Communism*, p. 113; cited by Guevara, *Guerrilla Warfare*, pp. 16, 32.
67. Ibid., p. 115 (cited by Guevara, *Guerrilla Warfare*, p. 17).
68. Andrés Pascal Allende, "Mensaje a los Miembros," p. 26.
69. "Guerra Popular en Centro América," *Tricontinental Magazine*, May–June 1970, pp. 92–105.
70. Mao Zedong, "De la Guerre Prolongée," cited by André Glucksmann, "El Discurso de la Guerra" (editorial), *Anagrama* (Barcelona), 1969, p. 330.
71. Vo Nguyen Giap, quoted by Guevara, *Guerrilla Warfare*, p. 9.

72. Ernesto "Che" Guevara, "Guerre et Population Paysanne" (July 1959), *Oeuvres V: Textes Inédits*, Francois Maspero, Petite Collection No. 101 (Paris, 1972), p. 12.
73. Ernesto "Che" Guevara, Preface to Vo Nguyen Giap, *People's War, People's Army* (first published in Cuba) in "Oeuvres V: Textes Inédits, Francois Maspero, Petite Collection No. 101, Paris, 1972, p. 51.
74. Irving Louis Horowitz, "The Political Sociology of Cuban Communism," in *Cuban Communism*, 3rd ed. (New Brunswick, N.J.: Transaction Books, 1977), pp. 47–65.
75. "Address by the President on Central America—Fact Sheet," Washington, D.C., May 9, 1984.
76. Eileen Skully, "The PLO's Growing Latin American Base," Heritage Foundation, Washington, D.C., August 2, 1983, p. 2.
77. Center for International Security, "The Sandinista–PLO Axis," p. 2, quoted in The Jewish Anti–Defamation League, "PLO Activities in Latin America New York," May 1982, p. 9.
78. "The Arab–Israeli Contest for Influence in Latin America," *Business Week*, May 3, 1983, p. 52, quoted by U.S. Department of State, *The Sandinistas and Middle Eastern Radicals* (Washington, D.C., 1985), p. 2.
79. Humberto Belli, in *Human Events*, November 25, 1978, quoted in "The PLO in Central America," p. 4.
80. Israeli Defense Force, "Report: The PLO and International Terror," March 1981, quoted in "The PLO in Central America," p. 4.
81. Jorge Mandi, quoted in *Al–Watan* (Kuwait), August 7, 1979; cited in David Kopilow, "Castro, Israel, and the PLO," Cuban American National Foundation, Washington, D.C., 1985, p. 13.
82. Hadar, *Jerusalem Post*, August 14, 1981, quoted in "The PLO in Central America"; White House *Digest*, July 20, 1985, Washington, D.C., p. 4; Borge, *Carlos*, p. 66.
83. Fonseca, *Bajo la Bandera*, p. 440.
84. Omar Cabezas, "Fire from the Mountain," in *The Making of a Sandinista* (New York: Crown Publishers, 1985), pp. 28–29.
85. FSLN Executive Secretariat of the National Leadership (Carlos Fonseca, Oscar Turcios, Efrain Sánchez Sancho, José Pérez Escobar), "The People's War Continues," *Tricontinental Bulletin*, July–August 1970, p. 33.
86. Nolan, "Ideology," p. 161.
87. *Tricontinental Bulletin* 1971, p. 47; February 1972, p. 39.
88. Nolan, "Ideology," p. 163.
89. Instituto de Estudio del Sandinismo, "Porque Viven Siempre entre Nosotros," Camilo Ortega Saavedra (Managua: Editorial Neuva Nicaragua, 1982), p. 101.
90. Fonseca, *Bajo la Bandera*, p. 440.
91. "Porqué Viven Siempre entre Nosotros," p. 99.
92. Fausto Amador, "How I Came to Be a Trotskyist," *Intercontinental Press*, June 27, 1977, p. 743. See also Fausto Amador, "Why Upsurge in Nicaragua Failed to Dislodge Somoza," *Intercontinental Press*, June 19, 1978.
93. "Porqué Viven Siempre entre Nosotros," p. 100.
94. Ibid., pp. 100–101.
95. "Latin America in the Struggle Against Imperialism for National Independence, Democracy, People's Welfare, Peace and Socialism," Declaration of the Meeting of Communist Parties of Latin America and the Caribbean (Moscow: Novosti Press Agency Publishing House, 1975).

96. Fonseca, *Bajo la Bandera*, p. 440.
97. See "Latin America in the Struggle" (note 95).
98. Ibid., p. 301.
99. Mandel, *Revolutionary Marxism*, p. 104.
100. Luis Sánchez Sancho, "Nicaragua Communist in the Van of the Liberation Movement," pp. 30–38.
101. Pedro Arauz Palacios, "Sobre las Circunstancias que Rodearon la Muerte del Comandante Carlos Fonseca Amador," Comunicado de la Resistencia Interna del FSLN en Lugar de Nicaragua, December 1976. This document was publicly distributed by the FER in the "Ruben Dario" Campus of the National University of Nicaragua in Managua in December 1976. The FSLN leadership has never given a public explanation of these changes addressed by Commander Pedro Arauz Palacios.
102. FSLN Direccion Nacional, *Nicaragua: On the General Political–Military Platform of Struggle of the Sandinista Front for National Liberation for the Triumph of the Sandinista Popular Revolution* (Oakland, Calif.: Resistance Publications, 1977).
103. Humberto Ortega, "Nicaragua: The Strategy of Victory" (Interview by Marta Harnecker in *Granma*, January 27, 1980) in *Sandinistas Speak*, pp. 53–84.
104. Ibid., pp. 57, 59.
105. FSLN Rigoberto López Pérez meeting of the Sandinista Assembly, "Analysis of the Situation and Tasks of the Sandinista People's Revolution" (the "72–hour Document"), September 1979, quoted by Shirley Christian, *Nicaragua. Revolution in the Family* (New York: Random House, 1985), p. 129.
106. FSLN Rigoberto López Pérez meeting, 1979, p. 5.
107. Ibid., pp. 5–6.
108. Douglas W. Payne, "The 'Mantos' of Sandinista Deception," *Strategic Review*, Spring 1985, pp. 18–19.
109. Ibid., p.
110. See Douglas W. Payne, "The 'Mantos' of Sandinista Deception," pp. 9–20.
111. Bayardo Arce Castano, "Secret Speech to the Political Committee of the Nicaraguan Communist Party (PSN) with Regard to the Elections of November 1984 in Nicaragua," quoted in Douglas W. Payne, "The Democratic Mask: The Consolidation of the Sandinista Revolution," *Perspectives on Freedom*, no. 3 (New York, 1985), pp. 90–95.
112. Luis Cardoza y Aragon, "La Revolución Guatemalteca," *Ediciones Cuadernos Americanos*, no. 43 (1955); quoted in Arnoldo Cardona, "Guatemala, Dogma, and Revolution," *Tricontinental Magazine*, September–October, p. 40.
113. Hu "Cuba: The Pursuit of Freedom" (New York: Harper & Row, 1971), p. 1373, quoted in "Soviet–Cuban Connection in Central America and the Caribbean," released by the State Department and Defense Department (Washington D.C., March 1985), p. 6; and Barbara Walters, "An Interview with Fidel Castro," *Foreign Policy*, Fall 1977, p. 32, quoted in ibid.
114. Edén Pastora Gómez, "A Revolution Betrayed," in *Crisis and Opportunity*, ed. Mark Falcoff and Robert Royal (Washington, D.C.: Ethics and Public Policy Center, 1984), pp. 404–405.
115. Karl Marx, "El Dieciocho Brumario de Luis Bonaparte," in *Obras Escogidas*, vol. 1 (Moscow: Progreso, 1973), p. 408.

5

Strategy, Flexibility, and Violence

Douglas W. Payne

The foregoing contributions to this volume make it clear that the phenomenon of revolutionary violence in Latin America must be perceived within a political force field of local, regional, and global components. Both the North-South equation and the East–West confrontation are operative and interconnected in a complex, shifting mosaic.

After Castro's victory in Cuba in 1959, a pattern of polarization evolved between revolutionary forces that seek a complete restructuring of Latin American social and political institutions, and traditional elements that seek to preserve them. Recently, however, those forces seeking reform through democratization, those historically caught in the squeeze, are achieving marked if wobbly success. It is now evident that the strengthening of democratic institutions in the region, in many cases with the assistance of the United States, is the greatest threat to the forces of revolution, who are constantly adjusting strategy and tactics in response to changing objective conditions in the region and the world.

The history of revolutionary forces in Latin America can be tracked in the evolution of strategy and tactics for the maximalist goal of seizure and consolidation of power and for the minimalist goal of power projection and influence in the region. What must be acknowledged is that the use of force, whether utilized by a revolutionary state such as Cuba, or by Nicaragua, which also seeks to achieve that status, or by an armed revolutionary group seeking the seizure of power, is only one element in an overall political strategy.

The Sandinistas have always referred to themselves as a political–military organization, and their seizure and consolidation of power was foremost a political victory, with a tactical armed component. Further, the Sandinista's sophisticated synthesis of guerrilla warfare and broad-front tactics marked a milestone in revolutionary strategy after the failure of rural and urban foco theory, and Cuba and the Soviet Union both share in that achievement. Both were instrumental in training and guiding the Sandinista Front in revolutionary strategy and ideology, and each provided and continues to provide hands-on support, surreptitious and otherwise, through the complex matrix of power projection built in the region by Havana since 1959 and by Moscow since the days of the Comintern.

In Havana in 1982, three years after the Sandinista victory, Manuel Pineiro, Chief of the Americas Department of the Cuban Communist Party, addressed a meeting of Latin American and Caribbean communist parties and armed leftist groups.[1] He keynoted the Sandinista milestone and elevated it to a broad model for the hemisphere. He declared the absolute necessity of hemispheric unity and coordination of action among his listeners. He acknowledged the need for violent tactics in many scenarios, but gave paramount status to the Leninist principle of forming temporary, tactical alliances with nonrevolutionary elements through various forms of political deception. He stated that any social or political groups that sought change, however minimal, in their national condition were subject to such engineering. He highlighted as targets reformist military sectors, social democratic and other center–left political parties, liberal and liberationist sectors of the Catholic Church, and labor and peasant unions.

To exert such influence requires power projection that is based on more than just force. It requires filling as many political spaces, legal and illegal, as possible. A legal communist party will not be scuttled during an armed insurrectional situation, and an armed group will not be abandoned after a failed offensive or the emergence of a democratic government. Each will be kept in place for use during whatever tactical moment, and each will seek to achieve the capability of altering appearances for tactical alliance purposes.

With a clear convergence of interests, Havana and Moscow operate on the theory that any type of presence in the region may ultimately be useful, depending on their reading at any given time of the correlation of forces in the region and the world, and especially with regard to the relative strength and strategy of the United States. The internal documents of revolutionary and communist groups throughout Latin America reveal nearly unanimous subscription to such a world view. The various elements of this fluctuating network are at times unstable, but the goals of Cuba and the Soviet Union converge in the attempt to manage and coordinate them to take advantage of opportunities that may arise. The goals are maximalist (the seizure and consolidation of power in a country by an allied group like the Sandinista Front) as well as minimalist (Cuba's use of armed revolutionary groups in Colombia, or the threat of such use in Mexico, as a foreign–policy leverage device).

The system is not a well–oiled machine, though that is an optimal goal, but it is complex, extensive, and at times alarmingly effective. Nonetheless, recent events tend to bear out Octavio Paz's perception that the only effective defense against totalitarianism is democratic legitimacy.[2] Revolutionary theorists like Manuel Pineiro point to intransigent authoritarian regimes as the most viable targets for revolutionary projection. Sandinista strategist Humberto Oretga has admitted that Somoza's *mano dura* (hard hand) was a key factor in the Sandinista victory,[3] and Fidel Castro has stated that the most likely place for success in Latin America today is Chile, where Pinochet regularly applies the *mano dura*.[4] Those who are skeptical of Paz's belief in democratization might look at the current situation in Central America, where guerrilla movements are shrinking with the advent of democratic process in both Guatemala and El Salvador. In fact, the only guerrilla force in that region that is growing is in Nicaragua, where the government is decidedly undemocratic.

Notes

1. Pineiro's 1982 address appears in English translation as "Imperialism and Revolution in Latin America and the Caribbean," in *New International: A Magazine of Marxist Politics and Theory*, Spring–Summer 1984, vol. 1, no. 3, pp. 103–130. The text was originally published in Spanish in *Cuba Socialista*, September–October, 1982.
2. See "Latin America and Democracy," in Octavio Paz, *One Earth, Four or Five Worlds: Reflections on Contemporary History* (New York: Harcourt Brace Jovanovich, 1985), pp. 158–188.
3. Interview with Humberto Ortega in *Sandinistas Speak: Speeches, Writings and Interviews with Leaders of Nicaragua's Revolution* (New York: Pathfinder Press, 1982), pp. 53–84.
4. Interview with Fidel Castro conducted by Robert McNeil in Havana 9 February 1985, and televised 11–15 February 1985 on the McNeil/ Lehrer News Hour.

PART II
THE PRACTITIONERS OF REVOLUTION

6

Communist Orthodoxy and Revolutionary Violence

Vladimir Tismaneanu

This chapter offers an assessment of the basic attitudes and reactions of Latin American communist parties to the issue of revolutionary violence. The emphasis is on the permanent and consistent correlation between the international politics of the Soviet Union and the strategic outlook of the pro–Soviet Latin American Communist or "orthodox" parties. The Cuban revolution and the continental political upheavals it engendered represented major challenges to the revolutionary paradigm espoused by most Soviet–line parties. The strategy of rural and urban guerrillas and the Castro-Guevarist celebration of armed struggle as the unique legitimate revolutionary approach were openly questioned and criticized by the exponents of "orthodox" Marxist–Leninist parties. This conflict was aggravated in the 1960s by the proliferation of Castroite groups that threatened the ideological monopoly of the existing communist bureaucracy and put forward daring revolutionary assumptions. The established communist apparatuses resented the voluntarism of the new revolutionary movements, excoriating their lack of discipline and organization. Harsh accusations were exchanged between the partisans of "mass struggle" and those of the violent approach, which culminated in Fidel Castro's unequivocal condemnation of the "reformist opportunism" of "orthodox" parties.

The Chilean drama and the failure of Salvador Allende's experiment confronted Latin American leftist groups with the need to reexamine most of their ideological tenets. The communist dogma of the "peaceful road to socialism," which had been vehemently attacked by Maoists, Trotskyites, and Castroites, turned out to be a rationalization of political impotence. With the Soviet Union increasingly involved in Latin American affairs, and persistence of the Cuban–Soviet rapprochement after 1968, the prophets of violence could launch a new offensive. The victory of the Sandinistas in Nicaragua was thus perceived as a turning point in the revolution of the Latin American Left.

Armed struggle could result in a victory for the revolutionary forces even in Central America, and the dream of a continental revolution, Che Guevara's utopian design, reemerged as an immediate objective. The evolution of the Communist Party of El Salvador is emblematic in this respect. After having deplored Salvador Cayetano Carpio's "adventurism" in the early 1970s, this party decided a decade later to embark on armed struggle and abandon the "mass struggle" strategy. Similarly, the Chilean Communist Party, long considered the avatar of the "reformist" ("moderate") strategy, seems to have engaged in direct military actions at the same time. These changes are indicative of a new attitude of orthodox parties toward the issue of violence, which was undoubtedly related to the Soviet–Cuban perception of Latin America as a potential battlefield and a promising ground for revolutionary opportunities.

This general shift does not exclude or deny the existence of a certain diversity in the attitudes of Latin American pro–Soviet parties with regard to violence. The communist–controlled Colombian FARC accepted a dialogue with the government in 1984, whereas communist parties in Brazil, Uruguay, and Venezuela clung to their electoralist practices. However, it appears that the violent approach tends to be reassessed, revalued and increasingly accepted by the pro–Soviet orthodoxy within the Latin American left. This is a logical outcome of a more general trend toward unification of traditionally opposed leftist groups in an effort to transcend ideological differences and establish a common revolutionary strategy.

Marxism, Leninism, and Stalinism in Latin America

Latin American communist parties, founded with direct Comintern support in the years that followed the Russian Revolution, faithfully reproduced and reflected the Leninist–Stalinist organizational pattern.[1] Until Fidel Castro engineered the metamorphosis of the Cuban Revolution into a one–party communist state, most Latin American communists, with the exception of the Chilean and briefly the Guatemalan parties, were sectarian minorities hindered from effective action by their total subordination to Soviet instructions. The Latin American communist parties were not interested in developing original theoretical and practical experiments. Their strategy and tactics were primarily and fundamentally dictated by the interest of Soviet foreign policy, and Latin American communist ideologues did their best to rationalize this lack of autonomy according to the prevalent Stalinist criterion of "proletarian internationalism." During their first decades of activity, these parties observed and followed all the turns and twists of the Soviet line without any significant attempt to transcend the ossified dogmas of Marxism–Leninism as codified by Stalin. There were some exceptions—one could again mention Chile, but also Brazil or El Salvador—when local Moscow-line parties decided to embark on semi–original platforms, but these endeavors collapsed dramatically, and the "general line" was even more drastically imposed and reasserted.

Factional struggles have always characterized the evolution of Latin American communism, but the dissident groups were themselves unable to go beyond the level of shallow Marxist–Leninist rhetoric and totally shared the Stalinist strategic view, in the times of both the Comintern and later Cominform. The influence the orthodox parties exerted was limited to intellectual circles, and communism was a predominantly intellectual affair. On the one hand, one should not underestimate their capacity to influence the universities and to create genuine fortresses of Marxist–Leninist subversion among the cultural elites. On the other hand, the radical phraseology of the "orthodox" parties had a certain appeal among union leaders (Mexico, Chile, Bolivia) and temporarily allowed the communist militants to gain significant positions within these organizations.

The communist political culture in Latin America was developed along lines similar to those in Europe. The basic value inculcated by the party was discipline, "democratic centralism" functioned as the guiding principle of party life, the harassment of real and/or imaginary dissidents (heretics) was a condition sine qua non for the "steeling", that is, the "Bolshevization", of the party. Convinced that they had to accomplish a historical mission, or in other words that they belonged to a universalist movement, Latin American Communists ignored the sociopolitical realities of the countries where they lived and borrowed and ruminated on the wooden vocabulary of Stalinist orthodoxy. They nourished a visceral hatred for their socialist rivals, particularly against the exponents of Aprism, the social–democratic ideology and movement founded by Victor Raúl Haya de la Torre.[2] It is noteworthy that Rodney Arismendi, the Uruguayan communist leader, published his main theoretical contribution in 1946 as a refutation of Haya de la Torre's "populist" ideology. In Arismendi's view, people like Haya de la Torre, Rômulo Betancourt, or José Figueres were exponents of the "big bourgeoisie" allied with imperialism and were not entitled to speak on behalf of the anti–imperialist "national bourgeoisie."[3]

Abiding strictly by Comintern directives, which did not consider Latin America a serious target for large-scale subversive operations, the "orthodox" parties were practically paralyzed until 1935. The Farabundo Martí violent episode in 1932 is indicative more of a local centrifugal attempt than of a general trend in the Comintern's Latin America strategy. Though politically insignificant—once again, the Chilean case is the exception, not the rule—these parties were perceived as alien elements without any organic links to the much-invoked proletariat and peasantry. They were the object of successive waves of repression on the part of authorities, particularly in the "pre–frontist" years. It would not be an exaggeration to say that Latin American communist parties, having adopted and unreservedly shared the basic tenets of Stalinism, actually enjoyed their hopeless isolation and uprootedness. Hardened communist leaders like Blas Roca in Cuba, Gustavo Machado and Jesús Faria in Venezuela, Luis Corvalán in Chile, Luís Carlos Prestes in Brazil, and Rodney Arismendi in Uruguay became members of the Comintern "aristocracy." They were educated in the Stalinist tradition, which they came to value more than anything else as the sole legitimate revolutionary theory and practice.

In this respect one can speak of the *totalitarian* character of Latin American communist parties, of their unreconstructed commitment to the Stalinist implementation of Leninism. Since real revolutionary confrontations were not on the Soviet agenda for Latin America during the Comintern years, "orthodox" groups were assigned the task of "debunking" the "internal enemies" infiltrated within the movement. The permanent purge of Trotskyites and other "deviationists" became an obsession for the Stalinist apparatchiks. At the same time, they encouraged the consolidation of a warm sense of fraternal community within the Communist Party and practiced the same pedagogy developed in Europe that aimed to transform the revolutionary organization into a substitute for the family or, to use a psychoanalytical concept, for the father figure.[4]

For Latin American orthodox communists, the party is a closed system, the military-political association of people unified by devotion to the same values, dogmas, and cause. Monolithic unity is unquestionable, and the supreme authority, that of the general secretary, is conferred by Moscow. Latin American "orthodox" parties are still among the most obedient with regard to Soviet interests and imperatives, always ready to espouse the most recent trend of the Soviet line. Their general political behavior is reactive, lacking propensity for dangerous actions or risky undertakings.

Any change in the Soviet line is automatically translated into a modification of the strategy promoted by Latin American communist parties. Their isolation was not overcome to any significant degree until the Seventh Congress of the Comintern, in 1935, when Stalin decided to replace the "class against class" strategy—the so–called Third Period strategy—with the "popular front" tactics of broad alliances and united actions of "all democratic and progressive forces" against the growing danger of "Nazism–Fascism". A typical example of the application of this new outlook by Latin American communists was the more conciliatory politics of the Chilean Communist Party in 1938, when Pedro Aguirre Cerda became the candidate of a heterogeneous Popular Front coalition. Qualified support for this coalition was accompanied by calls for the elimination of those who resisted the Communists' infiltration of the basic institutions and were committed to a more reformist program. The Chilean Communists were thus proclaiming the need to form a "true" Popular Front government through the elimination of those ministers who displayed a conciliatory, anti–Popular Front tendency, and their replacement by men who were prepared to support the Popular Front by speeding the implementation of an immediate plan of economic and social action, based upon the Popular Front program.[5] Concerning the Popular Front episode in Chile and the vacillations of the PCCh, it is useful to mention that in August 1935 the party's Central Committee had enthusiastically endorsed the Resolutions of the Seventh Congress of the Communist International: "The resolution of the Seventh Congress of the International, and the victories of the Popular Front in Spain and France, opened the way in our party towards the idea that the national bourgeoisie had a place in the national liberation movement. . . . The Popular Front is a broad alliance with the participation of: the workers in industry and on the land, the peasants, the intellectuals, the middle class and the national bourgeoisie."[6] Following Cerda's election victory on December 24, 1938, the PCCh decided not to accept ministerial jobs, and the Party's general secretary, Carlos Contreras Labarca, offered a strange justification for this position: "The Communist Party declares that its inviolable and exemplary fidelity to the people's front . . . has never been inspired by the wish to obtain any participation in the government, and that it has never had interests but of satisfying our people's noble desire. . . . The Communist Party considers that its responsibility in carrying out this programme can be fulfilled outside the government".[7] Behind this self–serving statement, one can easily detect a willingness to escape historical responsibility for an undertaking that the communists deemed unlikely to be successful. Furthermore, the PCCh preferred to maintain an "autonomous" position vis-à-vis the government in order to be able to openly criticize possibly unpopular economic decisions.

During World War II, Latin American communist parties expressed unconditional support for the anti–Fascist coalition. They benefited from the new relations between the Soviet Union and the United States and tried to present themselves as loyal elements within the national political spectrum. The formal dissolution of the Comintern in 1943, an astute political maneuver carried out by Stalin in order to persuade his Western allies that the Soviet Union had ceased to represent a center of international subversion ("the headquarters of world proletarian revolution") allowed national communist parties to pose as dedicated exponents of "patriotic interests". The prewar Frontist line was thus developed into a consistent legalist approach, and "Browderism," the attempt to transform the communist parties into larger *political associations*, was extremely influential among Latin American Communists. The prevalent catchword was "the struggle for democracy", and the insurrectional strategy, the main Leninist vestige in the communist revolutionary program, was temporarily abandoned. Luis Carlos Prestes, the long–lived Brazilian communist leader, described the aims behind the overcoming sectarian tendencies and developing a mass party committed to the legal struggle for "progress and democracy":

> Instead of the small, illegal party that carried on agitation and spread the general ideal of communism and Marxism, we now need a great party, authentically linked to the working class and the decisive forces in our country, a party that will include the best, the most advanced, the most honest intellectuals, a party that will draw in the best elements of the rural masses, a party that by virtue of its broad social composition will in fact have the necessary power and ability to lead our people in the fight for progress and independence, for liberty and social justice, for popular democratic government.[8]

When Stalin decided to unleash developments leading toward the Cold War and impose total Soviet domination over East Central Europe, Browderism was suddenly exposed as a "right-wing," "opportunist" deviation, and Earl Browder was expelled from his leading position as secretary general of the CPUSA. The publication of Jacques Duclos' criticism of Browderism in the April 1945 issue of *Cahiers du Communisme* was the pretext of a general reassessment of the political strategy adopted not only by North American Communists, but also by Latin American Communists. In February 1946, Blas Roca, the general secretary of the Cuban PSP, who under the impact of the so–called Teheran line had established close relations with Batista's government, affirmed that the Cuban Communists' "errors" were "the consequence of Browder's corrupted, anti–Marxist theories."[9] The new course had to be "theoretically" justified, and Earl Browder, as well as certain Latin American communist leaders, served as the scapegoats for what Stalin considered to be an obsolete strategy. What followed was a period of confusion, with the national leadership of Latin American communist parties' bewildered and totally unable to grasp Stalin's genuine designs. The result of these developments throughout the Cominform years, with the purges in the East European satellite countries and the aggressive Soviet foreign policy, was an increasing isolation and marginalization of the Latin American communist parties.

The "tough" line was again changed after the Twentieth Congress of the Communist Party of the Soviet Union (CPSU) and Khrushchev's proclamation of "peaceful coexistence" as the guiding principle of Soviet foreign policy. The frontist strategy, with all its "entryist" implications, was again on the agenda. Communist parties all over the world were encouraged by the post–Stalin Soviet leadership to resume dialogue with all the "democratic and progressive forces". The new line involved a resolute divorce from the insurrectional approach, which was perceived as a "petit bourgeois," "adventurist" temptation. Latin American Communists were perhaps the most committed to what one might call a strategy of "historical expectative", being convinced that only a "peaceful transition to socialism" would avoid disastrous military confrontations between the two superpowers. The proponents of violence were labelled "leftist deviationists", and as a result of this fascination with gradual reforms, Latin American communist political culture acquired a dimension of *pragmatic prudence* masterfully depicted by Peruvian writer Mario Vargas Llosa in his novel *Historia de Mayta*.[10] Piecemeal change, adjustment to the rules of the national political game, resignation to a permanent marginal status despite radical calls for involvement of the party in the actual political process—these seemed to be the main priorities of the strategy formulated by the Twentieth Congress. To launch guerrilla warfare against the state machine was deemed a manifestation of political insanity, a quixotic attempt to ignore or defy historical-political determinism.

From Leninism, Latin American communist parties borrowed the cult of discipline, the hierarchical obsession, the vertical structure, and the visceral allergy to any heretical proclivities. Stalinism did nothing but strengthen these characteristics while fostering the most "conservative," that is, dogmatic, exclusive and intolerant features within these organizations. The counterpart to this rigid internal structure was a stupendous lack of political initiative, and a boundless servility toward Moscow, as well as a clear inability to articulate a coherent and consistent long–term strategy. Though theoretically committed to the ideal of a socialist revolution, Latin American "orthodox" parties tended to play the game of the establishment and were increasingly perceived as belonging to the status quo. These political groups had long been bereft of "revolutionary fervor" and utopian ardor.[11] In order to better understand the "orthodox" communist reservations concerning the validity of armed struggle strategy in Latin America, it might be useful to mention some of the main political–intellectual characteristics of these groups:

1. Doctrinaire, theoretically rigid, sectarian.
2. Vertical structure, a strong sense of hierarchy, lack of internal democracy.
3. Preeminence of the bureaucratic apparatus, and reluctance to indulge in spontaneous actions, usually described as "democratic centralism."
4. *Ouvrièrisme* (reliance on selected sectors of the urban working class) and trade–unionism, which resulted in perpetual accusations of reformism (from Trotskyites, Castroites, and Maoists).
5. Subordination to the Soviet Union and support for the Soviet interpretation of Marxism–Leninism and "proletarian internationalism."
6. Political opportunism barely covered by revolutionary phraseology.
7. The parliamentary temptation and a boundless "flexibility" manifested by continuous readiness for tactical and strategic somersaults in accordance with changes in Soviet foreign policy. With the benefit of hindsight, these parties are always prone to put forward critical analyses, but with some exceptions they hesitate to challenge the legalist approach. They may posture as moderates, but they are still Leninists, i.e., their final objective is

seizing political power. For historical–political reasons, primarily related to the Soviet geopolitical designs, these parties seemed to postpone the confrontational moment *ad calendam graecas* and became masters of trafficking in an image of moderation and self–restraint.

8. Polycentric, neo–Marxist, and "Euro–Communist" leanings have not been particularly conspicuous among Latin American communist parties, Mexico and the Venezuelan MAS being the exceptions. Moreover, resistance to any genuine process of de–Stalinization seems to be a peculiar feature of their development. In a certain way, they seem to be relics of another age, revering obsolete dogmas and extolling compromised idols.[12] The Cuban Revolution gave "orthodox" parties the opportunity to eschew the process of de–Stalinization. The urgent imperative of solidarity with a beleaguered revolution excluded squabbles and debates that could only engender "anarchy and confusion".

The Cuban Revolution and Leninist Orthodoxy

With regard to the Cuban Revolution, Soviet–line parties were not able to put forward an articulate assessment of its long–term, strategic significance. Their dogmas were dramatically challenged, and armed struggle turned out to be more than a matter of theoretical debate. Not only the PSP in Cuba, but all Latin American "orthodox" parties were confused and disconcerted by the triumph of the July 26 Movement, a political–military organization that had nothing to do with the Leninist concept of the vanguard party. The emergence of Castroite splinter groups within the Soviet–line parties naturally threatened the political–ideological hegemony of the traditional communist elites. On the other hand, the communist parties were confronted with violence–oriented groups formed of radicalized elements within the youth organizations of Aprista and Christian–Democratic parties (Peru, Venezuela).

The victory of the Cuban Revolution has thus forcefully modified the whole spectrum of the Left in Latin America and has raised fundamental theoretical and practical questions with regard to the nature, methods, and pace of the revolutionary struggle on the continent. Furthermore, in the early 1960s Fidel Castro and his followers tended to transform Havana into a center of the continental revolution, a new capital city of "internationalism". Castro made no secret of his deep contempt for "scholastic Marxists", whose main concern consisted of the theoretical evaluation of the "objective conditions" for revolution. The Cuban leadership promoted and encouraged the development of military–political groups inspired by the Castroite example and ready to emulate it all over the continent. Armed struggle against the dominant oligarchies was proclaimed the main strategy, and violence was rehabilitated as a justified political weapon.

It took a long time for Latin American "orthodox" parties to understand all that the Cuban Revolution implied for the future of left-wing radicalism in

Latin America. The Sino–Soviet split and the polemics between the two communist giants further complicated the situation of the orthodox parties. The issue of the path to power was vehemently debated, and mutual accusations of "opportunism" and "adventurism" were exchanged by supporters of one or the other "superparties". Generally speaking, the primary attitude of the "orthodox" parties toward the strategy formulated by the Cuban leaders—which was later called Castro–Guevarism—was one of moderate and restricted support. The Communists were certainly critical of any form of "revolutionary impatience", and Lenin's theses against leftism as an "infantile disorder of Communism" were obsessively invoked. Some orthodox parties persisted in their commitment to the nonarmed road (Chile, Uruguay), whereas other Moscow–line groups decided to follow the Cuban exhortations of struggle (Colombia, Venezuela, Guatemala). A most important event in the history of the relations between Fidel Castro and the orthodox parties was the Conference of Latin American Communist Parties organized in Havana in November 1964. The main objective of the conference was to develop and enhance coordination and cooperation between Soviet–line parties and to strengthen the relations between them and Cuba.[13]

Among the parties which decided to embark upon violence, the Guatemalan PGT proffered an analysis of the armed path. The resort to violence was the consequence of the interpretation of the Guatemalan struggle as a part of the continental revolution unleashed by Castro's victory in Cuba. Guatemalan Communists admitted that "subjective conditions" had not fully matured, that is, the masses failed to support the revolutionary project of the left.

> However, they will develop in the process of the actual struggle. Armed struggle, it is true, cannot be launched unless a *minimum* of subjective conditions exist. But this does not mean that it is necessary to wait until these conditions have fully matured. If at the moment of *winning power* it is essential to have full maturity of both the objective and subjective factors of the revolution, this, we believe, is not an absolute must for *beginning the armed struggle*.[14]

This was a Guevara–type analysis and proved to be strictly temporary. The decision to espouse the armed struggle strategy in Guatemala was the result of dramatic ideological confrontation within the PGT. The party was clearly forced to respond immediately to the challenge represented by the Castroite group MR–13, founded by Marco Antonio Yon Sosa and Luis Augusto Turcios Lima: "*Outside* our Party, democratic organizations came into being which made it their aim to reply with violence to the violence of the reaction. Some of these organizations won prestige among the people who saw in their activities the best answer to the counterrevolutionary terror".[15]

The orientation toward armed struggle within certain Latin American communist parties was certainly catalyzed by Castro–Guevarism as well as by the influence of certain voluntarist theses developed by the Chinese Communist Party throughout the harsh public polemic with the CPSU. On the other hand, the paralyzing effects of geographic fatalism had been radically discarded by the Cuban Revolution. It was therefore increasingly difficult for Moscow–line parties to indulge in their fetishism of the peaceful way, which indeed expressed the opportunist syndrome so characteristic of those groups. Luis Corvalán, the general secretary of the PCCh, attempted to defend the old political paradigm, insisting that the non–violent way to socialism is the way of mass struggle. The main task of the Communist Party consisted then of the ideological and organizational activities bound to prepare the subjective conditions of the revolution. Clinging to traditional Leninist tenets, Corvalán criticized those who asserted the primacy of revolutionary voluntarism over "objective conditions":

> The objective conditions are determined by social development, while the subjective [ones] . . . are shaped by the revolutionary movement itself, above all by its vanguard. Consequently, there is no justification for sitting back and waiting for the subjective conditions to mature of themselves. But neither can their maturing (as regards time and form) be accelerated at will by ignoring the realities of the situation. These conditions will ripen only as a result of persistent working among the masses.[16]

The reference to the masses and the refusal of the elitist–conspiratorial approach was typical of this kind of reading of Lenin's view of the revolutionary situation.[17] Its only result could be continual clashes between the communist bureaucratized apparatus and the exponents of the new revolutionary wave—mutual recriminations, incessant polemics, and permanent internecine struggles within the radical Left. The orthodox parties were not ready to endorse and accept Fidel Castro's hegemony within the Latin Left and were opposed to the generalization of Castro–Guevarist strategy of rural guerrilla warfare.[18]

After intensely pondering the risks of a strategic shift toward armed struggle, Colombian Communists concluded that there was no contradiction between mass struggle and armed guerrilla struggle. They fully covered their about–face with compulsory references to the preeminence of mass activities, aiming to establish a bridge between the Castro–Guevarist approach and the traditional Marxist–Leninist view. On the other hand, they affirmed their commitment to the development of armed struggle:

> It would be negative and fatal for the Colombian revolutionary movement to stand by and watch the destruction of this [guerrilla] force while waiting for a revolutionary situation to mature before beginning the armed struggle. The armed aggression of the enemy must be met by guerrilla resistance and armed struggle in the countryside. When conditions permit, this should be spread to the cities and working–class areas.[19]

There were interesting developments within the Venezuelan Communist Party, which after having been involved in the armed struggle in the early 1960s decided to come back to legality. This turn was defined as "cowardice" and "opportunism" both by Castroite Venezuelan Communists like Douglas Bravo and by Fidel Castro himself.[20] According to Castro, the main errors of the Venezuelan party, which epitomized the weaknesses of traditional Marxist–Leninist "vanguards" in Latin America, consisted of (1) overestimation of urban struggle and underestimation of the peasantry as a revolutionary force; (2) lack of confidence in the guerrilla movement or, in Fidel's own words, "downgrading the guerrilla movement and pinning great hope on the military uprising"; (3) patronizing attitudes toward the guerrillas: "It is absurd and almost criminal . . . to try to direct the guerrillas from the city. The two things are so different, so distinct, the two settings so completely dissimilar, that the greatest insanity—a painfully bloody insanity— that can be committed is to want to direct the guerrillas from the city"; (4) skepticism with regard to the universal value and relevance of violent strategy: "What will define the Communist is his attitude toward oligarchies, his attitude toward exploitation, his attitude toward the armed revolutionary movement"; and (5) theoretical sclerosis and all–pervasive dogmatism: "Many times practice comes first and then theory . . . Whoever denies that it is precisely the road of revolution which leads the people towards Marxism is not a Marxist though he may call himself a Communist".[21]

The Tricontinental conference (1966) and the OLAS conferences of 1967 represented the height of Castro's attempts to promote his views on continental revolution and to establish organizational–institutional vehicles for their implementation. The OLAS conference, which proclaimed Guevara an honorary citizen of Latin America, consecrated the Castroite line, stating, "the guerrilla is the nucleus of the liberation armies, and guerrilla warfare constitutes the most effective method of initiating and developing the revolutionary struggle in most of our countries".[22]

Che Guevara's pathetic defeat in the Bolivian jungle exacerbated the polemics between Castro and the orthodox parties. For the traditional Marxist–Leninist parties, nothing seemed more dangerous or absurd than Guevara's strategy centered on the functional and political preeminence of the *foco guerrillero*. The debacle of many guerrilla operations, the military immaturity of some guerrilla groups, and their failure to attract significant peasant support were all regarded by orthodox communists as irrefutable evidence of the erroneous nature of the Castro–Guevarist approach and, ipso facto, a vindication of their mass–struggle strategy:

> Armed actions *not directly connected with the development of mass struggle* end in defeat—despite the heroism of a group of intrepid men. What is more, the armed struggle originating on the basis of class conflicts, or a democratic mass

movement, can "lose touch" with its base and in its development forfeit the active support of the masses because of such mistakes as underestimating the political struggle, or failing to take into account changes in the situation, or as a result of imperialism and local reaction achieving a temporary tactical–political superiority. Having lost touch with the class struggle and the support of the masses—*sympathy* alone is not enough—the group of heroes become a group again who do not add to their strength merely by proclaiming the anti–imperialist and socialist character of their struggle.[23]

This statement by Schafik Handal of the PCES can be read as a reply to the Guevarist theses as synthesized by Régis Debray. According to the French propagandist of Castro–Guevarism, traditional Marxist–Leninist parties are obsessed with legalism and can only hinder the development of effective guerrilla movements. In this respect, and in a Leninist framework, their function is "objectively" counterrevolutionary. They tend to exert control over guerrilla groups, but fail to assume "genuine" revolutionary goals:

Che Guevara wrote that the guerrilla movement is not an end in itself, nor is it a glorious adventure; it is merely a means to an end: the conquest of political power. But, lo and behold, guerrilla forces were serving many other purposes: a form of pressure on bourgeois government; a factor in political horsetrading; a trump card to be played in case of need—such were the objectives with which certain leadership were attempting to saddle their military instrumentalities. The revolutionary method was being utilized for reformist ends.[24]

Guevara's deadly fiasco in Bolivia and the increasing isolation of the violence–oriented Castroite groups all over the continent forced the Latin American Marxist–Leninist Left to proceed to a general reassessment of basic strategic assumptions. Another factor that counted in this process of general regrouping in the early 1970s was the bureaucratization and Sovietization of the Cuban Revolution.[25] Both strategies—Leninist–Stalinist and Castro–Guevarist—seemed to end up in blind alleys. The expectations and hopes aroused by the first revolutionary wave had been invalidated by stubborn political realities. The moment had come to reinterpret the revolutionary theory and to attempt the seizure of power *by peaceful means*. There were, of course, militants who could not accept the peaceful (evolutionary, frontist) road. In Central America these debates resulted in the decision of the PGT to endorse the armed struggle precisely in 1969 at the moment when both the FAR and the party have been thoroughly decimated by counterinsurgency operations. In the Communist Party of El Salvador, the orientation toward mass struggle was challenged by Salvador Cayetano Carpio, the party's general secretary, who after having broken with his former comrades established the guerrilla movement FPL in 1970.[26]

In sum, the main conflict between Castroist radicalism and orthodox Leninism stemmed from the divergent views on both the strategy and the possibility of revolution in Latin America. Castro and Guevara were perfectly aware of the historical anomaly that consisted in the usurpation by orthodox parties of the main claims of revolutionary legitimacy in the area. They had bitterly experienced not only the PSP's adversity during the anti–Batista struggle, but also the apparatchiks' typical lust for power in the first years after the victory of the revolution. The purge of Aníbal Escalante's "micro–faction" and the Marcos Rodríguez affair in 1966 were far more than domestic settlements of accounts. They were staged as symbolic examples to the whole Latin American orthodoxy, necessary caveats to the sclerotic bureaucracies that could, and actually did, oppose the amplification of the new movements.[27] In Castro's view, if the communists wanted to avoid the most traumatic schisms, they had to submit to his dictates. For the "orthodox" parties, this was an impossible requirement since their raison d'être was subordination to Moscow and not to a parallel (and sometimes rival) center.

The military coup in Chile in September 1973 ended Allende's experiment with the "peaceful road to socialism". Chilean communists, who had long promoted the strategy of the Popular Front and mass struggle, were among the staunchest critics of leftist adventurism as expressed in political statements made by certain socialist and MIR leaders. According to Volodia Teitelboim, leftist intemperance contributed to the deterioration of the political and social climate under Allende:

> Although there were some measures clearly decided during that period, the actual programme of Popular Unity was not always implemented according to plan. Sometimes its fundamental aims were paralyzed because of diverging interpretations within the Popular Unity groups, and largely because of extremist (i.e. MIR) tendencies they did not take into account the existing conditions and domestic balance of power.[28]

Toward a Unified Strategy

It has become increasingly clear, in the mid–1970s, that a consensus sui generis tended to gain support both from Castroites and orthodox parties. Cuba's rapprochement with the U.S.S.R., which followed the Soviet invasion of Czechoslovakia, and the collapse of the Chilean experiment with the "electoral way" could only facilitate the task for both groups. They have both decided to subdue ancient allergies and resentments and seek a common strategy against their perceived "common enemy" (the U.S.A.). A meeting of communist parties of Latin America and the Caribbean, significantly held in Havana from June 9 to June 13, 1975, expressed the compromise between Castro and the orthodox parties in its final declaration. "The use of all legal possibilities is an indispensable obligation of the anti–imperialist forces, and the defense of the right of the peoples to decide, through democratic means, the transformations they demand, is a constant principle of our struggle".[29] The concession to Castro and his followers was transparent in the following paragraph of the declaration: "Revolutionaries are not the first to resort to violence. But, it is the right and duty of all people's and revolutionary forces to be ready to answer counterrevolutionary violence with revolutionary violence and open the way, through various means, to the people's actions, including armed struggle, to the sovereign decisions of majorities".[30] The declaration and subsequent political documents advocated "joint actions of all anti–imperialist forces" and urged all the forces of the left to overcome previous divergences. The hour had arrived for reconciliation, and sectarian considerations had to be set aside: "As for the forces that call themselves the 'left', we urge unity without discrimination, excluding none but those who exclude themselves. Communists do not claim a monopoly in questions of unity, nor do they arbitrarily decide who is to join the anti–fascist front and who is to remain beyond its pale".[31]

Castro himself repeatedly called for unity of all leftist forces and resumed his relations with those parties he had violently excoriated in the 1960s. His main concern was now the preparation of a *new revolutionary offensive* which was to be launched in Central America. The victory of the FSLN in Nicaragua in 1979, the resurgence of guerrilla movements in Guatemala and Peru, and the development of the armed struggle in El Salvador, compelled many an orthodox party to reconsider its attitude toward violence. More than symptomatic, in this respect, is the evolution of the PCES.

After Salvador Cayetano Carpio's split over the issue of armed struggle, Shafik Jorge Handal asserted himself as a disciplined mouthpiece for Moscow's line which, in the early 70's, supported a reformist, "wait and see" position in Latin America. Later, a total reversal of strategic options on the Soviet–Cuban part engendered a fundamental overhaul of the "gradualist" tenets and led the PCES to armed struggle. What we might depict as a *new revolutionary wave* began with the unification of the three main groups within the FSLN as a result of Castro's personal intervention and the victory of the Sandinistas in Nicaragua. During a debate sponsored by the *World Marxist Review* in 1981, it was emphatically stated that the revolutionary development in Nicaragua should modify the traditional view on armed struggle and the violent road to socialism: "The Nicaraguan revolution has confirmed that *far from impeding armed struggle, as some petty bourgeois theorists contend with reference to the experience of the 1960s, the present international situation largely predetermines its favorable outcome*".[32] Furthermore, this tribune for the Moscow–line parties insisted on the necessity of continuing the two main strategic approaches and warned against unreserved commitment to one or another form of struggle: "The fact that so far this method (armed struggle) has been the only one to lead to victory in Latin America does not imply that other methods or combinations of them are alien to the revolution". Rodney Arismendi, CC First Secretary of the Communist Party of Uruguay was quoted with his conclusion that "what miscarried in

Latin America in the 1960s was not the possibility of guerrilla warfare as a method, but 'guerrillism'''.[33]

It is interesting to dwell upon some of the basic theses developed by Shafik Handal in support of the decisive reorientation of the PCES toward armed struggle. According to the general secretary of PCES, the significance of armed struggle in El Salvador definitely transcends a limited national framework: ''By fighting and winning, the Salvadoran patriots and the whole of our people are making a contribution to the continuity of the revolutionary process in Central America and the cause of Nicaragua's defense, so ultimately advancing the democratic and national liberation movement in Latin America''.[34] After long years of intramural squabbles, of internecine conflicts, after the denunciation of his forerunner, Salvador Cayetano Carpio, as a ''petty–bourgeois adventurer'', there is something of a historical irony in this candid acknowledgement of (1) the inevitability of armed struggle, and (2) the uninterrupted character of the Central American revolution. All this rhetoric sounds like an echo of long–abandoned OLAS myths, with the eloquent corrective that they are now being uttered by an archetypical Soviet–line apparatchik. Surprising as it may appear coming from Handal, his position confirms the axiom that nothing completely vanishes in the field of revolutionary ambitions and chimeras. Paradoxically, the case for armed struggle, once the attribute of heretic revolutionaries, is made by a commissar whose subservience to Moscow involves now the obligation of complying with Castro's strategic obsessions and tactical decisions.

The drama—inasmuch as it is a drama—of orthodox Leninist parties in Latin America is their despairing rootlessness. They benefit from a sham revolutionary legitimacy primarily related to their unconditional support for the Soviet Union. In emphasizing the violent road to socialism, Fidel Castro managed to stir certain emotional chords so characteristic of Latin American political culture, while the traditional lukewarm approach of the ''established'' communist parties could only engender contempt and mistrust. All their hostility to Castro notwithstanding, the Latin American communist parties benefited from his legend, particularly after the *líder máximo* decided to avoid openly his commitment to a rigid version of Marxism–Leninism. As for Salvadoran Communists, they had to go to Canossa and admit the legitimacy of the violent approach. One can conclude from the experience of PCES that all major strategic options of Latin American communist parties are subordinate to Soviet interests and more recently to Cuban political interests. In Handal's words, the new line was dictated by historical evolution which would have placed the issue of power on the immediate agenda. With oracular certainty, Handal suggests the capital objectives of the FMLN strategy:

> We have drawn a number of lessons from our experience, and they testify that
> the revolution can advance in the most difficult conditions if there is a united

vanguard closely linked with the masses, equipped with the right revolutionary line, and displaying an unbending will and resolve to fulfill its historical mission and win . . . We have become convinced that offensive is the substance of revolution as a historical process, and that the main task is the winning of power and its defense.[35]

Even more telling, the Salvadoran communist leader exposed his own former reformist illusions and indicated the true nature of the communist design: "Unless the vanguard carries the masses to higher stages of the struggle when the need for it has already matured, it ceases to be such a vanguard, and is faced with the threat of fragmenting into groups and factions, vegetating, and even integrating with the political mechanism supporting the system of 'one's own' and foreign exploiters".[36]

Handal's very terminology, his consistent call for unity, actually reflects a new Soviet–Cuban assessment of the revolutionary opportunities in Central America. Old ideological incompatibilities must be played down and mutual hostility must be abated in order to promote "revolutionary offensive". The most important event for the coagulation of the new line of the PCES, was the party's Seventh Congress in April 1979, a conclave that consecrated the turning point in the approach to armed struggle. The PCES has thus been potentially engaged in military operations since 1979, and it took part in what the Left described as the "final offensive" of January 1981. Since then, the FAL (Armed Forces of Liberation) have been integrated in the FMLN and were active in all major military operations under the FMLN umbrella.

According to Handal, the turning point in the strategy of Salvadoran Communists expressed the increasing awareness of the "masses" that only armed struggle could solve the country's problems. His claim is that it was after the 1977 fraudulent elections that the consciousness of the masses matched the existing revolutionary situation in that a propensity toward armed opposition to the established regime was irreversible. As a result, the PCES decided to carry out the historic turn to armed struggle, breaking with its previous theoretical and practical commitments. Handal maintains that this decision was made by the Seventh Congress in April 1979, but it was not made public until 1980 allegedly because of the "contradiction between the high requirements of this decision and the deep ideological and organic weaknesses" of the party. More realistically, the gap was due to the PCES participation in the November 1979–January 1980 government. The mystique of the electoral way was said to have led the party to abandon the efforts to develop the revolutionary violence of the masses and particularly "the self–defense against the repression and the build–up of the armed forces of the party".[37] The Fifth Congress (1964) was found guilty of renouncing the strategy of armed struggle and blamed for its exclusive orientation toward "mass struggle". Handal now admitted that this fault stemmed from a rigid, petrified view of the relationship between the two strategic approaches, an exaggeration characteristic of the polemics with the theory and practice of the foco guerrillero.

What is striking in Handal's "self–criticism" is his avoidance of any reference whatsoever to the international factors that in the mid–1960s determined the abandonment of the violence–oriented strategy on behalf of what he scornfully calls "reformism" and "economism". The truth is that Latin American orthodox parties could not tolerate the emergence of an alternative revolutionary center and the imposition of Castro–Guevarism as the revolutionary doctrine par excellence. The Soviet Union was not interested in supporting revolutionary exploits in Latin America, particularly at a time when Fidel Castro acted as a rather independent and nonconformist factor in the conflicts that devoured international communism. The orthodox parties were thus invited by Moscow to stick to the tenets of the doctrine of peaceful coexistence and repudiate any "Blanquist" (read Maoist) temptations. "Mass struggle" was the only answer these groups could offer to the romantic–revolutionary yearnings exploited by the Castroites. It was only after 1978–79 that a general strategic reassessment was undertaken, and the issue of violence received a different treatment in communist ideology. The reasons for the timing were Vietnam, Angola, Grenada, and Nicaragua—all perceived as examples of the U.S. global strategic threat.

In Handal's opinion, the main obstacles faced by the new strategic outlook within the PCES itself—and the case can be extended to other Latin American communist parties—were best defined as the lack of preparation, both on the organizational level and individual level. The cadres were not trained for guerrilla operations and were therefore reluctant to embark upon the new, reconstructed line. A central task was the establishment of the Military Commission of the party. The communist cells, the marrow of the Leninist party, were assigned direct military objectives: "Learning from the international experience, we oriented the cells to organize around themselves secret groups, that we called GARs (Groups of Revolutionary Action) . . . "[38] The GARs, which are assigned both political and military tasks, are supposed to penetrate and infiltrate various mass organizations.

The Leninist technique of infiltration and manipulation is thus capitalized in the attempt to create mass support for the military actions of the party. Concerning the GARs, Handal insisted:

> The development of war confers upon them an increasingly offensive character and a higher technical–military level; it is thus that the GARs of today carry out combative tasks similar to those accomplished by the guerrillas; they are secret [sic!] guerrillas, whose members fight and work, fight and study, are full–time combatants and do not need territories and a complex urban infrastructure in the area."[39]

The following level—or better, the superior organizational echelon of the armed struggle—is represented by the guerrilla units. The PCES was among the last leftist groups in El Salvador to set up its own military force (the FAL), which is still a relatively minor element compared to Joaquín Villalobos's

ERP (People's Revolutionary Army). A major handicap has certainly originated in the perennial communist ambition to acquire and exert control over leftist groups, such as the PRTC, particularly at those times when communist leaders choose to interpret political events as leading to a "revolutionary situation" (for instance 1979, 1981, both periods of strong PCES pressures for "unification" with PRTC and FARN).

Contrary to the openly elitist view, Handal called for the development of a Revolutionary Army as a *mass organization*, whose tasks, though primarily military, also include propagandistic and political objectives. With the zeal of the neophyte, Handal does not hesitate to formulate a theory of the revolutionary war: "One of the laws of all Revolutionary Popular Wars is that the Revolutionary Army can only be built during the development of the war".[40] Having once broached this issue, the Salvadoran communist leader postures as a military theorist and weighs the necessity and possibilities of developing the rear guard of the would–be Revolutionary Army. His answer materializes in the Bases of Support for the Revolution (Base de Apoyo para la Revolución), which are in fact another name for the "liberated areas" under guerrilla control, providing shelter and the main resource of the rebels.

It is significant that Handal is so interested in the development of the rear guard. It is more than a matter of conjecture to assume that he is aware of the advantages his party could draw from the establishment of "revolutionary institutions" in the so–called "liberated zones." More than any other guerrilla group, the communists are well–prepared for launching operations of mass–indoctrination, achieving political control over the population, and concocting propaganda myths for foreign observers. To conclude, Handal formulates the meaning of the popular revolutionary war, which would be "the continuation of armed struggle with political struggle, the latter consisting of all the non-armed forms which are coordinated with the unique process of the revolutionary struggle."[41] This is a rather facile definition, but Latin American communists have never been renowned for ideological subtlety. The important point for our discussion is the present rehabilitation, on the part of Moscow–line parties, of the strategy of violent opposition to existing governments in Latin America. As a corollary, one should notice the emergence of unified leftist organizations that have succeeded in grouping traditionally rival movements. The case of El Salvador is symptomatic of this tendency, an indication of the current ideological and political transfiguration of orthodox parties in the "hottest" areas of the western hemisphere. Professionals of propaganda, skilled maneuverers and apt politicians, orthodox Marxist–Leninists can furnish the necessary cadres for totalitarian institutions. Masters of political deception, combining the logic of subversion with that of survival, these organizers are ready now to shake hands with all those radical sects mobilized by resentment and frustration in order to accelerate the advent of what they regard as a superior social order. Unlike many utopian Catholics and urban declassé intellectuals, Latin American communists are well aware of the real stakes of the game. They know perfectly what it is all about. Their current support for violence, though qualified, localized, and sometimes half–hearted, signifies more than a mere ideological adjustment. It is, rather, a strategic transmutation, which says a lot about increased Soviet–Cuban interest in destabilizing established regimes in the Western hemisphere. This new strategic outlook can even be detected in the political platform of the Chilean Communist Party, whose views used to be considered a paradigm for the "peaceful road" approach. After 1980 at the latest, the PCCh joined the radical Left in maintaining that only a massive armed campaign would provide the resolution to the Chilean situation. Corvalán's party, once reputed for its "moderation", went so far as to establish an alliance with Andrés Pascal Allende's MIR and the "Stalinist" Almeyda faction of the Socialist Party. It is true that Corvalán himself never expressed support for the doctrine of armed struggle but he has openly referred to the right of rebellion and the possible use of violence: "Fascism is reactionary violence . . . We must put an end to this violence. To this end there are many ways of fighting. When reason is not enough, or this is ignored, we have to use force."[42]

Latin American orthodox parties, though far from being the most active and/or influential leftist groups in their countries, again tend to become a significant factor in the development of the new revolutionary wave. Their reexamination of the violent strategy, which in El Salvador—as well as Honduras and Guatemala—resulted in the party's direct engagement in guerrilla warfare, suggests a further redistribution of forces within the Latin American Left in accordance with the Soviet–Cuban assumptions about imminent "revolutionary crises" in the Western hemisphere.[43]

Notes

1. For a comprehensive historical–political approach to the nature and development of Latin American Marxist–Leninist movements and parties, see Boris Goldenberg, *Kommunismus in Lateinamerika* (Stuttgart Berlin Köln Main: Verlag W. Kohlhammer, 1971); another illuminating source is provided by Luis Aguilar's anthology *Marxism in Latin America*. Rev. Ed. (Philadelphia: Temple University Press, 1978); for the relationship between the orthodox parties and the Castroite movements (the "Jacobin leftists"), see Robert J. Alexander, "The Communist Parties of Latin America," *Problems of Communism*, July–August 1970, pp. 37–46.
2. For an assessment of Haya de la Torre's contribution, see Harold Eugene Davis, *Latin American Thought: A Historical Introduction* (New York: The Free Press, 1972), pp. 185–189; Carlos Rangel, *The Latin Americans. Their Love–Hate Relationship with the United States* (New York: Harcourt Brace Jovanovich, 1976), pp. 115–121.
3. See Sheldon B. Liss, *Marxist Thought in Latin America* (Berkeley: University of California Press, 1984), p. 196.
4. An excellent approach to the anatomy and psychology of communist apparatus in

a Western society is offered by Annie Kriegel, *Les communistes français. Essai d'ethnographie politique* (Paris: Ed. du Seuil, 1968); On the development of Trotskyism in Latin America, see Robert J. Alexander, *Trotskyism in Latin America* (Stanford: Hoover Institution Press, 1975); a well–informed sympathetic analysis of the revolution of Latin American communism and its relations with other leftist clans is provided by Donald C. Hodges, *The Latin American Revolution. Politics and Strategy from Apro–Marxism to Guevarism* (New York: William Morrow, 1974).

5. "A Program of Action for the Victory of the Chilean Popular Front," a document reprinted in Luis Aguilar, *Marxism in Latin America*, op. cit., pp. 162–166.
6. See Carmelo Furci, *The Chilean Communist Party and the Road to Socialism* (London: Zed Books, 1984), p. 34.
7. Ibid., p. 35. See also Robert J. Alexander, *Communism in Latin America* (New Brunswick: Rutgers University Press, 1957), p. 192. For a comprehensive account of the Popular Front experience in France, the country where the Comintern's new strategy was most extensively developed, see: Edward Mortimer, *The Rise of the French Communist Party* (London and Boston: Faber and Faber, 1984), pp. 226–267; for an insightful interpretation of the evolution of communism in Chile, see Ernst Halperin, *Nationalism and Communism in Chile* (Cambridge, Mass.: MIT Press, 1965).
8. Luís Carlos Prestes, "Brazilian Communists in the Fight for Democracy," (1945), Aguilar, *Marxism in Latin America*, pp. 173–178. It is symptomatic that it was precisely Prestes, the man who had led the legendary rebel column after the "Lieutenants' revolt" in 1924 and belonged to the communist hegemonic nucleus during the aborted insurrectional attempt in November 1935, who was chosen to voice the "moderate" strategy and the support for the idea of Pan–Americanism. One of the Comintern's pillars in Latin America, Prestes faithfully accepted and expressed the Soviet international line. More than an irony of history, therefore, is his recent divorce with the official leadership of the Brazilian Communist Party headed by Giocondo Días. A lifelong orthodox Stalinist decided to break ranks and commit the mortal sin of "factionalism". According to official PCB documents, Prestes and his supporters from the São Paulo state leadership "placed themselves outside the ranks". See Carole Merten, "Brazil", in Richard F. Staar, ed., *Yearbook on International Communist Affairs 1985* (Stanford, California: Hoover Institution Press, 1985), p. 52.
9. See Boris Goldenberg, *Kommunismus in Lateinamerika*, op. cit., p. 307. The communists' support for Batista had been rewarded first through the appointment of Juan Marinello (1943) and then of Carlos Rafael Rodríguez (1944) as ministers without *portfolio*, (ibid., pp. 304–305). For an analysis of the political meanderings of Cuban communism, see Andrés Suárez, *Cuba: Castroism and Communism* (Cambridge, Mass.: MIT Press, 1967); Theodore Draper, *Castroism: Theory and Practice* (New York: Praeger, 1965); Boris Goldenberg, "The Rise and Fall of a Party: The Cuban CP (1925–59)," *Problems of Communism*, July–August 1970, pp. 61–80.
10. Mario Vargas Llosa, *Historia de Mayta* (Barcelona: Editorial Seix Barral, 1984).
11. *International Communism After Khrushchev*, ed., Leopold Labedz. See Ernst Halperin, "Latin America," (Cambridge, Mass.: MIT Press, 1965). The commitment of these parties to the violent overthrow system is rather rhetorical, and armed struggle has often been branded as a harmful temptation. This persistent lack of active radicalism does not imply that Latin American "orthodox" parties are democratic: "They are totalitarian parties with a totalitarian system of organization and a totalitarian mentality, and whenever they have managed to maneuver

themselves into a position where they enjoy a share of real power . . . their totalitarianism at once becomes manifest in their behavior towards both their allies and their opponents''. (Ibid., p. 154).

12. One of the very few attempts to go beyond the Leninist–Stalinist organizational and ideological patterns was undertaken by the leaders of the Venezuelan MAS (Movimiento al Socialismo) and particularly by Teodoro Petkoff. Petkoff, a former member of the Politburo of the Venezuelan CP was involved in the guerrilla operations in the early 1960s. Later, he became an ardent partisan of the legalist approach and called for a general reappraisal of the Marxist–Leninist experience in Latin America. In the eyes of orthodox communists, he became a "renegade", primarily because of his opposition to the Soviet hegemony within the international communist movement and the "revisionist" theses stated in his main publications. With regard to the internal struggle within Venezuelan communism, see Teodoro Petkoff, *Socialismo para Venezuela?* (Caracas: Editorial Domingo Fuentes, 1970); Robert J. Alexander, *The Communist Party of Venezuela* (Stanford, Calif.: Hoover Institution Press, 1969); Benedict Cross, "Marxism in Venezuela," *Problems of Communism*, November–December 1973, pp. 51–70; Pastor Heydra, *La Izquierda; Una autocrítica perpetua* (Caracas: Universidad Central de Venezuela, 1981); David J. Myers, "Venezuela's MAS," *Problems of Communism*, September–October 1980, pp. 16–27.

13. For the complete text of the communiqué of this communist conclave, see William E. Ratliff, *Castroism and Communism in Latin America. The Varieties of Marxist–Leninist Experience* (American Enterprise Institute–Hoover Policy Studies, 1976), pp. 195–198.

14. Bernardo Alvarado Monzón, "Some problems of the Guatemalan Revolution," in *World Marxist Review*, Vol. 9, No. 10, October 1966, p. 41. Alvarado Monzón was at that time General Secretary of the Guatemalan Party of Labor. Referring to the experience of armed struggle in other countries of the area (the Dominican Republic, Cuba), Monzón defined revolutionary armed struggle as a basic strategy in the Caribbean area. Monzón mentioned the differences between the strategy in this area and that promoted by communist parties in the southern part of the continent and in Brazil: "In some of these countries capitalist relations are relatively highly developed, there exists a stronger and bigger working class, and they also have communist parties enjoying much influence among the masses. Owing to these circumstances the non–violent and legal forms of struggle predominate in these countries." (Ibid., p. 43).

15. Ibid., p. 41. In March 1965, the Central Committee of the PGT elaborated the strategic outlook concerning the development of armed struggle in Guatemala. According to this document, such a strategy will lead to a revolutionary people's war and not to a brief armed insurrection or the creation of pockets of guerrilla resistance doomed to isolation and final defeat: "A revolutionary people's war presupposes the existence of definite conditions which mature as the war develops and make it possible, organizationally, politically and militarily to prepare the popular forces for the eventual uprising and victory". (Ibid., p. 42).

16. Luis Corvalán, "The Peaceful Way—a Form of Revolution," in *World Marxist Review*, Vol. 6, No. 12, December 1963, p. 9.

17. Lenin's classical description of the revolutionary situation was formulated in his study "The Collapse of the Second International" (1915). According to Lenin, there are three major symptoms of the revolutionary situation. The first is the existence of a crisis among the "upper classes," a political crisis within the ruling group, leading to a fissure through which the discontent and indignation of the

oppressed classes burst forth. For a revolution to take place, it is usually insufficient for "the lower classes not to want" to live in the old way; it is also necessary that "the upper classes should be unable" to live in the old way. The second symptom is when the suffering and the want of the oppressed classes have grown more acute than usual. The third is when, as a consequence of the above causes, there is a considerable increase in the activity of the masses, who uncomplainingly allow themselves to be robbed in "peacetime," but, in turbulent times, are drawn both by all the circumstances of the crisis and by the "upper classes" themselves into independent historical action. See V. I. Lenin, *Collected Works*, Vol. 21 (Moscow: Progress Publishers, 1964), pp. 213–214. In Lenin's view, it was precisely the reliance upon the advanced class which distinguished Marxism from Blanquism. Latin American Soviet–line parties persistently invoked these Leninist theses while criticizing Castro–Guevarism and Régis Debray's elitist conception of the foco guerrillero as a substitute for the traditional vanguard party. See Hartmut Ramm, *The Marxism of Régis Debray. Between Lenin and Guevara* (Lawrence: The Regent Press of Kansas, 1978).

18. One of the best documented studies on the development of rural guerrilla groups in Latin America is Richard Gott's *Guerrilla Movements in Latin America* (Garden City, N.Y.: Doubleday & Co., 1971). Gott's book tends to share the revolutionary myths of the Far–Left, and its conclusions are highly debatable. Nevertheless documents published as appendixes or extensively quoted in the text highlight the oscillations of orthodox parties when faced with the necessity of reassessing their strategic options. An interesting case of fundamental strategic reorientation was that of the Colombian Communist Party who decided at its Tenth Congress (in January 1966) to embark officially upon a path of violence and organize its own guerrilla group, the Revolutionary Armed Forces of Colombia (FARC) under the leadership of Manuel Marulanda Velez. See Gérard Chaliand, *Mythes révolutionnaires du tiers monde* (Paris: Ed. du Seuil, 1979), pp. 85–105.

19. See Gott, op. cit., p. 519 (Chapter from the central report approved by the Tenth Congress of the Colombian Communist Party, January 1966); see also Jaime González, "The Armed Forces of the Revolution in Colombia," in *World Marxist Review*, Vol. 11, No. 2, February 1968, pp. 48–52.

20. See "The Venezuelan Communist Party Replies to Fidel Castro," in Aguilar, *Marxism in Latin America*, op. cit., pp. 391–395. Later Bravo will come to deplore Castro's realignment to the Soviet–line: see Douglas Bravo, "Differences with Fidel Castro Concerning a Bolivarian War of Independence," in Donald C. Hodges, *The Legacy of Che Guevara* (London: Thames and Hudson, 1977), pp. 122–124.

21. Castro's speech on March 13, 1967, in *Gramma* (Havana), March 14, 1967 (supplement); see also for the relation between Castro's views and Régis Debray's theses, *The Marxism of Régis Debray* op. cit., pp. 56–60. Castro's attacks on the leadership of the Venezuelan CP will reemerge in his speech at the closing session of the OLAS Conference on August 10, 1967. While singling out the Venezuelan "reformist" militants, Castro resolutely incriminated the general strategic outlook of Soviet–line parties. He was certainly informed of the tensions between Ernesto Che Guevara's group and the leadership of the Bolivian CP and regarded the orthodox parties as "objective" saboteurs of revolutionary elements. For the relation between Cuba and the PCV, see Agustín Blanco Múñoz, *La lucha armada: Hablan 5 jefes* (Caracas: Universidad Central de Venezuela, 1980), particularly the long conversations with Gustavo Machado, Pompeyo Márquez, and

Teodoro Petkoff. During an interview with this author in Caracas (February 1985), Teodoro Petkoff acknowledged that the conflict with Castro contributed to the crystallization of his new view of internationalism which was to lead eventually to the creation of MAS. This conflict acutely emphasized the organizational and intellectual debility of traditional Leninist parties.

22. See William E. Ratliff, *Castroism and Communism in Latin American*, op. cit., p. 206; for Guevara's own view, see *Che: Selected Works of Che Guevara*. R. E. Bonachea and N. P. Valdés, eds., (Cambridge: MIT Press, 1969); for the orthodox assessment of the Tricontinental Conference, see J. M. Fortuny, A. Delgado, N. Salibi, "The Tricontinental Conference," in *World Marxist Review*, Vol. 9, No. 3, March 1966, pp. 21–24.

23. See Shafik Handal, "Reflections on Continental Strategy for Latin American Revolutionaries," in *World Marxist Review*, April 1968, p. 56.

24. See Régis Debray, *Revolution in the Revolution?* (New York: Grove Press, 1967), p. 105.

25. With regard to the institutionalization of the Cuban Revolution, one should mention Jorge L. Domínguez's studies, among which "Revolutionary Politics: the New Demands for Orderliness," in Jorge L. Domínguez, ed., *Cuba. Internal and International Affairs* (Beverly Hills/London/New Age Publ., 1982). As for the process of Stalinization, it is important to point to Irving Louis Horowitz's illuminating contribution in his "Political Sociology of Cuban Communism." Professor Horowitz gives the following key criteria for grasping the Stalinist transformation of the once promising heterodox Cuban Revolution: (1) the bureaucratization of the Communist party machinery and subordination of society to the party–state; (2) the emergence of a leader and his small coterie as exclusive spokesmen for the party; (3) the promotion of inner political struggle as a substitute for class struggle, the politics of debate, and the passion for socialist democracy; (4) the elimination of all roads to socialism save one: the economic growth road set and defined by the maximum leader; (5) the nearly exclusive concentration on national rather than international problems. While it is true that Stalinism, with its theory of "socialism in one country" meant the antithesis of the Marxist messianic–internationalist vision, one cannot overlook the perverse confiscation of what might be called the language of world revolution and the transformation of the Comintern into an appendage of Stalin's foreign policy. In other words, Stalinist nationalism is not reducible to self–reclusion and isolationism, but rather involves permanent need of expansion. This is true of the Soviet Union, China, Vietnam, and other communist would–be "empires", including Castro's Cuba. The fate of Castro's internationalist ("Bolivarian") aspirations and beliefs could be a fascinating topic for an essay on the degeneration of radical idealism under totalitarian circumstances. See Irving Louis Horowitz, "The Framework of Cuban Communism" and "The Political Sociology of Cuban Communism," in I. L. Horowitz, ed., *Cuban Communism* (New Brunswick: Transaction Books, 1977).

26. For a historical–political perspective on the background of the far–left movements in El Salvador, see: Shirley Christian, "The Other Side," in *The New Republic*, October 24, 1983, pp. 13–19 and Gabriel Zaid, "Enemy Colleagues. A Reading of the Salvador Tragedy," *Dissent*, Winter 1982, pp. 13–39. More recently, similar internecine struggle in Honduras led to the expulsion of Rigoberto Padilla Rush from his post as General Secretary and from the Central Committee, in October 1984. See Thomas P. Anderson, "Honduras," in Richard F. Staar, ed.,

1985 Yearbook on International Communist Affairs, op. cit., pp. 100–101. More recently, Padilla's faction was publicly acknowledged by the Soviet–sponsored *World Marxist Review* as the legitimate voice of Honduran communists. See Rigoberto Padilla Rush, "Armed Intervention on the Pretext of Countering a Mythical Threat," *World Marxist Review*, Vol. 28, No. 7, July 1985, pp. 24–31.

27. For the conflict between Castro and the PSP "Old Guard," see Suarez, *Cuba: Castroism and Communism*, op. cit., especially the analysis of the Marcos Rodríguez affair; and Maurice Halperin, *The Rise and Decline of Fidel Castro* (Berkeley: University of California Press, 1976). For the relation between Castro and the Soviet Union, see Maurice Halperin, *The Taming of Fidel Castro* (Berkeley: California: University of California Press, 1981).

28. Volodia Teitelboim, interview, in Carmelo Furci, *The Chilean Communist Party*, op. cit., pp. 126–127. A sharp attack on the politics of the Chilean orthodox communists who allegedly would have followed the "Euro-Communist" strategy of "historic compromise" was formulated by Jorge Palacios, a Chilean leftist doctrinaire, in his book *Chile: An Attempt at "Historic Compromise"* (Chicago: Banner Press, 1975.

29. "Conference of Communist Parties of Latin America and the Caribbean, June 1975," in William E. Ratliff, *Castroism and Communism in Latin America*, op. cit., p. 229.

30. Ibid.

31. See Volodia Teitelboim, "For the Complete Independence of Our America," in *World Marxist Review*, September 1975, p. 40.

32. See "A Continent in Struggle. The International Factor in the Revolutionary Struggle of Latin American Peoples," in *World Marxist Review*, June 1981, p. 47. For Arismendi's statement, see *Estudios*, No. 73, 1979, p. 22.

33. Ibid.

34. See Shafik Jorge Handal, "Offensive: The Substance of Revolution," in *World Marxist Review*, April 1985, p. 38.

35. Ibid., p. 39.

36. Ibid., p. 40.

37. Shafik Jorge Handal, "Consideraciones acerca del viraje del Partido Comunista de El Salvador hacia la lucha armada," in *Fundamentos y Perspectivas*, San Salvador, No. 5, Abril 1983, p. 23.

38. Ibid., p. 29–30.

39. Ibid., p. 31.

40. Ibid., p. 39.

41. Ibid., p. 44.

42. "Declaracion del Partido Comunista de Chile," Santiago, 23 September 1980, quoted by Furci, *The Chilean Communist Party* op. cit., p. 167. Furci, who is a member of the Italian Communist Party, links this evolution to the general strategic change inaugurated by the victory of the Sandinistas: "The latest developments in the PCCh's political strategy may influence—and be influenced by—other Latin American leftist movements . . . If the U.S.S.R. endorses the strategy of armed struggle in Latin America, as the case of El Salvador may suggest, it will be fundamentally as a result of the triumph of the Nicaraguan revolution. At the same time, the PCCh's swing from the peaceful road to the armed struggle has created a new phase in Chilean politics." (Ibid.) Concerning the relations between the PCCh and the underground armed group "Manuel Rodríguez Patriotic Front" (FPMR) described by many observers as the party's military branch, Corvalán avoided the unequivocal: "The Communist Party is a political party and

the FPMR is an organization with military discipline which seems to have combat means. Although it is not a political organization in the full sense of the word, we maintain with the FPMR a fraternal relationship based on a common cause." (See "Interview with PCCh Secretary General Luis Corvalán," *El Mercurio* (Santiago), August 11, 1985, in FBIS, (Latin America), 20 August 1985, p. E6).

43. The imperative of unity was clearly expressed by Manuel Pineiro Rosada, the chief of the Department of the Americas within the Central Committee of the Cuban Communist Party: "The unity of the revolutionary movement inside the borders of a country is a contribution to the broader unity on a continental and world scale. In regard to our region, the historic and economic factors, the confrontation with a similar enemy, and the political interrelation of our societies foster an identity in proposals and reciprocal solidarity of the left". (See Manuel Pineiro, "Imperialism and Revolution in Latin America and the Caribbean", *New International*, Vol. 1, No. 3, Spring–Summer 1984, p. 124).

7

Revolutionary Elites

Michael Radu

Despite the abundant literature on the revolutionary phenomenon in Latin America since the Cuban Revolution, the study of revolutionary elites on the continent remains in its incipient phase. One reason for this is the fall from scholarly fashion of the older theories of the elite. A far more important reason is the growing influence of Marxism in Third World and Latin American studies. Because it tends to minimize and underestimate the role of individual or small groups to the advantage of social classes or economically discrete social strata, Marxism carries an inherent and all pervasive bias against the analysis of revolutionary elites. Even non-Marxist scholars underestimate the role of the elite for the sake of economic and social macroanalysis. Concerning Latin American revolutionaries, conceptual and ideological biases are reinforced by scant background data and obfuscated by their abundant rhetoric and the presumption of an organic link between the revolutionary elites and their followers. This link is considered natural because the phenomenon of revolution in Latin America is itself deemed a necessary and inevitable corrective to what is widely described as social inequality, economic exploitation, and unfair distribution of scarce national resources. If the revolution is "inevitable", it matters little who the leaders are, how they became leaders, or what role they play in the orientation, program, or tactics of revolutionary movements.

Any serious analysis of the nature and role of Latin American revolutionary elites must dispel this maze of widespread misperceptions, neglected facts, and preconceived notions. It is possible, however, to approach the topic in a preliminary manner by comparing certain long-available data with dominant academic and political perceptions in Latin America and the West. Such an approach cannot replace an intensive study, but it can underscore the need for one, the general lines it should follow, and the main issues it should examine. The present chapter proposes to reach these goals.

The Conceptual Framework

In the context of this chapter the term "revolutionary elite" is defined as the group of individuals who have political, military, or ideological control over decision making within revolutionary movements. "Revolution" is summarily defined as a political, economic, ideological, and social project, not necessarily fulfilled but characterized by one overall goal: the radical and usually violent restructuring of the entire society, from the distribution of wealth and property to the level of individual mentalities (i.e., "cultural revolution" or the creation of a "new man"). This concept of revolution is totalitarian. The project aims for absolute change which, following political and/or military success, focuses on total control over popular and individual beliefs, and then on permanent social and ideological control over the entire population and to the forcible imposition of a well–defined ideology, mostly international in nature, over the society as a whole. Within these constraints the term "revolutionary" applies only to groups and organizations proclaiming allegiance to various forms of Marxism–Leninism. The active, radical, and outspoken representatives of "liberation theology" form a limited exception. They are Catholic, but they speak the social, political, and economic language of Marxists–Leninists, often act like and continually support them, implicitly or explicitly. In a nutshell, "Latin American revolutionary elites" are Marxist–Leninist groups who control basically Marxist–Leninist organizations whose goal is the usually but not always violent replacement of existing governments in Latin America with totalitarian regimes.

At one time the term "communist" would have characterized these groups, but today in Latin America and throughout the world the term has lost its original clarity. The confusion is the result of negative connotations of the term in the West (indirectly related to the abuses of the McCarthy era, which resulted in a widespread dislike of the term "anticommunist") and, more important, of empirical realities in Latin America and the rest of the world. In a strict sense, the term "communist" defines a person directly and formally associated with the existing communist parties in Latin America. However, these parties are now universally and correctly seen as only the third largest Marxist–Leninist element in Latin America, after the Castroites and a large number of independent ideological fellow travelers and "heterodox" Marxists (Trotskyites, Maoists, etc.). Consequently the term "communist" has lost its descriptive value. Moreover, the ideological and often military competition among Marxist–Leninist groups, many of whom dismiss the communist parties as irrelevant or even traitorous, further demonstrates the emptiness of the term "communist" in Latin America.

The practical meaning of the terms "communism" or "communist" in Latin America, and the Third World has nothing to do with Marxism–Leninism. It does have a great deal to do with Leninist totalitarianism, however. Since no Latin American revolutionary movement since the Cuban Revolution of 1959 has ever claimed anything but Marxist–Leninist goals—except the Nicaraguan insurgents presently operating under the umbrella of the *Nicaraguan Opposition Union (UNO)*—the term "revolutionary" in Latin America appears to be empirically associated with Marxism–Leninism. For this reason, the use of the term "revolutionary" in this chapter should be seen as tantamount to "Marxist–Leninist". Whether applied to the Chilean MIR, the Argentine ERP or Montoneros, the Uruguayan Tupamaros, the Colombian M-19 or FARC, Peru's Sendero Luminoso and MRTA, or the plethora of Guatemalan, Salvadoran, and Honduran guerrilla groups, the conclusion remains the same. All are fundamentally Marxist–Leninist, even though they may have started from different parts of the political spectrum and each may consider its ideological approach "more" Marxist–Leninist than anyone else's.

The leadership of revolutionary movements or groups throughout Latin America always claims to represent "the people" or the "masses", which may seem incompatible with their definition as elites. After all, one of the essential characteristics of any elite is its clear demarcation from the populace as a whole. How can a group "representing" the populace be an elite? The answer is found in the peculiar Leninist meaning of the term "representation" and the nature of the Latin American revolutionaries' modus operandi.

The Background of the Revolutionaries

In their *Leaders of the Revolution*, Mostafa Rejai and Kay Phillips defined "the principal leaders" as "persons who risk their lives by playing a *prominent, active, and continuing* role throughout the revolutionary process".[1] To a decisive extent this definition applies to the revolutionary elites of Latin America, although it must be expanded to include not only the top leaders of each organization but also the entire core of militants. In other words, revolutionary elites are ideologically aware, decision–making, revolutionary *professionals*. This latter characteristic separates them neatly from the rank and file of their followers. They are occupied full–time with political and/or military activities with a revolutionary aim. While many have degrees in law, history, or the liberal professions or were longtime students, their formal professions act more as a useful cover for their actual occupation.

"Rolando Morán," the supreme commander of the EGP, Guatemala's largest guerrilla organization, is an example of the degree of professionalism of eminent Latin American revolutionaries. Morán is the nom de guerre of Ricardo Ramírez de Léon, the most prominent Guatemalan ideologue and theoretician of guerrilla warfare. He was most influential in Latin America during the 1960s under the aliases of Orlando Fernández and Arnoldo Cardona Fratti.[2] Under these guises he contributed significantly to the conception of Régis Debray's "Critique des Armes."

According to his own statements[3] Morán was born in 1932. In 1949 he fought an alleged coup against then–president Arévalo. Later he was "a union organizer and student leader." He was still a "student leader" at the time of Arbenz's fall in 1954. While taking refuge in the Argentine Embassy he met Ernesto ("Che") Guevara. He was sent to Argentina with Guevara and then "worked in the student movement, traveled, read voraciously and studied other revolutionary experiences." He arrived in Cuba as a reporter for a student magazine and stayed for a while. In 1959 he returned to Guatemala as a member of the youth section of the PGT, tried unsuccessfully to become involved in the aborted November 1960 leftist military coup, and became a liaison between the guerrillas and the PGT. Between 1966 and 1972 Morán lived in Cuba and actively represented the Guatemalan revolutionaries in Havana. In January 1972 he returned to Guatemela and became leader of the newly established EGP.

Certain aspects of Morán's life are striking and highly typical of many Latin American revolutionary leaders. First, he never held a regular job; after his seventeenth year he was involved solely in politics. Second, although he never obtained a degree he remained a "student" from 1950 to 1962. At San Carlos University in Guatemala the average period between enrollment and graduation for a law student is more than ten years.[4] This university is by far the largest in the country and typical of most public universities in Latin America. It is not surprising that the role of perennial student is often cover for the professional revolutionary. Moreover, in most Latin American revolutionary organizations (at least in those about which there is reliable information) there are many more "students" at the leadership level than professionals, that is, many more dropout "perennial students" than graduates. For instance, in 1970, fifty–five guerrillas from the Uruguayan Tuparamos were captured. Fifteen were students and four were seminary students, compared with seven liberal professional practitioners and one priest.[5] Also, before 1972, students clearly outnumbered professionals among captured Tupamaros, often by a large margin—38.9 percent to 22.2 percent in 1966–1969, 35.1 percent to 23.4 percent in 1970.[6] Among the present leaders of the Salvadoran insurgency, many if not most are former activists in the AGEUS, including such figures as Joaquín Villalobos, the supreme leader of the ERP, Roberto Roca of the PRTC, Schafik Handal of the PCES, Fermán Cienfuegos of FARN, and most likely Leonel Gonzales of the FPI.

The highly disproportionate role and influence of university "students" in the leadership of Latin American revolutionary movements should also be seen and understood in conjunction with the role of the faculty and graduates of universities. (In all instances, the term "university" will refer only to public institutions). It is significant that in 1979–1980 a study of the patterns of political allegiances in Venezuela demonstrated a considerable difference in orientation between the technical and business schools, which are overwhelmingly private, and university and teachers' colleges, all public. In the states of Lara and Monagas, during the fall of 1978, polls indicated that 7 percent of technical and business school faculty and students, compared with 19 percent of those at university and teachers' colleges, preferred the Left.[7] An even more skewed pattern was found prior to the 1985 Guatemalan presidential elections. There a huge majority of San Carlos students voted for the small Social Democrat Party and the Christian Democrats, while the overwhelming majority of students at the private and highly competitive Francisco Marroquín University preferred the right–of–center National Liberation Movement or parties of the same orientation.[8]

In most Latin American public universities the faculty is dominated by the Left. This is true not only in such universities as Mexico, San Carlos, San Marcos in Lima, and the National University in El Salvador, but also in many Catholic universities, which are generally run by the clergy (mostly Jesuits) but are essentially subsidized by the government. One significant example is the University of Central America (UCA), "José Siméon Canas," of San Salvador, a Jesuit–run institution. UCA played the main programmatic and ideological role in the leftist coup of October 1979 in El Salvador and provided most of the first post–coup regime's leaders—two of the five junta members (Guillermo Ungo and Román Mayorga Quiroz, both former rectors), a majority of ministers, and fourteen out of twenty–nine members of the government.[9] In addition, Fabio Castillo Figueroa, until recently a political leader of the PRTC, was a former National University rector, a communist–backed member of the short–lived 1961 junta, and a presidential candidate a few years later.

Students have played the essential role in the past and present Sandinista leadership in Nicaragua. The three founders of the FSLN, Carlos Fonseca Amador, Silvio Mayorga, and Tomás Borge, were all "student" leaders as well as leaders of the PSN youth branch. Omar Cabezas, currently chief of the secret police in the Interior Ministry, was *agitador estudiantil* (student agitator) in León; Carlos Núñez was a liaison between radical students and the FSLN in the 1960s. The Ortega brothers, Humberto and Daniel, were both active in the FER. The list of past and present Latin American revolutionary leaders associated with universities, particularly the public and Catholic institutions of higher education, is infinite. All of these institutions share certain characteristics: dependence on the government for operating budgets, admission and graduation standards, as well as nominal tuition costs.

The concept of higher education throughout Latin America fosters the relationship between the universities and the revolutionary leadership. With the possible exceptions of Chile, Uruguay, Argentina, Venezuela, and Costa Rica, admission to a university is the result or the beginning of a privileged life. University studies in largely illiterate societies provide immediate and rewarding social status. In other words, a university student in Latin America belongs to a remote group in possession of learning; he or she is one of the actual or potential ruling elites. In addition, faculty members are even more part of the elite. They transcend the rest of the population with their knowledge and garner respect from the illiterates, expressed by their awe for titles like *licenciado* (esquire/lawyer). Respect for university graduates or students, great in largely illiterate societies, easily transfers itself to following the ideological and political aims of educated elites. Also, in political terms, these university graduates or potential graduates are the present–day technocrats and future leaders of the country. Moreover, the overwhelming majority of teachers in Latin America come from public universities and teachers' colleges. Hence, the radical bias of teachers ensures the radical nature of higher education at the public or state level. Parish priests even hold up the teacher as *the* role model for ambitious rural or proletarian youths.

The impact of the youth on Latin American revolutionary groups and politics cannot be overestimated. Latin American societies are composed largely of the young with one–third or more of the population under the age of fifteen. In addition, the youth's political socialization starts at the high school and even secondary school level. The role of Guatemalan, Salvadoran, Mexican, and Colombian high school students in demonstrations, often violent and always in support of the revolutionary Left, is only one instance supporting the argument that the youth are a significant and potentially dominant element in the leftward shift of Latin politics. "Rolando Morán" began his political activities in Guatemala during the late 1940s at the age of seventeen. He was a typical product of the radicalism dominant in Latin America's universities. Radicalized teenagers aim toward politics, rather than learning; their primary purpose is to radicalize their colleagues in the universities.

The Revolutionary Elites as Elites

Because the bulk of the Latin American revolutionary leadership comes from university students and graduates, those involved are largely middle–class or upper–class elements, who could afford higher education, or the most brilliant lower–class elements, who could receive scholarships (only a small minority). The extent to which the revolutionary or potentially revolutionary Left enjoys popular support for its aims is also significant insofar as it demonstrates class differences between self–appointed vanguard groups and the populace at large.

A number of university students are members of the privileged class even before university admission. Many prominent revolutionary leaders in Latin

America come from the upper classes. Their names span the continent: Camilo Torres in Colombia; Luis Carrión and Ernesto Cardenal in Nicaragua; "Gaspar Ilom," the nom de guerre of Rodrigo Asturias, the son of Nobel Prize laureate Miguel Angel Asturias in Guatemala, who is now the main leader of ORPA; and Andréas Pascal Allende, the main leader of the MIR in Chile and nephew of the late president Salvador Allende is the successor of Miguel Henríquez, the organization's founder, who was himself the son of a general. Nowhere is the bourgeois or even haut bourgeois character of revolutionary leadership as prominent as among the present Sandinista *nomenklatura* in Nicaragua. The Sandinista regime is controlled by numerous members of the old aristocratic families of Granada, most of whom come from the same street (Atravezada) in that town: Cardenal, Chamorro, Gabuardi, Aguerro, Cuadra, and Lacayo. National Bank Director Joaquín Cuadra Chamorro is a typical example. Before the revolution he was a very wealthy man and a financial expert; his son, Joaquín Cuadra Lacayo, is chief of the general staff of the army; his three daughters are married to Carlos Núñez, one of the nine Commanders of the Revolution, Hugo Torres, the army's main political commissar, and Oswaldo Lacayo, another prominent army man, respectively.[10]

While the Grenada aristocracy is extensively represented in the Sandinista nomenklatura, the relative upstarts, including those of the nine members of the National Directorate who are of lower bourgeois origin and often from Matagalpa, tend to marry women from the traditional elites. Núñez is one case; Jaime Wheelock Román, a member of the Directorate and agriculture minister, married Vanessa Castro Cardenal, a member of the Cardenal family, which also provides the government with two ministers (the brothers and ex–priests Ernesto and Fernando); President Daniel Ortega married Rosario Murillo, a direct descendant of another prominent family.

In El Salvador the most famous revolutionary leader and theoretician of the Left, Roque Dalton, was the scion of a wealthy family; two sons of the present mayor of San Salvador, Antonio Morales Erlich, are guerrilla militants, as are many former UCA professors, such as Salvador Samayoa, a former education minister. The first head of the guerrillas' political front, the FDR, was Enrique Alvarez, a prominent member of the "fourteen families" who allegedly controlled the country.[11] In Guatemala, the leadership of the Left and the bourgeoisie have often been indistinguishable since the first generation of post–World War II Communists. José Manuel Fortuny, a founder of the PGT and its first general secretary, was the son of an attorney and a former law student; Bernardo Alvarado Monzón, Fortuny's successor as party leader, was the son of a minister and rector of San Carlos; Carlos Pellecer Durán, the PGT's most active and brilliant representative during the Arbenz period, was from a middle–class family and a former military academy student.[12] Of the main Tupamaros leaders, Jorge Pedro Zabalza Waksman was the son of a senator, and Pedro Ignacio Dubas Díaz was the son of a former congressman.[13] Such examples abound.

The privileged social origin of guerrilla leaders throughout Latin America is matched only by their claims to intellectual accomplishments. The list of real, claimed, or self–described "poets" and other types of literati among Latin revolutionaries is also endless: Otto René Castillo in Guatemala, Ernesto Cardenal and Daniel Ortega in Nicaragua, Roque Dalton in El Salvador, Javier Héraud in Peru, and so on. The ideology, if not the talent level, of these revolutionary artists varies only between Otto René Castillo's "tomorrow, when they don't intervene in Korea/to surround the smiles with shadows/and they no longer wish to detain the red star/the quetzal wears on its breast/then the poets shall sign their songs with roses,"[14] and the far more famous *Poemas Clandestinos* of Dalton, which include "Old Communists and Guerrilleros," "The Central Committee as Sentinel," "Hitler Mazzini: Comparison Between Chile in 1974 and El Salvador in 1932."[15]

Elites and Internationalism

The importance of internationalism here relates less to its doctrinal implications than to its role in spawning revolutionary leaders in Latin America. Obviously, access to foreign publications, travel, or study abroad, let alone living there—as have all the leaders of the traditional pro–Soviet communist parties at various times—are part of the privileges of Latin revolutionary elites. Equally important is the ability of revolutionary elites not only to communicate with each other across national boundaries but also to associate freely with foreign members of the same ideological group. Examples abound, but for the sake of simplifying the argument, consider Enrique Schmidt Cuadra, the highest ranking Sandinista leader killed so far by the anti–FSLN insurgents. Born in Corinto to a family that through his mother was related to the Cuadras of Granada, Schmidt joined the FSLN in 1970 at the age of twenty–one. He became the business manager of Siemens–Nicaragua, formed the Sandinista intelligence system in 1975, and was an active member of the FSLN group that joined the PLO in Jordan and then in Lebanon (others included in that group were Pedro Arauz, René Tejada, Patricio Argüello, and Luis Enrique Romero). Between 1977 and 1978 Schmidt organized Sandinista support networks in West Germany and Spain; became an essential factor in the organization of the Interior Ministry after the FSLN victory, particularly as police chief in Managua; was awarded a honoris causa doctorate by the University of Bremen and found time to be president of the National Basketball Federation. He was killed in a clash with the insurgents on November 5, 1984, while serving as the secret police's chief of "special operations."[16]

To the Latin American revolutionary, the word "internationalism" does not only connote certain beliefs in continental or global strategic aims for the revolution, but it also refers, concretely, to prolonged stays and activities in other countries—as fighters in Lebanon, Jordan, Vietnam, or the Portuguese colonies in Africa (like the late Hugo Spadafora, former Panamanian deputy health minister, colleague of Pastora against Somoza and, since 1982, against the FSLN), or as students or residents in Moscow or Prague (like Dalton or Henry Ruiz), or in Cuba like most of them. In Havana, the Latin revolutionary leader or potential leader becomes a part of the continental revolution, of a global movement with a common enemy—the United States. The revolutionary leader is thus cosmopolitan by experience, belief, and most often training; not only has he lived abroad, but he is often a citizen of another country, with family there. Or, the Latin revolutionary finds it easy to take up residence in another Latin American country. The Montoneros' leaders lived in Nicaragua, as did those of the Argentine ERP many Nicaraguan revolutionaries, including Sergio Ramírez, now vice–president, and Miguel D' Escoto, now foreign minister, lived in Chile under Allende. This phenomenon is nothing new. Fidel Castro spent years in Colombia and Mexico; Che Guevara did the same in Guatemala and Mexico. The latter, an Argentine by birth, became Cuban minister and "Bolivian" leader of a failed insurrection.

More often than not the revolutionary is also familiar with faraway countries—mostly East or West European. Dalton spent some of his post–student years in Prague sipping Pilsner with fellow Latin "freedom fighters"; Carlos Fonseca Amador, the founder of the FSLN, visited Moscow in the late 1950s and later wrote an apologetic tract, "A Nicaraguan in Moscow". Montonero and Tupamaro leaders traveled to Mozambique and Angola, Ethiopia and the Middle East, North Korea and Vietnam. They are all citizens of the revolutionary world, not merely fighters for revolutionary change in and for their own countries. Often they play significant roles in foreign countries, whether as ministers, like Guevara, or as prominent spokesmen for transnational organizations, like the Maryknoll Miguel d' Escoto of Nicaragua, formerly an editor of the Maryknoll Orbis Publishing House in New York State. D'Escoto and fellow Nicaraguan Sergio Ramírez were professors in Chilean universities during the Allende years; Guatemalan Social–Democratic presidential candidate of 1985, Manuel Solorzano, also taught at the Gonzalo Facio University in Costa Rica.

Internationalism as a reality also explains the transnational impact of revolutionaries. Salvadoran Communists like Miguel Mármol, Abel and Max Cuenca, or Virgilio Guerra played an essential role in founding the PGT, as did Chileans Virginia Bravo Letelier, César Godoy, and Manuel Eduardo Hubner. The formation of the Salvadoran and Honduran communist parties during the late 1920s was largely due to the activities of Guatemalan and

Mexican Communists. And Farabundo Martí, scion of a wealthy Salvadoran family,[17] played a significant if unsuccessful role in trying to attract Augusto César Sandino to the goals of the Comintern while he was his secretary in the mountains of Nicaragua.

Internationalism as action illuminates the active and effective role of Argentine terrorists like Santiago Irurzún in killing Somoza in Paraguay in 1980; of an Oscar Turcios of the FSLN fighting in Guatemala during the 1960s; or of ideological adventurer Spadafora offering his services from Guinea Bissau during the 1960s, to Nicaragua in 1979, and against the FSLN in the same country after 1982.[18] Even Costa Ricans, generally seen as the least fanatical of Latin Americans, did fight and sometimes die for foreign causes: Popular Vanguard leaders José Romero Campos and Yamileth López Ballestero were killed by Nicaraguan insurgents in August 1983 while in the FSLN forces.[19]

Priestly "Internacionalistas"

The enormous role of radical priests in Latin America on the side of the Marxist–Leninist guerrillas is beyond dispute, and most were not nationals of their countries of operation. For a Jesuit, Maryknoll, or Capuchin priest or nun, internationalism is the natural and logical result of training, and cross–national connections are part of their impact as members of a global organization—the Roman Catholic Church. The international nature of the training and background of the Latin American radical priests (most of whom are not Latin Americans but Spaniards, North Americans, or West Europeans) facilitates their empathy, both personal and intellectual, with the professional revolutionary, which underpins their cooperation. Again, a Nicaraguan case is typical in this respect—that of Foreign Minister Miguel d' Escoto Brockman, a member of the Maryknoll order and scion of one of Somoza's most prominent and wealthy associates, Miguel Gerónimo Escoto Múñoz. Miguel d' Escoto was the godfather of one of the first Somoza's sons and ambassador to Spain, the United Kingdom, Italy, and France, among other countries. His son Miguel was the happy sender of congratulations to the last Somoza on the occasion of his "triumphal election" in 1967, after respectfully sending condolences to the first Somoza's widow, a university teacher in Allende's Chile, and the overweight spokesman for the present regime in Managua, trying to shed his surplus weight through a "political" fast in 1985.[20]

As for those non–Latin American priests associated with the revolutionaries, from Rogelio Póncel of El Salvador (Belgian), "Guadalupe" Carney, S.J., of Honduras (American), and dozens of others, they all appear to have shared Carney's opinion regarding their own societies and social background:

"For me, bourgeois living is at best half–way Christianity. After what I've seen of worldwide reality, I have to rebel against that".[21] Carney, following his own precepts, joined, as second in command, the PRTC's foco in Honduras' Olancho department in the summer of 1983. Together with his leader, Che Guevara's former colleague in Bolivia, Reyes Mata, Carney was a "victim" of the group's annihilation by the army.

Coming from Western societies, most foreign "liberation" priests and nuns are even more alien to Latin America's realities than are its own revolutionary leaders, and thus they are even more inclined to avoid a rigorous analysis of the reasons for poverty and passivity by blaming social ills on their own societies. Most or almost all of those priests and nuns were anticapitalist, antidemocratic, and anti–Western even before they left their countries of origins with Carney a perfect example in this respect. In many ways, the "liberation theology" priests and nuns resemble Latin American intellectuals. Some are just fellow travelers, choosing to support the revolutionaries from their highly priced ivory towers, like Gabriel García Márquez, the Colombian Nobel Prize laureate and informal spokesman for the Cuban regime's most outrageous foreign policy claims. Some are courageous supporters, prepared to pay for their beliefs, like Peruvian philosopher and sociologist Abimael Guzmán Reynoso the supreme leader of the murderous Shining Path (Sendero Luminoso) of Peru.

The Military

During the late 1950s and early 1960s, before Latin American armies had largely eliminated ideologues and romantic revolutionaries from their junior ranks, they had provided large contingents of would–be revolutionaries, particularly in Guatemala, Venezuela, Brazil, and to some extent in El Salvador.[22] Like their educated civilian counterparts the revolutionary officers were privileged elements of their own societies, more often than not trained abroad (Marcos Antonio Yon Sosa and Luis Turcios Lima, founders of Guatemalan guerrilla movements, in the United States or by U.S. forces in Panama). They had traveled abroad and had come to see the world as cosmopolitan travelers and multilingual trainees. Equally important, a disproportionate number of military leaders of the Latin American Left are, like many of the civilian revolutionaries, members of ethnic minorities (Yon Sosa was half Chinese) which are often regarded as alien intrusions upon the Latin American body social.[23] Some of these military men, like Carlos Prestes in Brazil, have successfully made the transition to civilian political leaders; most, like Brazilian Carlos Lamarca, Yon Sosa, or Turcios Lima, were even more typically victims of the Left's cult of violence than their civilian counterparts and never managed to become more than episodic characters in desperately violent movements with no clear political goals.

Minorities Within A Minority

One of the striking characteristics of the revolutionary leadership in Latin America is the disproportionate number of members of ethnic minorities, mostly of non–Spanish European descent in their ranks. It is not a coincidence that some of these minorities originated in Eastern Europe (Croatians and Jews) and arrived in Latin America at the start of this century, with strong leftist or radical nationalistic leanings, continued by their sons today. Others came from the Middle East, mostly Palestine and the Levant, and became radicalized later, sometimes under the influence of events in their ancestral lands.

Particular mention should be made of the Jewish presence among the revolutionaries, which far exceeds the minimal proportion of Jews among Latin American populations. Mauricio Rosencoff Silberman of the Tupamaros and Volodia Teitelboim of the Chilean Communist Party, both Jewish revolutionaries, are among their groups' main ideologues; Teodoro Petkoff in Venezuela and Abraham Guillén, the ideological father of the Tupamaros and the Brazilian guerrillas of the 1960s, are other examples among many of the continuity of the strong Jewish leftist tradition. Their involvement is the result of traditional Jewish leftism that originated in the East European roots of many South American Jews.

The unorthodox, highly rebellious, and violent nature of most Basque immigrants to the New world is as important as the recent heavy influx of Basque "liberation theology" clergy in explaining the disproportionately high number of Basques in the ranks of the revolutionary elites in Latin America, whether clergy, lay people, Argentine, Chilean, or Uruguayan.

None of these alone explains the nature of the revolutionary Left elites in Latin America, but seen in light of previously mentioned elements, they help define the revolutionary elites as a combination of ethnically different, intellectually and socially distinct, and often self–proclaimed superior elements who are privileged educationally, materially, and politically. In simple terms the Latin American revolutionary elite is little more than a collection of what Lenin described as "traitors to their own class"—members of the bourgeoisie with all its arrogant pretensions of intellectual superiority and a better knowledge of the "people's" interest, individuals with only marginal ties to the productive process or to the actual way of life of the masses.

Insertion into the Society

Were the Latin American revolutionary elites merely rebel scions of the upper classes, bourgeois youth unable or unwilling to follow their successful parents, then their impact would be limited. Where this is the case, revolutionaries are in the same pathetic situation as the Peruvian Castroites of the mid–1960s. Mostly Lima intellectuals and poets, the Castroites believed in a foco guerrillero that would suddenly make the "people" rise up and defeat the class they held responsible for all real or imagined Latin American ills— their own class. Peruvians Luis de la Puente Uceda and Javier Heraud paid for this illusion with their lives.

The success of the Latin revolutionaries, however, lies in the attraction they hold for the alienated beyond their class and social stratum, which ensures the rank–and–file membership in their movements. Even so, membership in these groups is quite small. It is the revolutionary elites' ability to insinuate themselves into their societies that makes them more than a social embarrassment. That the Latin American middle and upper classes are, and have been since the late 1950s, the leaders of Leninist revolution only demonstrates the deep gap between the elites in general and the population as a whole.

The urban proletariat, lumpenproletariat, and the peasantry have long been the major targets for recruitment by the revolutionary elites. In neither case were the elites on familiar ground—hence their limited success.

The revolutionary's social background, training, mentality, and claims of understanding the social realities and needs of the "masses" practically ensures his isolation from the population at large. The gap between the self–styled "vanguard" and the masses it pretends to lead is often profound. The Popular Revolutionary Alliance ARP of Argentina, which included almost all groups of the Marxist–Leninist Left, received next to no support from the "masses". Its base of support was linked directly with the degree of privilege. In a survey taken before the March 1973 elections, the ARP received 20.6 percent of the upper–class support, 27.6 percent of the upper middle–class but only 3.3 percent of the lower classes, the "people" it claimed to represent.[24] Most often the gap is filled by mythology, and the wider the gap the more improbable the mythical claim. The revolutionary acts as if persistent incantatory references to "the people", the past, or "progress" will bring unity between himself and the population.

In their revolutionary mythology of Latin America, the elites refer to a past that is alien to them as well as to the population, convinced that the magic of words will translate into an active following. How else can one explain Mario Roberto Santucho's attempt to attract a following in the late 1950s through the "Indoamerican Popular Revolutionary Front" in Argentina, an ethnically European country. For Santucho, who later created the Trotskyist ERP and was killed soon after the 1976 military coup, the Indian may have been the symbol of America's ultimate unity, the vehicle for continental unification. For the ordinary Argentine, however, whose forefathers came from Spain and Italy, the Indian meant nothing. Similarly, in Uruguay, another ethnically European country in the Western hemisphere, the name Tupamaros (from the Peruvian Tupac Amaru, a pre–Independence Indian rebel against Spain) was chosen as a symbol of solidarity with the rebel, as an archetype. In sophisticated

Montevideo such romantic notions only looked and sounded out of place. In Peru the Tupac Amaru Revolutionary Movement, the most recent terrorist group, also claims roots in the Indian past. But those making the claim are former military officials and intellectuals from Lima and the coastal regions, not the Aymara or Quechua indigenous peoples. When the sophisticated son of a Guatemalan Nobel Prize winner takes as his nom de guerre the name of an obscure Indian rebel of the eighteenth century, ("Gaspar Ilom") he too, tries to join the people through what he assumes is a common past, in order to bring them on his side for the future.

The revolutionary is and sees himself as a citizen of America if not the world, but he knows that nationalism is strong in Latin America and that internationalism as a matter of public rhetoric would only increase his isolation. Hence the ubiquitous essence of such words as "national" in the titles of so many insurgent groups. The revolutionary is also aware that he belongs to the privileged class, so he strives to deny this shameful background in the hope that repeated denial and consistent association with "the poor" as in Guerrilla Army of the Poor will obscure his original remoteness from the "masses."

Despite striving for an organic unity with "the people," the revolutionary "knows," in his mind at least, that he is different and in fact better. The Argentine ERP may have demanded informally that its members engage in manual labor, and they may have claimed that those who did so had more influence in the organization;[25] but if that demand would have been truly mandatory, the organization would not have been led by a Santucho or Gorriarán.

Tomás Borge, Nicaragua's interior minister and one of the nine leaders of the FSLN, touched on the issue of the revolutionary elite's claim to be the "vanguard of the people", and his remarks appear valid for most Latin American revolutionary groups. For Borge, "It was the Sandinista National Liberation Front, it was Sandinism that knew how to apply the theory of revolution to the concrete reality of Nicaragua . . . The Sandinista Front is the living instrument of the revolutionary classes, is the guide leading toward a new society . . . It had the wisdom and the courage . . . It knew, and it will know, the role of the revolutionary classes . . . It knows the point when it is necessary to have qualitative changes".[26] He thus claims that the FSLN leadership, with its scions of the middle and upper classes, has a right to rule because of its superior knowledge, a gift that presumably raises it above the rest of the society. This knowledge, obtained through study, but more often through Marxism–Leninism and its "scientific theory", as well as through action, is allegedly what sets the FSLN apart. Superior knowledge, the result of being an elite, is offered as a reason for remaining an elite in control. The argument is circular, but it is firmly believed by those who can profit from it.

Revolutionaries also claim action as another reason why they should be the vanguard of the people. Action is the start of the revolution. It lies at the root of Guevara's guerrilla foco theories. "Che" believed that the actions of a few "chosen" men would start the avalanche of national revolution. This belief motivated his imitators of the 1960s, from Venezuela to Argentina and from Guatemala to Chile. By "acting" they may have shared the opinion of Juan García Ellorio, Argentine priest, scion of an upper middle–class family, and spiritual founder of the Montonero organization: "Either I fought or I was a phony".[27] One is not "real" until and unless one engages in violence. The answer to everything is the machine gun or help to its admirers. For a Roque Dalton, the cult of the "deed" is also a recipe for political support from the masses: "In a land like ours where everything's at hand and concentrated where the historical accumulation is so dense, ultraleftism that doesn't stop at words and has the wherewithal to be ultraleftist in deeds will always go deeper penetrating the popular heart that still beats on the ultraleft of the chest".[28]

One also may argue that violence provides other kinds of satisfaction, a "mental scheme" implying "the assumption of one's own capability to kill, wound, or humiliate, as a source of jubilation and pleasant emotions".[29] Whatever the case, action is what makes a revolutionary, at least in his own eyes. As Castro once said, the duty of the revolutionary is to make revolution.

The revolutionary mythology of action goes even deeper than the cult of the deed; it necessarily involves the cult of the martyrs. The martyr not only provides inspiration and a model, he also satisfies the revolutionary's thirst for belonging to an unbroken continuum from the heroic past. Farabundo Martí, Augusto Sandino, Guevara, Torres, Dalton—the list of martyrs is infinite. They are the dead past artificially kept alive. The longer they are kept alive the better, for they accumulate characteristics of the changing times; they grow after death; their failures become successes; their words become slogans, often mindlessly recited. In this, as in many other respects, the Latin revolutionary strengthens his own resolution by referring to past martyrs of political violence; the noninvolved feels a vicarious pride in being associated with the terrorist. It was said of the Tupamaros at the beginning of the 1970s that in middle class avant–garde circles of Montevideo society . . . it is chic to boast of a young student cousin, or nephew, who is "almost certainly one of them".[30] Violence is middle class chic. It becomes in vogue to join or at least support "them". At this level the Latin American elites are no different from West European and U.S. vicarious revolutionaries among the intellectuals and spoiled sons and daughters of the middle classes.

An Aristocracy of "Popular" Revolutions

The nature of the Latin American revolutionary elites generally is characterized by their isolation from the reality of national aspirations, their closed ranks at the national and continental level, their self–assumed duty to change a society about which they know little other than what is filtered through books, all in the name of an abstract "people" they ultimately despise for lack of political "consciousness". It is far more likely for a Sandinista to befriend (or marry) a Montonero or Tupamaro than to understand a Miskito Indian in his own country. It is regarded as more "natural" to assume the mantle of past heroes than to support present national aspirations, because no nation is seen as great enough for the revolutionary's ego. The Tupamaros and Montoneros believed that they advance their own cause by financing and fighting alongside the Sandinistas in Nicaragua, or the ERP by aiding them through the murder of Somoza in Paraguay. In a way they do indeed fight their own struggle, whether in Uruguay or Nicaragua, Guatemala or El Salvador. In this they are all direct descendants of the conquistadores, and they manifest the same disregard for borders (and for economic activities) that the latter did. Like the conquistadores, they do not mix with the plebes but try to "civilize" them. The new aristocracy is continental in its aspirations, international in its personalities, and at the same time profoundly bourgeois in its narrow–mindedness and petty factionalism. The alienation of this group from its class and national origins is almost complete, and this serves to strengthen its dedication to the only profession it masters—the politics of violence. This fundamental alienation is often perceived, but only as it relates to others, who are accused of losing touch with the "masses". When applied to oneself, it is obfuscated in the dense fog of revolutionary mythology or by desperate attempts to belong to exotic causes. Roque Dalton, a dropout of San Salvador's best private school, who "worked" in a bicycle factory in Hanoi but never had a job at home, is an example.[31]

The revolutionary, whether atheistic Leninist or "liberation theology" practitioner, is separated even from the faith of the "masses". His beliefs, a surrogate religion of sorts, are perhaps best demonstrated by Dalton's "Credo of Che": "Che Jesus Christ was taken prisoner after finishing his sermon on the mountain (to a background of rattling machine guns) by Bolivian and Jewish rangers commanded by Yankee–Roman chiefs".[32]

The strength of such beliefs, including the cult of martyrs, the demonology of Yankee interventionism, the surrogate nationalism centered around figures like Sandino or Tupac Amaru, and an escapist yearning for the "purity" of the poorly known pre–Colombian times (of which Sendero Luminoso is the best example today) is reinforced continuously. Their continuous repetition eliminates the need to face the compexities of real life. On the other hand, the simple–mindedness of revolutionary slogans, in Latin America and elsewhere, is also related to the need to attract support from the uninitiated, the "people", who may not be sophisticated enough to understand "scientific socialism" in all its tortuous details.

The very nature of the revolutionary elites, as described so far, should demonstrate the fallacy of believing in alliances with them whether against a

Somoza or toward electoral victory. Outsiders are not welcome and can never be allowed to understand, let alone participate in revolutionaries' decisions—a fact that democratic leaders like the Robelos or Cruzes of Nicaragua have discovered too late. In this respect it should come as no surprise that, once they have a chance, the aristocrats of revolution aim at total power. It is all they ever wanted.

Notes

1. Mostafa Rejai with Kay Phillips, *Leaders of Revolution* (Beverly Hills, London, and New Delhi: Sage Publications, 1979), p. 13. Emphasis in the original.
2. See Introduction to Ricardo Ramírez, *Lettres du Front Guatémaltèque* (Paris: François Maspero, 1970), p. 9.
3. Interview with Rolando Morán, commander–in–chief of the Guerrilla Army of the Poor, in *Companero: The International Magazine of Guatemala's Guerrilla Army of the Poor*, vol. 2 (San Francisco: Popular Press, n.d.), p. 33–44.
4. Information provided to the author in Guatemala in November 1985.
5. Alain Labrousse, *Les Tupamaros* (Paris: Ed. du Seuil, 1971), p. 174.
6. Arturo C. Porzecanski, *Uruguay's Tupamaros* (New York: Praeger, 1973), p. 29.
7. *Venezuela at the Polls: The National Elections of 1978*, ed. Howard R. Penniman (Washington, D.C., and London: American Enterprise Institute, 1980), p. 83, tables 3–11.
8. Informal poll at Francisco Maroquín, made available to the author by the university.
9. See Castro Morán, *Función política del ejército Salvadoreño en el presente siglo*, (San Salvador: UCA Editores, 1984), p. 276.
10. For a fascinating description of the family ties between the Nicaraguan aristocracy and the *nomenklatura* of the regime, see *Quiubo* (Panama City), translated in FBIS–LAM, June 21, 1982, pp. 8–10.
11. For a good analysis of the personal and social background and infinite ties between the leaders of the two sides in El Salvador's civil war, see Gabriel Zaid, "Enemy Colleagues," *Dissent*, Winter 1982.
12. Ronald M. Schneider, *Communism in Guatemala, 1944–1954* (New York: Praeger, 1959), p. 90–94.
13. *Las fuerzas armadas al pueblo Oriental*, vol. 1, *La subversión* (Montevideo: República Oriental del Uruguay, Junta de Comandantes en Jefe, 1976), p. 106, 108.
14. Otto René Castillo, "Tomorrow Triumphant," in *Guatemala: The People Unite!* Unitary statement from the Guatemalan National Revolutionary Unity–URNG, (San Francisco: Solidarity Publications, Popular Press, 1982), p. 2.
15. See Roque Dalton, *Poemas Clandestinos* (San Salvador: Editorial Universitaria Centroamericana, 1982).
16. *Intercontinental Press*, December 10, 1984, p. 716.
17. See Arias Gómez, *Farabundo Marti* (San José: EDUCA, 1972), pp. 15–16.
18. The role of the Cuban *internacionalistas* in Guevara's failed attempt to conquer Bolivia in 1967, of the Brazilian, Argentine, and Uruguayan revolutionaries in strengthening or radicalizing Allende's regime in Chile in 1970–1973, and of the

Salvadoran and Guatemalan leftists in supporting the FSLN during its struggle against Somoza are well publicized already.

19. See *New York Times*, "Two Costa Ricans Killed This Month Fighting Beside Sandinista Troops," August 30, 1983.
20. See *Foro Centroamericano*, October 1985, p. 2.
21. Padre J. Guadalupe Carney, *To Be a Revolutionary* (San Francisco: Harper & Row, 1985), p. xvii.
22. Personalities like the founders of the Guatemalan guerrilla movements of the 1960s—Marcos Antonio, Yon Sosa, Alejandro de León, Luis Turcios Lima, Luis Trejos, all leaders of the Castroite failed coup of November 1960, Carlos Lamarca and long before him, Carlos Luís Prestes in Brazil, as well as Venezuelan junior officers of 1960. The same applies to officers in El Salvador in the early 1980s, like Captain Mena Sandoval or even Colonel Alfonso Adolfo Majano, the former even betraying his colleagues and killing his commanding officer during the guerrillas' January 1980 "final offensive". These are only some of the many available examples—and most failed to reach much more than an inglorious death in the obscurity of the mountains.
23. Handal in El Salvador, Saad in Ecuador, Alvaro Fayad in Colombia, all of Palestinian origin; certain leaders of Sendero, and the Brazilian revolutionary Left of the 1960s (Japanese by origin); and the abundant Croatian immigrants who played essential roles in Chile from fellow traveler Christian Democrat Radomiro Tomic to Communists Jaime Faivovich and Pedro Vuscovic, the Argentine Mario Firmenich, or in Uruguay, Raúl Sendic, are the most prominent.
24. José Enrique Miguens, "The Presidential Elections of 1973," in *Juan Perón and the Reshaping of Argentina*, ed. Frederick C. Turner and José Enrique Miguens (Pittsburgh: University of Pittsburgh Press, 1983), p. 162.
25. See *Gorriarán: Democracia y liberación* (Buenos Aires: Ediciones Reencuentro, 1985), p. 40. This is an extensive interview with ERP leader Enrique Gorriarán Merlo.
26. Role of the Workers in the Nicaraguan Revolution," May Day speech by Commander Tomás Borge, in *Intercontinental Press* (New York), May 31, 1982. Emphasis added.
27. Cf. Richard Gillespie, *Soldiers of Perón: Argentina's Montoneros* (Oxford: Clarendon Press, 1982), p. 59.
28. Roque Dalton, "Ultraleftists," in *Poemas Clandestinos*, tran. Jack Hirschman (San Francisco: Solidarity Publications, 1984), p. 111.
29. Pablo Giussani, *Montoneros: La soberbia armada* (Buenos Aires: Sudamericana Planeta, 1984), p. 89.
30. Gerald McKnight, *The Terrorist Mind* (Indianapolis and New York: Bobbs–Merrill, 1974), p. 93.
31. See Margaret Randall, Introduction to Dalton's *Poemas Clandestinos*, p. viii.
32. Ibid., p. 49.

8

The Appeals of Revolutionary Violence: Latin American Guerrillas and American Intellectuals

Paul Hollander

> *Among these fully awake men, at the height of their powers, sleeping doesn't seem like a natural need, just a routine of which they had more or less freed themselves . . . [They] exercise a veritable dictatorship over their own needs . . . they roll back the limits of the possible.*
>
> —Jean–Paul Sartre[1]

> *In Cuba hatred runs over into the love of blood; in America all too few blows are struck into flesh. We kill the spirit here . . . We live in a country very different from Cuba . . . You [Castro] were aiding us, you were giving us psychic ammunition . . . in that desperate silent struggle we have been fighting with sick dead hearts against the cold insidious cancer of the power that governs us, you were giving us new blood to fight.*
>
> —Norman Mailer[2]

> *We choose as a culture—and our press chooses as a profession—not to know of the blood of mothers and children in the revolution and what is called progress . . . For these murderers on the left, there are always, in our universities and churches and entertainment and opinion industries, . . . lionizing folk eager to mythologize the cruel and violent as virtuous. Their reputations somehow remain untouched by the rivers of blood that flow right past them.*
>
> —Martin Peretz[3]

Norman Mailer's admiration of authentic political violence—such as the one he detected in revolutionary Cuba—aptly captures the emotions and the approbation that Latin American guerrilla violence has evoked in many American intellectuals. Such violence was admired and approved of because of its passionate and spontaneous nature ("the love of blood") and because of its revolutionary legitimation. For Mailer and other romantics, passion proved authenticity and good intentions, strong feelings themselves were proof of a good cause. Perhaps, as the early Bolsheviks felt, "soiling one's hand" with violence provided the ultimate proof of authentic commitment. "He is indeed an 'egoist' who refuses the small sacrifice of dirtying his person for the sake of the salvation of humanity".[4] Cuban–style (guerrilla) violence stood in dramatic contrast to Mailer's vision of American repression: silent, cold, colorless, indirect, unspontaneous, inauthentic, routinized, lacking in passion.

Of late such sentiments have been transferred to the Nicaraguan revolution and its leaders. A remarkable illustration of the continuity of such attitudes was provided by the statements of many American (and other) writers attending the 1986 PEN Congress in New York. Omar Cabezas, former guerrilla leader, currently the Nicaraguan Deputy Minister of the Interior (i.e., police), was an invited "guest of honor." Norman Mailer's sympathies were once more in evidence as he "openly encouraged . . . a petition in support of the Nicaraguan position." As another observer noted, "At PEN, Nicaragua was the hot issue. The most popular statement of the week expressed 'acute distress at U.S. Government intervention in Nicaragua' . . . " The political attitudes and double standards of many participants were underlined by the protest against U.S. Secretary of State Shultz addressing the Congress, as against the warm welcome given to Cabezas who, in his capacity of Deputy Minister of Interior, has been directly involved with censorship—a matter supposedly of great concern to the writers attending. Apparently most of those present had no difficulty believing that—as Cabezas said—there was only "a little" censorship, reluctantly exercised, in Nicaragua, but even for this little censorship, the United States was responsible.[5]

It is a major proposition of this essay that the appeals of Latin American guerrilla violence and the associated idealization of the guerrilla fighter are forms of social criticism directed at the United States. In the eyes of their American admirers, the Marxist guerrillas are surrogate avengers of the evils that American capitalism perpetuates. The admiration of the guerrillas is closely linked to the endorsement of the social–political values they represent and the political system they seek to establish. In turn, the perceived authenticity of guerrilla violence—a major source of its attraction—reflects a more diffuse longing for authenticity on the part of the social critics. This longing for authenticity has in fact been a main theme of social criticism in American society since the 1960s. While it may be argued that Mailer expressed these sentiments in a more extreme and forceful way than that entertained by other American intellectuals, such attitudes have been widespread and have produced noteworthy double standards in judging political violence. While such double standards are not new—insofar as most people are always willing to condone questionable means to ends they consider laudable—the applause for

Latin American guerrilla violence is among the most striking expressions of this age–old phenomenon in recent times.

Generally speaking, estranged intellectuals tend to look on revolutionary violence as invigorating and redeeming, or at least acceptable and justifiable, possibly a regrettable necessity but hardly a cause for moral indignation, let alone outrage. The appeals of violence and revolution are inseparable. Nonrevolutionary violence lacks the legitimacy, while revolution without violence is inconceivable and would not be authentic.

The myth of the revolution, as Raymond Aron observed well before the recent popularity of Latin American revolutionaries, consists of "foster[ing] the expectation of a break with the normal trend of human affairs . . . Revolution provides a welcome break with the everyday course of events and encourages the belief that all things are possible."[6] In the same spirit, many American intellectuals since the 1960s have been searching for relief from what they perceived to be the meaninglessness and the deadening routines of their modern capitalist–industrial society. Visions of authentic violence appear to gratify such needs. Again as Aron pointed out, "He who protests against the fate meted out to mankind by a meaningless universe sometimes finds himself in sympathy with the revolutionaries, because indignation or hatred outweigh all other considerations, because in the last resort violence alone can appease this despair."[7] Peter Berger cautioned that those who applaud purifying violence from a distance rarely acknowledge that "the reality of revolution, as against the romantic fantasies about it, is as ugly as the reality of war and in some instances uglier."[8]

That intellectuals supposedly dedicated to rational problem solving and peaceful conflict resolution are attracted to and even fascinated by certain types of political violence suggests that the appeals of "good" violence are difficult to resist. Even more striking, churchmen of many denominations have also been eager to condone revolutionary violence, sometimes barely able to contain their enthusiasm for it, as will be shown below. Their endorsement may even extend to nonrevolutionary violence and coercion, provided it is exercised by a revolutionary or formerly revolutionary regime. Thus, for example, Bishop James Armstrong and the Rev. Russell Dilley of the United Methodist Church wrote: "There is a significant difference between situations when people are imprisoned for opposing regimes designed to perpetuate inequities (as in Chile and Brazil, for example) and situations when people are imprisoned for opposing regimes designed to remove inequities (as in Cuba)."[9]

The appeal of the Latin American guerrilla for American intellectuals can best be understood as part of the broader phenomenon of estrangement from American society which became widespread in the 1960s and has persisted into the 1980s, notwithstanding certain political changes at the national level. The connection between admiration of the guerrilla and rejection of American society is captured by an American social critic: "An honest man today must consider the liberal as the true enemy of mankind . . . He must agree with Che Guevara that the only hope the peoples of the world have is to crush American imperialism by defeating it on the battlefield, and the only way to do that is to coordinate their attacks and launch them wherever . . . men are suffering as the result of American interests . . . The poor and honest of the world must arise to launch simultaneous Vietnams."[10]

Correspondingly, the idealized image of the Latin American guerrillas and their brand of violence has reflected the political values and aspirations of estranged intellectuals and the spirit of our times. The culture heroes of the period—Che Guevara, Fidel Castro, Mao Tse–tung, Ho Chi Minh, and possibly Frantz Fannon—have all been associated with guerrilla warfare.[11] Of one such culture hero, probably the foremost, it was observed that "Che Lives— sprawled out in four colors across the paperback bookstand of your nearest Safeway . . . soon to be crucified by the Hollywood spectacle–mongers. Not even a communist revolution in Bolivia could save him from being a North American culture hero."[12] Even literary representatives of righteous political violence attracted a following, as indicated by reports of professors of literature at an elite university who "found that students respond to those works of authors such as Conrad and Dostoevski which are concerned with terrorists . . . They personally identify with and often admire terrorists."[13]

The guerrilla shared attributes of other fashionable culture heroes of the times. In the words of Tom Wolfe, "Radical chic invariably favors radicals who seem primitive, exotic and romantic, such as grape workers who are not merely radical and 'of the soil' but also Latin; the Panthers with their leather pieces . . . and shootouts and the Red Indians." The fashions of the times also mirrored the admiration for such culture heroes: "Middle class students . . . would have on guerrilla gear . . . berets and hair down to the shoulders, 1958 Sierra Maestra style and raggedy field jackets and combat boots and jeans."[14] Probably tens of thousands of posters of Che Guevara and an armed Huey Newton decorated the walls of college dormitories in the 1960s and 1970s.

Latin American revolutions and revolutionaries also evoked associations of joyous fiestas for North American onlookers. Tad Szulc reported from the early days of the Cuban revolution: "The Cuban events . . . had an extraordinary impact . . . not only because they represented such an appealing social revolution but also because of their unusual, romantic, picturesque features. There was a touch of the glorious, inebriating fiesta about everything the victorious rebels did."[15] The triumph of the Sandinista revolution likewise brought with it a "holiday mood" in Nicaragua, as witnessed by an American social scientist.[16] According to a *Playboy* magazine reporter, the festive mood persisted past the revolution: "Wherever we went, people were young, singing political folk songs and chanting 'Power to the People!' One night there was even a Pete Seeger concert in town!"[17]

Reaching out to admire and idealize revolutions and revolutionaries was part of a broader quest for alternatives to a social system perceived as unjust, oppressive, inegalitarian, aesthetically deficient, and generally unstimulating ("the talk of revolution offers a vicarious identification with adventure, strength and moral purity").[18] Focusing on the Latin American guerrillas—concurrently with or after the eclipse of the Vietcong—had its own logic. These guerrillas and the social forces they supposedly represented could be regarded as victims of the United States, and this made them all the more deserving of sympathy and support. An important early representative of this school of thought was C. Wright Mills. In the words of his biographer, Irving Louis Horowitz, "Latin Americans for Mills seemed . . . to represent the 'ideal–typical' oppressed region, whether in Spanish Harlem or in Playa Girón."[19]

Particular embodiments of guerrilla virtue and heroism—Castro, Che Guevara, Tomás Borge, Villalobos of El Salvador—catered to the revolutionary romanticism of the critics of American society. Latin American guerrillas were seen not only as fighters for the best of all possible causes, but also as exceptional men touched by the peculiar charm of Latin American culture, climate, language, and tradition. They partook of exotic qualities that set them aside from other specialists of political violence. For example, Nicaraguan guerrilla leader Omar Cabezas was said to personify "both Quixote and Crusoe . . . Throw in a dash of existential anguish, two drops of Augustinian faith and Thomistic teleology, a measure of Marxist analysis . . . and a full ounce of Latin American, Nicaraguan, Sandinist brio and consciousness, and the result is strikingly humorous and forcefully dramatic."[20]

It should be noted here that the propensity to idealize left–wing guerrillas has not been limited to those of Latin America. During the Vietnam War, similar attitudes toward the Vietcong and its revolutionary violence were evident. Occasionally anti–Israeli Arab guerrillas also received respectful treatment, if not outright admiration, in the same circles. Nonetheless, Latin American guerrillas, since the rise of Castro and Che Guevara, have been embraced with a particular warmth and intensity and, for obvious historical reasons, for a longer period of time, up to the present. Their appeal had two major components: the guerrilla way of life and violence, on the one hand, and their ideological orientation, on the other, especially their adoption of Marxism–Leninism. It was the combination of these elements—and especially the proper theoretical legitimation of otherwise less acceptable violence—that lent the guerrillas their unique attraction (besides living in countries supposedly victimized by the United States).

The attitude of the same intellectuals toward the anti–Sandinista guerrillas provides substantiation of the point made above. The latter, as far as their brand of violence and way of life was concerned, were no different from the Marxist guerrillas who fought Somoza or the guerrillas operating in El Salvador. Yet the so–called Contras have been held in contempt among these intellectuals because they were fighting *without* Marxist credentials and legitimation *against* a Marxist regime.[21] Jeffrey Hart also noted: "Guerrillas . . . become fashionable only when they are communist and anti–Western."[22]

None of this is to suggest that the attributes and appeals of the Marxist–Leninist guerrillas in Latin America had no historic precedent or parallel. For example, it has been argued that these guerrillas had certain traits in common with the early Fascists of Mussolini's Italy, in particular the leader–worship and belief in the redeeming qualities of authentic violence. James Gregor wrote:

> When Lee Lockwood asked a survivor of the guerrilla band that Castro led in the Sierra Maestra whether he had ever concerned himself with political ideology he could only respond with a guffaw. He replied that under the circumstances there was no time for that, and concluded "We let Fidel do our thinking for us."
>
> This was precisely the style of the Fascist *squadristi*, the street fighters of Mussolini. They were the vanguard of the Italian people, a "new and heroic generation", "unconditionally dedicated to the Cause", and "devoted to its supreme leader." . . . For *squadristi*, violence was the school of revolution . . . They were committed to the "moral regeneration" born of violence that would dissipate bourgeois apathy and egotism.

Pride in youthfulness and nationalistic self–assertion represented further shared attributes: "In the case of Castroism, the emphasis on youth, generational conflict, action as antecedent to thought, on the transforming function of military conflict, on the invocation of nationalist sentiment are all instances of Fascist *style*."[23]

It is important to point out that whatever the similarities between the styles of Latin American guerrillas and the early Fascist fighters, the appeal of Fascism for Western intellectuals was limited and short–lived, whereas the appeal and idealization of Latin Amercian guerrillas have been tenacious, persisting over almost three decades, and show no sign of fading away. Instead, each new wave of left–wing revolutionary violence is greeted with delight, rapidly gains an enthusiastic following, and creates new, if temporary, culture heroes as American intellectuals move from the reverential identification with Castro and his guerrillas to those of Nicaragua or El Salvador. For a while the admiration persists even after the conquest of power, as the cases of Cuba and

Nicaragua. The attributes of the guerrillas continue to provide a revolutionary glow and legitimation to the new regimes.

Whether these intellectuals are more attracted to the guerrillas fighting for power or to those who are securely entrenched and engaged with gusto in social engineering (or postrevolutionary violence) is not entirely clear, but it is beyond doubt that "there has to be at least one approved insurgent movement on the Left at any given time" and that "the faithful do seem to need a place to which their faith can attach itself."[24]

A closer examination of the attractions of the guerrilla and his various contemporary Latin American incarnations will shed further light on the roots of the tenaciousness of the phenomenon here discussed. Such an examination of the appeal of the guerrilla image can be a guide to the dreams and frustrations of many contemporary American intellectuals. Their dreams have a venerable ancestry and echo the predicaments of intellectuals of other times, and other societies as well.

The single major benefit that the attempted identification with the guerrilla, especially the guerrilla leader, yields to the intellectual is the resolution of the theory–practice dilemma. Intellectuals have traditionally been thinkers and not doers and are often painfully aware of the distance separating their ideals from fulfillment. Idealistic intellectuals at various times longed for effective political action but were incapable of moving from the plane of theory to that of action. The deeper their commitments to political change and social justice, the more acutely their impotence is felt—whether it is due to social isolation, occupational segregation, lack of organizational experience and leadership, or some flaw of personality. In recent times, many Western and particularly American intellectuals have concluded that voicing social criticism, however eloquent, was an inadequate expression of their political commitment. Yet it has been difficult to find practical opportunities, political allies, or inspiring role models in their own society that would have made possible the transition from ideas to action. The working classes in the United States have been notoriously unrevolutionary and repulsively content with the status quo (from the standpoint of such influential radical intellectuals as Herbert Marcuse). Black revolutionaries were few in number and unfriendly toward white middle–class people, including the militantly estranged intellectuals.

By contrast, Latin American guerrillas were more successful in making common cause with the masses and making "the passive peasantry to understand the nature of the wrongs they [were] obliged to suffer."[25] The proper relationship between the guerrillas and the masses has been a major preoccupation both of the theorists of guerrilla war and of their distant admirers. "The guerrilla, who is often an educated man of middle–class origins, will use his superior learning to enlighten the peasants, while the peasants will show him the *reality* of their social condition."[26]

Latin American guerrillas, beginning with Castro and Che Guevara, possessed these qualities that American intellectuals in search of role models—or objects of idealization and identification—were looking for. Many of these guerrillas, and certainly their leaders, appeared to be fellow intellectuals of a vastly improved variety who heralded the end of the baleful separation between theory and practice. That these guerrillas were doers could hardly be doubted. Castro and his followers seized power and ran a state, as did the Sandinistas twenty years later. Their colleagues in El Salvador controlled parts of the country and were active enough to engage the sympathetic attention of the news media. There was a good chance that they too would seize power.

C. Wright Mills was probably the first well–known American intellectual to discover and testify to the authenticity of Castro and his fellow leaders and bring back the good news that they were not only fighters but also thinkers, true intellectuals who at long last succeeded in uniting theory and practice. They were exceptional individuals, equally at home in the world of weapons and the world of books. Castro confided to Mills that his book *The Power Elite* ''had been a bedside book of most *guerrilleros* in the Sierra Maestra.''[27] Especially impressive were the accomplishments of Che Guevara (even before his martyrdom), who was both a theoretician and an accomplished practitioner of guerrilla warfare. The intellectual credentials of the Sandinistas were also satisfactory; they included poets, writers, theologians, graduates of various universities (including Columbia University in New York and Patrice Lumumba in Moscow).

The theoretical prowess of Latin American guerrilla leaders rested on their Marxist–Leninist qualifications, which enabled them to articulate their objectives and legitimate their methods in ways that were familiar and pleasing for Amercian radical intellectuals. They were good Leninists zealously seeking theoretical guidance and legitimation for the actions they were going to take in any case.

The appeals of guerrilla violence were also related to the social situation of its admirers. American intellectuals, and in particular the academics among them, have for some time been suffering from what might be called ''excess security'', a condition that extended to the economic, political, and occupational spheres alike and led to a measure of discomfort and unease. Theirs was an unadventurous life free of any danger other than an automobile accident or delayed promotion. Deeply committed social critics found it especially galling that their criticism did not bring persecution. It was difficult for American radical intellectuals to live dangerously in the service of a good cause. Guerrilla violence meant living dangerously for a good cause; the attendant adventure and excitement was legitimated by higher purpose. A further attraction of this violence was its communal character. Unlike the lone assassin, a more familiar embodiment of political violence in the United States, guerrillas practiced their craft in cohesive, communal groups.

Guerrilla authenticity—including the use of authentic violence—thus had several components. Uniting theory with practice was the most important component, but not the only one. It was also important that these guerrillas were not dogmatic or weighted down by the past and its alleged "lessons". As C. Wright Mills put it, using a Cuban guerrillas as his mouthpiece,

> We are revolutionaries of the post–Stalin era; we've never had any "God That Failed". We just don't belong to that lineage. We don't have all that cynicism and futility about what we're doing, and about what we feel must be done . . . .
>
> We are without any of that ideological background; so we've had the courage for revolution; it wasn't destroyed by the terrible history of the world decline of the old left. We are people without bad memories.[28]

It is difficult to know whether any flesh and blood guerrilla had really said any such thing, but this is how Mills perceived the guerrillas—their unique and refreshing orientation and freedom from the guilt and the inhibitions of a chastened Old Left. Mills' guerrilla doubled as a spokesman for the New Left that Mills was propagating and projecting. (Twenty years later the same refreshing spirit of youthfulness, undogmatic idealism, and pragmatic quest for social justice was projected on the Nicaraguan guerrilla leaders by their American supporters.) In the same spirit John Gerassi, admirer of both the Vietcong and Latin American guerrillas, had praised "the spontaneity, existential commitment, and will" associated with the "original *barbudos*".[29]

It should be pointed out that during the 1960s the action–orientation and apparent spontaneity of the guerrillas were probably more important for their American supporters than their capacity to theorize. American intellectuals at the time were more interested in deeds than in thoughts—which also helps explain the attractions of guerrilla violence. Throughout the period under discussion, from the late 1950s to the present, two images and attractions of the guerrillas vied with each other: the spontaneous noble savage and the thoughtful philosopher–king, the latter usually projected on the leaders, the former on the rank and file.

Carlos Rangel's comments further clarify the attractions of the guerrilla image.

> The emergence of revolutionary Cuba had a double meaning: it demonstrated the resilience of Leninism, and, more important, it briefly renewed the old socialist hope of a regime that could combine Communism and human decency. Old dreams were rekindled . . . [of] an island uncontaminated by civilization and original sin, peopled with noble savages free from ambition, cruelty, and envy . . . The revolutionary mystique as it had developed since 1917 . . . now assumed a new form. The noble savage became a virtuous revolutionary uncontaminated by Stalinism . . . And what more suitable cradle could this virtuous revolution have than a tropical island?[30]

The guerrillas' bonds with nature have been a significant if implicit part of the noble–savage image. Guerrillas were generally seen as children of nature, of the countryside. The guerrilla was most readily envisioned as a denizen of impenetrable jungles and inaccessible mountains, at one with nature as he was with the simple people inhabiting such areas. He was both protected and nurtured by nature; its hardships steeled, energized, and made him superior to the corrupt, enervated troops of the government he was fighting who lived in more comfortable settings. Guerrilla warfare was primarily an outdoor activity involving a great deal of hiking, some mountain climbing, river crossing, hunting, and fishing—a whole range of wholesome physical activities that urban intellectuals felt deprived of but heartily endorsed. The intimate relationship with nature was an important expression of the autonomy and authenticity of the guerrilla fighters; it was a major source of his self–sufficiency.

The natural setting in which the guerrilla operated was conceived by American intellectuals and rendered by reporters almost invariably as rugged, but attractive, and sometimes outright idyllic. The intimate contact with nature also made this mode of warfare more appealing—lurking in the jungles of Central America and scaling forbidding peaks was by itself a heroic activity, even without fighting. It required good physical conditioning, toughness, determination, and survival skills, which urban intellectuals did not have but secretly longed for. The harmonious relationship between the guerrilla and nature fit into the anti–industrial, antiurban world view of many North American intellectuals. The guerrillas roamed the countryside like free spirits, they were not confined to suffocating and corrupting cities, they were free of the demeaning routines of urban and suburban life. Visiting intellectuals were invariably impressed by the purity and sparseness of such a way of life. The guerrillas owned little; they carried what was necessary for survival and had no interest in objects that Western society viewed as essential. The bonds with nature thus connected with the puritanical ethos of the self–denying guerrilla fighter. Such puritanical attributes were the hallmark of the "New Man" that the guerrilla fighter represented: "These pure, ascetic revolutionaries, hardened by danger and privations, were expected after conquering power to exercise it with the same goodness, the same fervor, that they had displayed in gaining it; they were expected to communicate their fervor and altruism to the masses, and thus bring about 'the advent of the new man' through an unprecedented sociological mutation".[31]

The self–conception of the guerrillas was no less exalted. According to Omar Cabezas,

> The Frente Sandinista [de Liberación Nacional-FSLN] was developing . . . a spirit of iron, a spirit of steel, a contingent of men bound with a granite solidity, a nucleus of men that was morally and mentally indestructible . . . The genesis of the new man was in the FSLN . . . an open, unegotistical man . . . who sacrifices himself for others, who suffers when others suffer . . . The new man was born in the mountains.[32]

The uplifting qualities of the guerrilla way of life were also given expression by Régis Debray, French theorist and occasional practitioner of guerrilla warfare, himself much admired by American intellectuals as a personifier of the unity of theory and practice. Debray wrote:

> In the mountains . . . workers, peasants and intellectuals meet for the first time. Their integration is not easy at the beginning . . . Mistrust, timidity, custom have to be gradually vanquished. . . . Since they must all adapt themselves to the same conditions of life, and since they are all participating in the same undertaking, they adapt to each other. Slowly the shared experience, the combats, the hardships endured together weld an alliance having the simple force of friendship . . . Bureaucratic faintheartedness becomes irrelevant. Is this not the best education for a future socialist leader or cadre?[33]

The apotheosis of the veneration of the ascetic, saintly guerrilla leader was reached in the Che Guevara cult. The recollections of I.F. Stone were typical:

> He was the first man I had ever met whom I thought not just handsome but beautiful. With his curly, reddish beard, he looked like a cross between a faun and a Sunday School print of Jesus . . .
>
> In Che, one felt a desire to hear and pity for suffering . . . It was out of love, like the perfect knight of medieval romance, that he had set out to combat with the powers of the world . . .
>
> In a sense he was, like some early saint, taking refuge in the desert. Only there could the purity of the faith be safeguarded.[34]

Another admirer wrote of Guevara's image in death: "I remain with my eyes fastened on the *guerrillero's* face, the magnificent face of this Christ of the Río Plata."[35]

It is not surprising that Guevara also earned the praise of Sartre, who described him as "the most complete man of his time, one who can easily be compared to the giants of the Renaissance for the stupendous many–sidedness of his personality: doctor and economist, revolutionary and banker, military theoretician and ambassador, deep political thinker and popular agitator, able to wield the pen and the submachine gun with equal skill."[36]

Che Guevara symbolized the transformation of political violence into a more lofty calling: "The *guerrillero* was the saint of the revolution, superior to other men not only because of his personal worth and his revolutionary conscience but also because of his charity and willingness to take on himself the sufferings of the oppressed. A disciple of El Che, the Colombian guerrilla–priest Camilo Torres, went so far as to say that 'if Christ had lived in Latin America in our time he would have been a guerrilla fighter.' "[37]

It was of course easier to idealize (and virtually canonize) Guevara than most other guerrilla leaders, because of his martyrdom—his capture and execution in Bolivia. He was spared the moral ambiguities that attend the safe and durable possession of power, the transformation of this guerrilla fighter into party functionary. While Guevara has become the most prominent embodiment of the guerrilla as saint, he himself had earlier popularized a saintly conception of the guerrilla. As one of his biographers put it,

> Che gave an almost celestial vision of his perfect hero as "a sort of guiding angel." Thus the guerrilla fighter is nearly divine, an unearthly gift dropped from the heavens, a Robin Hood or a savior, knight of chivalry who is magnanimous even to his enemies. If these visions are added to the technical, cultural, moral and ascetic qualities also defined by Che as necessary for the guerrilla, then the image of the guerrilla has replaced that of the saint.[38]

An important attribute and appeal of guerrilla violence is its irregular and unconventional nature. Because guerrilla warfare and guerrilla violence are not routine and they resist routinization, they present a welcome contrast to modern mass society and its bureaucratized violence, that Norman Mailer, among others, denounced. The violence of the guerrilla is an integral part of his way of life. It is more spontaneous, impulsive, exciting, adventurous, and, again, authentic. The authenticity comes from the simple fact that the guerrilla fights for a good cause—not for any personal gain, interest, or advantage but for the liberation of others. For that reason the sympathetic intellectual can endorse this kind of violence without hesitation; it is virtually self-legitimizing. In the eyes of these sympathetic beholders, guerrilla violence differs profoundly from the warfare and violence that standing armies engage in. For example, two American scholars wrote: "The government tries to vaporize the 'water,' the people, through sheer terror. In contrast, the violence of the revolutionaries must be measured, clear, and precise."[39] Another apologist of guerrilla violence, Philip Berryman, who is associated with the American Friends Service Committee, also insisted that "there were clear differences in the way violence was used by the army and by the guerrilla groups . . . The army practiced systematic torture and terrorism . . . and was largely indiscriminate in its violence, whereas guerrilla violence was targeted . . . [Guerrillas] made every effort not to endanger innocent bystanders."[40]

Such views no longer go completely unchallenged, even among those seeking sympathetically to understand guerrilla violence, at any rate in El Salvador, where both *New York Times* reporters and the vice-chairman of Americas' Watch have noted a rise in the human rights violations committed by Salvadoran guerrillas.[41]

The moral superiority of guerrilla violence is also seen as connected to the pattern of recruitment. Becoming a guerrilla is supposed to be truly voluntary. Ideal-typical guerrillas are neither conscripts forced to enlist nor mercenaries who fight for money. "Unlike the government soldiers, the rebels weren't paid for fighting—they fought for something they believed in . . . their leaders were men of outstanding ability—inspiring, humane and master strategists.''[42] (Idealism does not always suffice to meet the manpower needs of guerrillas. It has been reported recently from El Salvador that guerrillas forced peasants to join them.) Still, the basic image of the guerrilla is that of a person who makes an existential choice as he decides to put his life on the line for a cause and thus demonstrates the authenticity of his commitment to translating his political ideals into action.

American intellectuals rarely have this option. They must as a rule confine themselves to signing petitions, writing articles or books, making speeches— however passionate, articulate, and illuminating—or participating in demonstrations. Even if arrested for, say, blocking entrances to a military base, they are likely to be released on bail or perhaps detained for a short time—a far cry from the hardships, joys, and risks of stalking the enemy with gun in hand. While few American intellectuals, including radical social critics, would claim that the United States is ripe for guerrilla warfare, they tend to sympathize with the handful of small groups (Weathermen remnants, the Black Liberation Army, Puerto Rican independence fighters, etc.) who seek to introduce guerrilla warfare into the United States.

The appeals of guerrilla violence are also the appeals of smallness against bigness, of a heroic, poorly equipped David against the Goliath of a technologically and numerically superior army. Wrote C. Wright Mills:

> So here's the story of the insurrection in one sentence: a handful of men on a mountain top, half starving at that, defeated a 12,000–man army paid by Batista and largely supplied and trained by Yankees . . . [The] truth is that guerrilla bands, led by determined men, with peasants alongside them, and a mountain nearby, can defeat organized battalions of the tyrants equipped with everything up to the atom bomb.[43]

In another account with distinctly religious undertones, Castro and his small band are seen as sustained by their unshakeable faith in their mission: "With these twelve men on the top of the mountain that Christmas of 1956, Fidel Castro still believed he could make his revolution. He had every reason to despair . . . instead he was buoyant, optimistic, confident."[44] Similar notions dominated the perception of the Sandinistas: "The FSLN won the war not because of its military superiority, but because it was convinced of the rightness of its cause . . . The combination of a lean but well–trained and dedicated guerrilla army and massive urban insurgency was more than Somoza's corrupt and demoralized army could withstand."[45]

The myth of the poorly equipped yet invincible guerrilla has been popular ever since the Vietnam War. At the time, Western sympathizers insisted that the Vietcong were hopelessly outgunned by the United States, but they had overrated the importance of heavy weapons in guerrilla warfare and overlooked the successful efforts of the Soviet Union and China to provide the

Vietcong with all the essentials of guerrilla warfare. More recently, Salvadoran guerrillas and their U.S. supporters have insisted that they were not supplied with weapons from the outside and claimed that they were poorly equipped, relying primarily on captured weapons or those bought on the black market.[46] In each instance the myth of the underarmed guerrilla facing a materially and numerically superior enemy has served the purpose of highlighting the heroism of the guerrilla fighting seemingly overwhelming forces yet sustained by his spirit and superior values. Such a scenario also had the benefit of making it possible to identify the embodiments of good and evil respectively with the underdog and top dog and to draw on the sympathy generally reserved for the underdog.

The moral superiority of guerrilla violence is predicated as noted before, not only on the ends pursued but also on its allegedly more humane character, which is contrasted to the methods used by the adversary. Thus critics of the United States and its allies fighting Marxist guerrillas are repelled by the use of massive firepower, not only because of its potential threat to civilians but also because of a deep–seated hostility to such applications of modern technology *and* a more general aversion to modern technology per se. The attitude alluded to here is part of the David versus Goliath syndrome, combined with the preference for simplicity over complexity and the aversion to powerful machines of any kind. For example, much has been made of the repugnant impersonality of dropping bombs on people from a high–altitude bomber, very much in the spirit of Norman Mailer, who favored passionate face–to–face confrontations with blows struck into the flesh over more impersonal modes of combat. Never was it made clear why, for instance, it was morally preferable to kill (in Vietnam) one's enemies with concealed bamboo spikes smeared in excrement (to encourage blood poisoning) over burning them with napalm bombs, or why the assassination by communist guerrillas of assorted civilians in the employ of the government was qualitatively different from the army killing civilians supporting the guerrillas. As a rule, these divergent judgments were rooted in approval or disapproval of the objectives that they claimed to serve. Often, doubts were put to rest by pointing out that guerrilla violence supported change whereas counterinsurgency sought to maintain the status quo.

As noted earlier, sometimes even the postrevolutionary violence could be assimilated into the moral universe of the intellectuals who were supportive of such regimes. It was often claimed that even the "worst criminals" opposed to the new regime were treated humanely and with consideration.[47] Most frequently, postrevolutionary violence can be justified as defensive: Cuba defending against American subversion, and Nicaragua; resisting the "Contras"; Staughton Lynd, a former partisan of the Vietcong, perceived Sandinista violence in such charitable terms:

> That leadership was merciful to National Guardsmen captured during the insur-
> rection. It abolished the death penalty and has not reinstated it. It has confessed
> error in its policy toward the Miskito Indians . . . Surely the best way to dis-
> cover what these people [the Sandinista leaders] are really like would be to re-
> move the external harassment our Government has imposed on them.[48]

In this, as in many other instances, the assessment of guerrilla (or former guerrilla) violence was based largely on misinformation and supportive sentiment. In fact, the Sandinistas executed many former National Guardsmen but succeeded in convincing segments of American public opinion that this was not the case.[49]

Generally speaking, the information available on Marxist guerrilla violence in the United States has been limited. In turn, there has been reluctance on the part of the sympathizers to process the available information that conflicted with their predisposition. There is little doubt that the idealization of Latin American guerrillas and their violence has been made easier by the nature of the media coverage. This has been noted also by Peruvian writer Mario Vargas Llosa:

> The violations of human rights that occur . . . in democracies like Peru and
> Colombia when they have to respond to guerrilla actions or terrorism are always
> emphasized in the press, whereas one has to search long and hard in the same
> organs to find any comparable reporting on the violation of human rights in
> countries where they murder in the name of the revolution and openly proclaim
> that pistols and bombs—rather than ballot—are the appropriate instruments of
> political life.[50]

The favorable media coverage itself results from a climate of opinion jointly created by journalists and academic intellectuals who share many political values and beliefs.[51]

The tradition of favorable media coverage of left–wing guerrillas in the American mass media probably began with Herbert Matthew's glorifying accounts of Castro and his group in the Sierra Maestra in the late 1950s. Subsequently, throughout the 1960s the Vietcong benefited from a similarly selective and benevolent coverage. Guerrilla violence, as far as most American reporters and television cameramen were concerned, was virtually invisible and thus remained an abstraction for the American public, including intellectuals. Many of the latter probably shared Mary McCarthy's stated preference to believe that only the United States and its allies commit atrocities, as she made clear in her comments on the Hue massacre.[52]

The sympathetic media coverage continued in Nicaragua, greatly benefiting the Marxist–Leninist revolutionaries seeking to influence American public opinion.[53] Shirley Christian, one of the few American journalists who do not invariably give the benefit of doubt to the Sandinistas, wrote:

Reporters covering the war saw Somoza's opponents, the Sandinistas, through a romantic haze. This romantic view of the Sandinistas is by now acknowledged publicly or privately by virtually every American journalist who was in Nicaragua during the two big Sandinista offensives, the general strikes and the various popular uprisings. Probably not since Spain has there been a more open love affair between the foreign press and one of the belligerents in a civil war.[54]

Christian's study, based on scrutiny of several hundred news stories on Nicaragua published in the *New York Times* and the *Washington Post* and broadcast over the CBS network during the period from January 1, 1978, to July 21, 1979, established a clear pattern of selectivity in the reporting of revolutionary as opposed to counterrevolutionary violence. She wrote:

> There were almost no reports . . . of unjustified or noncombat brutality by Sandinista forces against government supporters. One paragraph in a story mentioned a charge [of] . . . Sandinista . . . reprisals . . . but reported no investigation of it. There were also brief mentions of "government informers" being killed or threatened.[55]

Being deprived of visual images or detailed reports of Sandinista political violence strengthened the predisposition to take a benevolent, nonjudgmental view of such violence. In the eyes of sympathetic American intellectuals, little brutality had been committed by the guerrilla, and what there was had excellent justifications. In any event, it was easier to overlook the unappealing aspects of guerrilla violence when it did not have to be confronted on the television screen or through other detailed accounts.

The Salvadoran guerrillas went to great lengths to influence American public opinion and representatives of the media by, among other things, taking journalists and various delegations on tours of rebel–held territory. For example:

> As soon as the American visitors rolled into town . . . more than 300 peasants walked around a corner chanting slogans broadcast by two men with microphones reading from a script: "Bombs no, medicine yes, bombs no, schools yes."
>
> The peasants followed along but one group got mixed up and began chanting "Bombs no, medicine no, schools no" until corrected by a leader.
>
> Asked why they had walked in from all over the northern part of . . . Morazan, several peasants said they had been told by the rebels to demonstrate for the visitors . . .
>
> A rebel camera team filmed the peasants' demonstration and the arrival of the American visitors, which one rebel with a loudspeaker called "a great gain" for the guerrillas.[56]
>
> [It was also reported of the same visit that] the rebels spared no effort to impress the American visitors, providing ample meals of steak, fresh orange juice and

baked bread, as well as beds, a video television screen and trucks for transportation. A well–known revolutionary priest, Miguel Ventura, offered mass in the local, bullet–pocked church. A rebel chorus sang hymns of liberation theology.[57]

In Nicaragua the guerrillas had a long–standing policy of deception aimed at outsiders.[58] These policies continued after the seizure of power and are exemplified by the treatment of visitors from abroad often attended to by Tomás Borge himself. He made it a special point to take important visitors on tours of model prisons in yet another demonstration of the humaneness of his regime. He also took the trouble to have a special office for receiving delegations from abroad, as was reported by a former high–ranking official in the State Security apparatus:

> Borge has two different offices. One . . . is located in the Silvio Mayorga building where he meets religious delegations and delegations from democratic political parties. In this office Borge has photographs of children, gilded, carved crucifixes, and a Bible or two. Before Borge meets with religious delegations he usually memorizes Bible passages which he can quote . . . Borge's real office, where he fulfills his duties as Interior Minister, is located . . . in Belo Horizonte . . . In that office there are no crucifixes or Bibles—only Marxis, literature and posters of Marx, Engels, and Lenin.[59]

Perhaps the best explanation of the favorable predisposition of both the media and intellectuals toward Latin American guerrillas and the causes they were fighting for was offered by Jeane Kirkpatrick. She wrote:

> One reason some modern Americans prefer "socialist" to traditional autocracies is that the former have embraced modernity . . . a profession of universalistic norms; an emphasis on science, education and progress . . . They speak our language.

> Because socialism Soviet/Chinese–Cuban variety is an ideology rooted in a version of the same values that sparked the Enlightenment . . . it is highly congenial to many Americans at the symbolic level. Marxist revolutionaries speak the language of a hopeful future, while traditional autocrats speak the language of an unattractive past. Because left–wing revolutionaries invoke the symbols and values of democracy . . . they are again and again accepted as partisans in the cause of freedom and democracy.[60]

She also observed an affinity between liberalism, Christianity and Marxist socialism displayed most vividly by "left–leaning clerics whose attraction to a secular style of 'redemptive community' is stronger than their outrage at the hostility of socialist regimes to religion."

These attitudes have been revealed most strikingly by authors and "activists" associated with the American Friends Service Committee, which has long been committed to the legitimation and support of revolutionary violence. Their justification rests on three premises: (1) guerrilla violence is restrained and selective; (2) without violence no beneficial change is possible; (3) guerrilla violence is the violence of good intentions and laudable objectives. Such onlookers can neither imagine nor believe that guerrilla violence too can be ugly, brutal, and excessive. If given specific examples of its incidence, they either question the credibility of the source reporting it or reduce its moral significance by asserting that such violence is atypical and rare, or that it results from exceptionally provocative and outrageous acts by the enemy. Above all, such sympathizers are morally disarmed by the claim that all acts of guerrilla violence were designed to hasten the demise of a highly repressive and unjust social system. As Philip Berryman put it, "A Christian must see such regimes as embodying 'systems of sin.' "[61] That being the case, taking up arms against such a system is easily justifiable. Once again the mystique of revolution and revolutionary violence offers legitimation, even though the terminology is different, appropriate to the religious discourse:

> The signs of grace in a revolutionary *proyecto* would be that the life of the poor is enhanced, their dignity respected; that there is an overall movement toward equality, a willingness to accept austerity in the interests of all, a conscious effort to build a society on cooperation and common effort—all qualities that have their analogues in the ideal vision of the church and Christian life in the New Testament . . . Hence the revolution could be regarded as a bearer, or mediation, of grace.[62]

Other clerics went further, claiming: "To be a Christian is to be a revolutionary." Padre Guadalupe Carney wrote:

> We Christian Revolutionaries of Central America believe that the basis of the new Christian Socialist system will be a spirit of equality and brotherhood, rather than seeking personal gain. This search for personal gain, inculcated continuously by . . . structures of capitalism, is a main cause of the injustices which we suffer at every level of life . . .
>
> We Christian Socialists want to help liberate people from this consuming drive for person gain . . .
>
> I have a deep desire (which I am convinced comes from the Spirit of Jesus) to completely join the Honduran guerrillas . . .
>
> There is no contradiction whatsoever between being a Christian, and a priest, and being a Marxist revolutionary.[63]

Such statements lead us to ponder once more the attractions of revolutionary violence, and especially the sources of the susceptibility to its appeals and the attendant suspension of disbelief appropriate enough for clerics less for intellectuals (or for clerics assuming the role of intellectuals) in full command of their critical faculties.

Susceptibility to the attractions of revolutionary violence, at home or abroad, and the corresponding willingness to give every benefit of the doubt to its perpetrators, flourish among those most thoroughly disenchanted with their own society, that is, members of the intelligentsia. The admiration and legitimation of such violence is an integral part of the emotional support given to the goals the violence is supposed to bring about. As noted earlier, however, the use of violent methods in itself evokes admiration when viewed as proof of authentic commitment and personal courage. In the 1960s, American social critics envisioned the possibility of successfully introducing such cleansing, revolutionary violence in their own society, but with the decline of such expectations there has been a shift to a greater identification with revolutionary movements and causes abroad, and especially in nearby Latin America and its central regions. Since Cuba has ceased to be a revolutionary society, and hence is no longer a setting for the display of exotic revolutionary violence (though it may still be admired on other grounds), the Marxist–Leninist guerrillas of Nicaragua and El Salvador have come to embody the virtues of righteous revolutionary violence. Once again the ready acceptance of the claims, promises, and methods of these movements raises questions about the deeper and possibly less political (or nonpolitical) roots of their attraction. Could such factors play a part in the perceived attractiveness of revolutionary violence, in addition to its putative role in bringing about a better society?

There are a number of suggestive observations in Stanley Rothman's study of the radical youth of the 1960s that may be helpful in understanding the recurring admiration and sympathy that guerrilla violence evokes in many American intellectuals. Extrapolating from Rothman's findings, it would appear that the appeals of guerrilla violence discussed here are rooted in the pleasure of vicarious participation in righteous violence, or "the romance of cleansing violence":

> Feelings of shared oppression provide the contact point for identification with a revolutionary brotherhood. A young middle–class student [or not–so–young adult intellectual] can thus consider himself the brother of oppressed peoples the world over, projecting his new–found feelings of solidarity onto peasants or proletarians . . . He becomes a self–chosen representative of the oppressed, a patron to the powerless. This identification helps to deny his own aggressiveness . . . By assuming the mantle of revolutionary agency, he gains self–aggrandizement . . . and achieves a sense of self–denial through his subsumption into a brotherhood of equals . . .

> For these middle–class students [and once more, we might add, intellectuals] revolutionary violence gradually came to be seen as a logical extension of long and arduous effort to overcome their origins . . . This goal led them to . . . identification with the world's outcasts and victims, whom they viewed as sources of both moral and physical strength.[64]

[In another context Rothman observes:] For alienated quasi–intellectuals like Meinhof, terrorism represented a final opportunity to reject the seductive material advantages and the spurious moral standards of an evil system. Her new role as revolutionary outlaw combined self–denial with self–assertion.[65]

The latter may be a crucial point: the irresistible appeals of a social role that combines ascetic, puritanical self–denial (Guevara–style) with robust self–assertion in the form of ideologically sanctioned release of aggression. Rothman argues that for the young middle–class radicals—and we may add again, also for the not–so–young intellectuals—guerrilla violence abroad (or black violence at home) was attractive because of its compensatory aspects. The admirers felt powerless and were obstructed from embracing political violence by both structural and psychological factors.

The admiration of guerrilla violence also had much in common with the admiration of certain types of criminal violence and the idealization of some criminals in the United States, seen as Robin Hood types visiting retribution on an immoral, flabby society, or as cultural heroes rebelling forcefully against an unjust system. The prototype apotheosis of the violent criminal turned social critic was provided by Norman Mailer's campaign for Jack Abbott, former convict turned author, who after a short spell of freedom and celebrity status in New York was returned to prison for a new murder committed after his release.[66] The phenomenon had its equivalent in France, where left–wing intellectuals embraced "another convict turned writer", "an outlaw hero, a poet, a kind of updated François Villon", Roger Knobelspiess, once pardoned by President Mitterrand. He too insisted on being "a victim of the police and an unjust society".[67]

For those incapable of performing heroic deeds themselves but longing for masculine self–assertion, identification with the guerrillas, especially victorious guerrillas, held great attraction, as for example Abbie Hoffman's comments on Castro's triumphant entry into Havana suggest:

> Fidel sits on the side of the tank rumbling into Havana on New Year's Day. . . . Girls throw flowers at the tank and rush to tug playfully at his black beard. He laughs joyously and pinches a few rumps . . . The tanks stops in the city square. Fidel lets the gun drop to the ground, slaps his thigh and stands erect. He is like a mighty penis coming to life.[68]

At last the support for guerrilla violence among American intellectuals associated with hero–worship also raises questions about certain alienating aspects of modern society that may create a more general predisposition to such hero–worship. Several decades ago Hans Speier addressed this issue, drawing attention to the growing need, at least among some groups in modern society, for what he called "freely chosen risk", a form of adventurous and exciting self–assertion associated with physical combat. He argued that modern urban, industrial, and highly bureaucratized society makes life for some overly secure, predictable, and boring, removing the possibilities of "elementary experiences of physical risk":

> A truly bewildering specialization of work . . . has created a web of interdependence which all of us help to spin and in which each of us seems caught . . . We are divorced from the naive and full assertion of life . . .
>
> Modern hero worship is a safe and underhanded way of obtaining vicariously what life refuses to give freely. Hero worship is a worship of active unbridled life . . .
>
> Worship of the heroic may be a substitute for action from which they [the worshippers] are barred by circumstances, fear and convention.

Speier also noted among the components of modern hero worship "the primeval veneration of strength and freely chosen risks in defiance of Christian and middle class ethics . . . a life experience in which aspirations are curbed, desires censored . . . [and] the passivity which modern civilization promotes."[69]

It is at the confluence of such generalized discontents of modern life and the more specific critiques of pluralistic capitalism that we find the breeding ground that nurtures the admiration of many American intellectuals toward Latin American guerrillas and their political violence.

Notes

1. Jean–Paul Sartre, *Sartre on Cuba* (New York, Ballantine Books, 1961), pp. 44, 102, 103.
2. Norman Mailer, *The Presidential Papers* (New York: Berkley Publishing Corp., 1968) pp. 69–70.
3. Martin Peretz, "Washington Diarist", *The New Republic*, May 2, 1983.
4. Nathan Leites, *A Study of Bolshevism* (Glencoe, Ill.: The Free Press, 1953), p. 114.
5. See *New York Times*, January 11, 1986; ibid., January 15, 1986; ibid., January 20, 1986; and ibid., January 22, 1986.
6. Raymond Aron, *The Opium of Intellectuals* (London: Secker and Warburg, 1957), pp. 35, 43.
7. Ibid., pp. 48–49.
8. Peter Berger and Richard J. Neuhaus, *Movement and Revolution* (New York: Anchor Books, 1970), p. 51.
9. Quoted in *A Time for Candor: Mainline Churches and Radical Social Witness* (Washington, D.C.: Institute on Religion and Democracy, 1983), p. 81.
10. John Gerassi, "The Political Activist Pivot," in *Latin American Radicalism: A Documentary Report on Left and Nationalist Movements*, ed. I. L. Horowitz, José de Castro, and John Gerassi (New York: Random House, 1969), p. 493.
11. See also Ronald Berman, *America in the Sixties* (New York: The Free Press, 1968), esp. chap. 11.

12. Steve Weissman, "The Prophet, Armed", *Ramparts*, August 24, 1968, p. 59.
13. *The Rationalization of Terrorism*, ed. David C. Rapoport and Yonah Alexander (Frederick, Md.: University Publications of America, 1982), p. 19.
14. Tom Wolfe, *Radical Chic and Mau–Mauing the Flack Catchers* (New York: Bantam Books, 1970), pp. 49–40, 152.
15. Tad Szulc, *The Winds of Revolution* (New York: Praeger, 1963), p. 120.
16. Thomas W. Walker, "Images of the Nicaraguan Revolution," in *Nicaragua in Revolution*, ed. Thomas W. Walker (New York: Praeger, 1982), pp. 82–83.
17. *Playboy*, September 1983, p. 58.
18. Berger and Neuhas, *Movement and Revolution*. For an excellent update on these attitudes, see "The Myth of Revolution," editorial *The New Republic*, April 29, 1985, pp. 7–10.
19. Irving Louis Horowitz, *C. Wright Mills: An American Utopian* (New York: The Free Press, 1983), p. 300.
20. Carlos Fuentes, "Foreword" to Omar Cabezas, *Fire from the Mountain: The Making of a Sandinista* (New York: Crown Publishers, 1985), pp. XI-XII.
21. See, e.g., Alexander Cockburn and James Ridgeway, "Reagan's 'Secret War' in Jalapa: Eyewitness to Terror," *Village Voice*, 2, 1983.
22. Jeffrey Hart, "Guerrilla Chic: What Is and Isn't Fashionable", *Washington Times*, June 27, 1983.
23. A. James Gregor, *The Fascist Persuasion in Radical Politics* (Princeton: Princeton University Press, 1974), pp. 302, 308, 309.
24. Peter Shaw and S. M. Lipset, "Two Afterthoughts on Susan Sontag", *Encounter*, June–July 1982, p. 40; and Walter Goodman, "Hard to Digest", *Harper's*, June 1962, p. 6.
25. Richard Gott, *Guerrilla Movements in Latin America* (London: Nelson, 1970), p. 359
26. Andrew Sinclair, *Guevara* (London: Collins, 1970), p. 350.
27. K.S. Karol, *Guerrillas in Power* (New York: Hill and Wang, 1970), p. 58.
28. C. Wright Mills, *Listen Yankee: The Revolution in Cuba* (New York: Ballantine Books, 1960), p. 43.
29. John Gerassi, "The Spectre of Che Guevara," *Ramparts*, October 1967, p. 30.
30. Carlos Rangel, *The Latin Americans: Their Love–Hate Relationship with the U.S.* (New York: Harcourt Brace Jovanovich, 1977), pp. 128–129.
31. Ibid., p. 129.
32. Cabezas, *Fire from the Mountain*, pp. 85–87.
33. Régis Debray, *Revolution in the Revolution?* (New York: Monthly Review Press, 1967), pp. 110–111.
34. I. F. Stone, "The Legacy of Che Guevara", *Ramparts*, December 1967, pp. 20–21.
35. Eduardo Galeano, "Magic Death for a Magic Life", *Monthly Review*, January 1968, p. 13.
36. Quoted in Michael Lowry, *The Marxism of Che Guevara: Philosophy, Economics, and Revolutionary Warfare* (New York: Monthly Review Press 1973), p. 7.
37. Rangel, *The Latin Americans*, p. 129.
38. Sinclair, *Guevara*, p. 42.
39. James Kohl and John Zitt, *Urban Guerrilla Warfare in Latin America* (Cambridge, Mass.: MIT Press, 1974), p. 24.
40. Philip Berryman, *The Religious Roots of Rebellion* (Maryknoll N.Y.: Orbis Books, 1984), pp. 209–210.
41. Aryeh Neier, "Abuses by Salvadoran Guerrillas", *New York Times*, July 26,

1985, Op–Ed page. See also Lydia Chavez, ''1500 in Salvador Flee Rebel Area'', *New York Times*, June 7, 1984; Warren Hoge, ''Rebel Tactics Enrage Some in El Salvador'', *New York Times*, March 16, 1982; James LeMoyne, ''Salvador Rebels Reported to Execute 9'', *New York Times*, November 4, 1984; and ''Peace Hope Dies for Salvadorans'', *New York Times*, October 14, 1985.

42. Leo Huberman and Paul Sweezey, ''The Conquest of Power,'' *Monthly Review*, November 1960, p. 63.

43. Mills, *Listen Yankee*, pp. 50, 114.

44. Huberman and Sweezy, ''Conquest of Power,'' p. 55.

45. Thomas W. Walker, *Nicaragua: The Land of Sandino* (Boulder, Colo.: Westview Press, 1981), p. 93.

46. See, e.g., Edward Schmacher, ''Salvador Guerrillas, in Interview, Say They Are Short of Weapons'', *New York Times*, 22, 1981; and Raymond Bonner, ''With Salvador Rebels in combat Zone,'' *New York Times*, January 26, 1982.

47. See, e.g., Carleton Beals, ''Terror in Cuba?'' *The Nation*, January 24, 1959, p. 64.

48. Staughton Lynd, ''The High Cost of Fighting Our 'Contras' '', Correspondence page, *New York Times*, November 3, 1985.

49. See e.g., Humberto Belli, *Christians Under Fire* (Garden City, Mich.: Puebla Institute, 1984), esp. pp. 57–64, 132–137; and Humberto Belli, *Breaking Faith: The Sandinista Revolution and Its Impact on Freedom and Faith in Nicaragua* (Westchester Ill.: Crossway 1985).

50. Mario Vargas Llosa, ''Latin America: A Media Stereotype,'' *The Atlantic*, February 1984, p. 22.

51. See, e.g., S. Robert Lichter and Stanley Rothman, ''The Media Elite and American Values,'' Ethics and Public Policy Center, (Reprint), Washington, D.C., 1982; see also by the same authors, ''Personality, Ideology, and World View: A Comparison of Media and Business Elites'', *British Journal of Political Science*, no. 1, 1984; and Leopold Tyrmand, ''Media Shangri–la'', *American Scholar*, Winter, 1975–1976.

52. Quoted in *Commentary*, January 1974, p. 36.

53. For a discussion of such manipulations, see Paul Hollander, ''The Newest Pilgrims,'' *Commentary*, August 1985.

54. Shirley Christian, ''Covering the Sandinistas: The Foregone Conclusions of the Fourth Estate'', *Washington Journalism Review*, March 1982, p. 34.

55. Ibid., p. 37.

56. James LeMoyne, ''The Rebels Give Show in Salvador,'' *New York Times*, July 8, 1985.

57. James LeMoyne, ''Salvador Rebels Vow to Spread War,'' *New York Times*, July 7, 1985. A discussion of similar Nicaraguan political hospitality, i.e., techniques for impressing visitors, may be found in Paul Hollander, ''Sojourners in Nicaragua: A Political Pilgrimage,'' *National Catholic Register*, May 29, 1983; and Paul Hollander, ''Political Tourism in Cuba and Nicaragua,'' *Society*, May–June 1986.

58. See, e.g., Douglas W. Payne, ''The 'Mantos' of Sandinista Deception'', *Strategic Review*, Spring 1985.

59. ''Nicaragua's State Security: Behind the Propaganda Mask *An Interview with Álvaro José Baldizón Aviles*,'' Briefing Paper, Institute on Religion and Democracy, September 1985, p. 2.

60. Jeane J. Kirkpatrick, ''Dictatorship and Double Standards'', American Enterprise Institute, Washington, D.C., 1982, pp. 44–45.

61. Berryman, *Religious Roots*, p. 382.

62. Ibid., p. 389.

63. Padre J. Guadalupe Carney, *To Be a Revolutionary* (San Francisco: Harper and Row, 1985), pp. 438–440. After moving from Honduras to Nicaragua the author wrote: "I have been very restless here in Nicaragua . . . because there is no longer any persecution here. There is no need to denounce and fight against injustices here . . . In Nicaragua there are no repressive authorities." p. 430.

64. Stanley Rothman, *Roots of Radicalism: Jews, Christians, and the New Left* (New York: Oxford University Press, 1982), pp. 166, 188, 198.

65. Ibid., p. 365.

66. See, e.g., M. A. Farber, "A Killing at Dawn Beclouds Ex–Convict Writer's New Life," *New York Times*, July 26, 1981; and Naomi Munson and James Atlas, "On Norman Mailer and Jack Abbott. The Literary Life of Crime," *The New Republic*, September 9, 1981.

67. John Vinocur, "Convict–Poet, Idol of France's Left, Is Fallen," *New York Times*, June 14, 1985.

68. Abbie Hoffman, *Revolution for the Hell of It* (New York: Dial Press, 1968), p. 13.

69. Hans Speier, *Social Order and Risks of War* (New York: Stewart, 1952), pp. 123, 127–128.

9

Toward A Reassessment of Insurgency, Violence, Revolution, Communism, and Assorted Ailments

Irving Louis Horowitz

Instead of responding to each chapter in this volume separately, I want here to address some general implications that emerge from themes developed by each author. The chapters that make up this volume are serious and significant unto themselves, but they nonetheless raise troubling theoretical problems for researchers. They are indicative of a division increasingly characteristic of the field of international relations—between those who operate at structural levels of analysis and those who operate at motivational levels. Let me try to be more specific.

The first and most serious problem that the chapters evince is a shift in emphasis from social stratification to social psychology. There is a serious break in these six chapters between scholars who analyze events in terms of classical issues: the structure of communist guerrilla insurgency, the uses of organized violence to gain revolutionary ends, and the issues of strategic response on the part of democratic nations to such developments. This is the familiar turf of international relations in the contemporary epoch, as common to *Foreign Policy* as it is to *Foreign Affairs*.

In the chapters by Paul Hollander and Michael Radu especially, there is a search for psychological meaning (each in quite distinctive ways, it should be added). Political psychology, a classical tradition that dates back to LeBon, Michels, and Sorel, attempts to locate political behavior in the longing for utopia and in the symbols, signs, and myths that fuse with collective action to bring about often unintended but still quite dramatic consequences in the body politic. But it is one thing to identify parallel trends, and quite another to fuse or synthesize them to make a convincing paradigm.

In my editorial role at *Transaction*, I have been fortunate enough to publish as well as to become increasingly acquainted with the towering work of Paul Hollander. His distinctive efforts to explain the attachment of the Western intellectual to the appeals of ''socialism'' have been fully documented, and his efforts to study acquiescence in evil, sometimes passively, other times actively, are unique for their probing intensity into the behavioral basis of communism. In the chapter in this volume, he shows that American intellectual acquiescence in totalitarian regimes dates back to the origins of the Bolshevik Revolution itself and is not simply a matter of recent political pilgrimages. Americans going overseas to bear witness to what the revolutionary regime wants the individual pilgrims to see and say is also a problem of religious ideology, a longing after perfection, an ideal that permits the installation of a heavenly order onto a disordered universe.

While this represents a new development—a further evolution in Hollander's work—problems remain: above all, the relationship of the sacred and the profane. We need to constantly re–examine the connections between religion and politics—the search for divine meaning no less than practical redemption in this world. Increasingly, from Iran to Poland, there is a revolt against secular modernity, or at least an intellectual demand for a set of symbols that are less corroded than those of modern communism or classic capitalism. The resistance of Baptists in the Soviet Union and the continued strength of Catholicism in China both attest to the power of symbols, even in the Second World. They are to be mocked only at the peril of the researcher. These symbolic identifications are certainly crude and puerile, but they are authentic, and it is this latter aspect—authenticity of religious experience—that seems to have escaped Hollander's efforts to explain the appeals of revolutionary violence.

Many chiliastic statements by presumably secular commentators and scholars are easy targets for mockery and jest. In retrospect they seem particularly unconvincing, that is, in light of the real evolution of totalitarian regimes. Nonetheless, there is a need to examine compassionately and carefully the restoration of metaphysical beliefs and teleological longings in the political process. There are new domain assumptions that form part of the baggage of everyday politics—east and west, north and south. The tasks of social research in the face of Moslem, Jewish, or Christian fundamentalism are extremely complex and require the ethnographic skills of the cultural anthropologist as much as the cutting edge of the philosophical rationalist. This sensibility is missing in Hollander's work on Western elites who embrace totalitarian dogma. But it is worth noting that it was the same fervent desire for political perfection that led a Jean–Paul Sartre to repudiate, no less than embrace, a Fidel Castro—however tardy and tawdry that repudiation might have been.

The demands of the masses are often and increasingly at loggerheads with the political persuasions of their own elites. This is as true in Europe as it is in the United States. The teleological beliefs of the masses contrast with the narrow positivism and scientific rationalism of educated elites. Crudities aside, the need to explain the consequences as well as the causes of this break between mass sentiments and elite sentiments is a paramount task of a political psychology of meaning. But to do so means to put aside the notion that irrationality is a unique characteristic of North American leftists or Latin American revolutionaries. Cultural figures increasingly share a search for meaning or purpose neatly disguised in intellectual circles by appeals to normative or evaluative criteria for decision making.

In a practical setting, a more expansive vision is of great consequence in how we look at the world, for if chiliastic visions of Western intellectuals sometimes lead to sanctioning anti-Americanism, so too does this same vision lead Third World masses to anti–Sovietism. Otherwise, national liberation struggles in places as remote from each other as Afghanistan, Angola, or Cambodia become meaningless. It is true that the *politics* of liberation theology is often anti–American, but its *eschatology* is anti–industrial and antibureaucratic. In this, the potential for resisting Soviet blandishments is at least a real factor in policy equations. However, to emphasize relentlessly only the excremental outpourings of fringe intellectuals is to miss the trees for the forest, to substitute an all–too–easy intellectual rationalist conceit for the even longer longing after paradise that is part of our common culture since Moses and Augustine.

Michael Radu has clearly also thought deeply about these nonrational, or Paretan, aspects of mass behavior. In this, he seeks to move the discussion from a political psychology of antidemocratic thought in general to a profiling of forms of revolutionary behavior in particular, or the on–sight betrayal of democratic values in favor of a culture of violence. I have not come across the equal of Radu's profile of the terrorist. Having tried to accomplish a similar chore some years ago, I know how difficult his job was and how remarkably textured his resultant analysis is. But the issue remains: does this allow us to move to a higher intellectual ground?

The task of analysis itself remains open to question. Profiling terrorists of Latin America, however worthwhile, is only part of Radu's effort. Ultimately, the goal is to develop a system of cauterizing regimes against such terrorist infections. Yet problems arise. What may be true in one context or country may not be so in another. Radu makes a point about the numbers of Jews and ethnic minorities located in revolutionary groupings, which is quite correct. But as a profile it is incomplete, because the Jews are also overrepresented in the business sectors of Latin America. What is decisive is the underrepresentation of Jews (and other minority cultures and ethnic groups) in the political process. In a world of *caudillos* and *caciques*, the opportunity for democratic participation is extremely limited. Jewish longings for democracy thus get recycled and rechanneled, often with tragic consequences, into revolutionary clusters. But a mere profile, however accurate, would not lay bare such underlying causative agents, so we are back to structuralist analyses of political events; and no less to the place of political theology in our age.

I am attracted to the kind of analysis that Tismaneanu presents in his effort to make sense of communist orthodoxy in unorthodox contexts, and to disentangle the relationship of Castroism as an ideology to its Marxist–Leninist pedigree. Indeed, his is one of the better such efforts, perhaps endowing the Castro regime with greater intellectual acumen and foresight than it actually possesses. But here my problem is less with Tismaneanu's diagnostic than with his taxonomy. We have taken to using radical ''isms'' in a dangerously cavalier, interchangeable way. Socialism, communism, Marxism, Leninism, Stalinism, totalitarianism—are all beginning to blend into a pastiche of sight, sound, and color and in the process are becoming dangerously impressionistic. Despite his remarkable sophistication, Tismaneanu seems to have fallen prey to configurations at the ideological level that have the net effect (unintended, I am sure) of leaving structures unexamined for their uniqueness and difference at the policy level.

Perhaps we should each begin to ask what it is in the political environment that we are least happy with or, in the vernacular of the Marxists, what is the ''main danger'' or the ''primary contradiction'' that requires our focus. This will at least permit a clear sense of goals and, moreover, a precise policy response. Is the issue primarily one of social systems or of political repression? Is the issue one of violence or of the collapse of democratic opposition? These are no mere exercises in communist catechism. Since China presumably shares with the Soviets the same ''economic system'', is the issue of moment overthrowing communism as such? If one answers yes, then China and the Soviet Union are equally ''enemies'' of the democratic West. While there are some who take just such positions, by far the majority of strategists make a sharp and clear distinction between the Soviet Union and the People's Republic of China on a wide variety of fronts—social, cultural, and military. Long–range trends that one sees in China vis–a–vis the Soviet Union will determine attitudes even more than structural or systemic features of each nation's brand of communism.

Without engaging in a Sorelian defense of violence, it is clear too that the issue is not opposition to violence—even guerrilla insurgency as such—so much as opposition to certain forms of insurgency. Thus, one can be perfectly at ease defending Jonas Savimbi and his UNITA movement in Angola or the Contras in Nicaragua, even though the levels of violence or guerrilla terror involved may be no less than those engaged in by their enemies. And we are not necessarily talking about the democratic transition versus the arbitrary seizure of power, for the Chinese revolution of 1949 was certainly as militaristic and autocratic as anything seen in the Soviet Union thirty years earlier. Political figures tend to be more concerned about outcomes than about inputs, and if this betokens a break between ''means'' and ''end'' it may just be that the pragmatic continuities of means and ends, inputs and outputs, exhibit more of those qualitative breaks than doctrinaire advocates of pure democracy are ready to acknowledge.

I suspect that in a crude or at least reflexive way we make sharp and clear distinctions between Soviet communism and the rest of the ideological baggage carried about by lesser regimes, or rather regimes of less global magnitude. There are, after all, both pro–Soviet and anti–Soviet forms of Marxism. Perhaps the latter are less evident in the mid–1980s than they were a decade earlier. But major distinctions among varieties of Marxism still may be as contextually decisive as distinctions between Marxian and non–Marxian systems. Admittedly, there are critical points when differences between democratic and dictatorial modes of belief and behavior clash, and bitterly so. But for the short–run (which may mean for decades not just days) the disentanglement of taxonomies and ideologies must be performed in real–world contexts where more is at stake than ideological purity—indeed, where what is at stake is survival of the democratic West.

It might be worth noting that democratic systems also have powerful, built–in ideological contradictions. For two hundred years the United States has endured as a solitary, unified republic, despite differences between the Jeffersonian and Hamiltonian visions of everything from law, order, and taxes to the good society. Nations do not break apart because ideological systems of seemingly sharp distinction cohabit in the same turf. Such prosaic, nonideological matters—for instance, the economic well–being of the masses, political participation, health and welfare for families, economic advancement through education, in short, the entire panoply of opportunity networks that characterize viable societies, whatever their ideological proclivities—must be reviewed and dealt with if the work of social and political scientists is not to degenerate into political sloganeering that pampers our egoes and satisfies our own sense of the perfect society at the expense of the clumsy, cluttered world of compromises and concessions that constitute real societies.

This last point is not meant to be a criticism of the three chapters, but rather a general observation on the limits of the ideological line of analysis mapped out as the proscribed limits (for these chapters of conference chores). Indeed, I suspect that Hollander, Radu, and Tismaneanu have considerable sympathy with this sort of distinction between analytical purity and the practical impurities of the political process. The trick—a neat one at that—is how to factor or weigh both the pure and the practical, the sacred and the profane, into types of analysis that will yield a rich vein of new research opportunities, and do so while still aiding the ongoing search for political frameworks that advance the cause of democracy and widen the spider's web of autocracy.

About the Contributors

Michael Radu is a Research Associate at the Foreign Policy Research Institute in Philadelphia, and contributing editor of *Orbis*. He is the editor of *Eastern Europe and the Third World*, and co–author of *Latin American Insurgent and Guerrilla Organizations*.

Ernst Halperin is Professor of Political Science at Boston University and Adjunct Professor of International Politics at The Fletcher School of Law and Diplomacy, Tufts University. His extensive writings on communist governments and ideology have appeared in such journals as *Survey*, *China Quarterly*, *Current History*. He is also the co–editor of *Hydra of Carnage* (1986).

Paul Hollander is Professor of Sociology at the University of Massachusetts, Amherst, and a Fellow at the Russian Research Center at Harvard. Among his areas of expertise are comparative Soviet and Western social behavior and the role of the intellectuals in politics. Among his many books is *Political Pilgrims*.

Irving L. Horowitz is Hannah Arendt Distinguished Professor of Sociology and Political Science at Rutgers University. He is president of *Transaction/Society*. Among his many publications is *Cuban Communism*.

Douglas Payne is Assistant to the Director of the Center for Caribbean and Central American Studies of Freedom House. His latest publications include *The Democratic Mask: The Consolidation of the Sandinista Revolution*.

William Ratliff is Senior Research Fellow at the Hoover Institution and Latin American editor for the *Yearbook of International Communist Affairs*. Among his publications is *Castroism and Communism in Latin America*.

Vladimir Tismaneanu is a research associate at the Foreign Policy Research Institute and contributing editor of *Orbis*. He has published extensively on communist affairs in *Problems of Communism*, *Survey*, etc., and is co–author of *Revolutionary Organizations in Latin America: A Handbook*.

Antonio Ybarra–Rojas is associated with the University of Iowa at Ames. His research fields include agricultural development in Latin America, the role of women in the labor force in Latin America and Nicaraguan contemporary developments, in which he was personally involved.